MARGARET FULLER

Margaret Fuller

Writing a Woman's Life

Donna Dickenson
Lecturer, The Open University
Milton Keynes

St. Martin's Press   New York

First published in the United States of America in 1993

Printed in Hong Kong

ISBN 0-312-09145-1

Library of Congress Cataloging-in-Publication Data
Dickenson, Donna.
Margaret Fuller : writing a woman's life / Donna Dickenson.
p.   cm.
Includes bibliographical references and index.
ISBN 0-312-09145-1
1. Fuller, Margaret, 1810–1850—Biography.   2. Women and
literature—United States—History—19th century.   3. Authors,
American—19th century—Biography.   4. Feminists—United States–
–Biography.   I. Title.
PS2506.D45   1993
818'.309—dc20
[B]   92-33474
                                                                                  CIP

To a 'Man of the Nineteenth Century',
My grandfather, Donald M. Dickenson
(1899–   )

Contents

Acknowledgements

The author and publishers wish to thank Yale University Press for permission to quote extracts from Larry J. Reynolds and Susan Belasco Smith (eds), 'These Sad but Glorious Days': Dispatches from Europe, 1846–1850, by Margaret Fuller, © 1991, Yale University Press.

Every effort has been made to trace the copyright-holders of all copyright material quoted in this volume but if any have been inadvertently overlooked the publishers will be pleased to make the necessary arrangements at the first opportunity.

List of Plates

Preface

This is the story of an unrepresentative woman: one who had to script a new woman's life. Yet it is also the narrative of *the* emblematic woman of her time. After Margaret Fuller's death in 1850, even the male writers with whom she was friendliest – Emerson and Hawthorne – made her life and work a No Man's Land, denigrating it consciously or unconsciously, in the ways documented in a later generation of male writers by Sandra M. Gilbert and Susan Gubar.[1] What befell Fuller's reputation has happened to that of many other women writers, but it happened to her first.

Fuller wrote her own life by living it. She wove it into a tapestry of epic deeds and proportions, a new Aeneid of Rome's refounding by an outsider. But after her early death alterations were made: the garment of her life was refashioned by male tailors – Emerson and the editors of her posthumous *Memoirs* – to suit the prevailing female fashion. The mode which they chose was actually less than flattering: the prevailing styles on which they modelled her garb were the female invalid, the cerebral spinster, the vestal devotee. Later Henry James fashioned even more ephemeral garments for her use – and Hawthorne, in posthumously published slanders, stripped her naked.

Yet Fuller's life and death were heroic. She made her life not into the Gothic tale which women's novels of the time portrayed, but into a Latin epic, a *Boy's Own* story. Beginning from a youth steeped in the Latin texts from which most girls were barred, she spent the three last and most vital years of her life supporting the Roman revolution and running a hospital for the wounded during the siege of Rome. Earlier, she had edited the magazine which was to epitomise the Transcendentalist movement (*The Dial*), written criticism and social policy articles for the *New York Tribune*, worked with prostitutes in Sing Sing, and visited the Indian women on Mackinac Island. Her most influential publication, *Woman in the Nineteenth Century* (1845), sold out within a week and helped to set the tone, if not the agenda, for the Seneca Falls convention of 1848 and the American woman's movement. Her personal life, too, was heroic in the best woman's way: caring for her mother and seven younger siblings, then later enduring her own first childbirth without family support in Italy, with no one who could so much as speak her language. Even her death – in a hurricane, only 50 yards off the coast of Fire Island, returning to America from Italy with her Italian husband and twenty-two-month-old son – was tragic rather than merely poignant.

This critical study of Margaret Fuller begins, then, with the treatment of her life after her death. My unconventional way of proceeding – last things first – is intended to highlight the contrast between the script written for her to play from the unmarked grave, and the one she actually wrote for herself by living it. Putting things this way round also states *my* purpose and plot: not to write this life in the usual linear way. (A full chronology is appended to make good any omissions.)

The first chapter concentrates on 'the Margaret myth', Henry James's term – and also partly his creation. The remaining chapters contrast the legend with the life. The paltriness of the downgraded life of the myth contrasts consistently with the life as she actually wrote and lived it.

Why it should have been necessary to downgrade Fuller – perhaps unconsciously, perhaps 'in her own best interests' – is considered in light of Sandra M. Gilbert and Susan Gubar's *No Man's Land*; Elaine Showalter's speculations[2]; and Carol Gilligan's work on female moral development.[3] The informing model for the claim that Fuller wrote her life as a quest plot is, of course, Carolyn Heilbrun's *Writing a Woman's Life*,[4] as this book's subtitle reflects. These works have been of immense assistance in helping me to refine views towards which I was working in my earlier studies of Emily Dickinson (1985)[5] and George Sand (1988)[6]. I have also drawn extensively on recent feminist political philosophy, particularly Carole Pateman's *The Sexual Contract*.[7] Pateman's work has helped me see why Fuller so long mistook a liberal individualistic dream of freedom – one which only accommodated men – for a reality which she, as a woman, might live.

Thus my version of Fuller's life is informed by the insights of many of the major recent works in women's studies. Conversely, I argue that Fuller's life is an excellent case for exemplifying and better understanding some of those theoretical insights. The point of view is, needless to say, feminist, but it is a feminism which draws extensively on the composite, eclectic, comprehensive theoretical framework provided by the last twenty years of women's studies. It locates Fuller within the context of other gifted women, and of women's studies, as much as within history.

The voices of feminist theory do not muffle Fuller's own; rather, they amplify it. Throughout, I try to let Fuller speak for herself, primarily through extensive use of her letters, now available in an edition restored by Robert N. Hudspeth after the depredations of Fuller's posthumous editors. In preparing her *Memoirs*, these men took their tailor's shears to Fuller's original words, throwing away large pieces of fabric but adding bits of lacy trim. This critical biography draws entirely on the restored texts of the letters, Fuller's life as *she* wrote it. (To those who want to read more of what Fuller wrote, outside of her letters, I would recommend my forthcoming collection of Fuller's works in the Oxford World's Classics paperback series, *Woman in the Nineteenth Century and Other Writings*.) At the time of writing I was able to use the first five volumes of the *Letters*, which had appeared in print, and the sixth and final volume in a typescript which Dr Hudspeth generously made available to me. I owe him an enormous debt of gratitude.

My thanks, too, to Elaine Showalter, David Watson and Mary Fainsod Katzenstein for discussion of the ideas behind the manuscript at an early stage, and to Robert Hudspeth and Elaine Showalter for their help also at the halfway-through-the-first-draft point. I have also benefited throughout the writing of this book from conversations with Jean Grimshaw, Morwenna Griffiths, Gwen Adshead and other members of the Society for Women in Philosophy. I would like to acknowledge the great helpfulness of the staff at the Houghton Library of Harvard University, particularly Elizabeth Falsey, Acting Curator of Manuscripts.

To Fayetta McKown I am grateful for the critical perspicacity and teaching skills which informed my first exposure to Hawthorne, Thoreau and Emerson. To my husband, Christopher Britton, and my children, Anders and Kirsten Lustgarten, I am obliged for their willingness to somewhat rewrite their own lives temporarily, in order to accommodate my writing Fuller's.

Donna Dickenson
Oxford, March 1992

1

'My God, How I Hated Her!'

'My dear Sir,' I exclaimed, 'if you'd not been afraid
Of Margaret Fuller's success, you'd have stayed
Your hand in her case and more justly have rated her.'
Here he murmured morosely, 'My God, how I hated her!'[1]

Margaret Fuller was privileged in her lifetime, from 1810 to 1850 – as a woman editor, essayist, political journalist and arts critic in an otherwise largely male domain – because she was one of the first of her kind. When women began entering the literary lists in greater numbers – after Fuller's death and partly through her inspiration – she became a greater threat, to be excoriated and exorcised. Yet throughout her life she herself was ambivalent about her critical and creative abilities, saying of herself that 'I have no art'. Such diffidence was further ammunition against her after her death: she was taken at her own modest word by male successors who 'came to praise but also, perhaps unconsciously, to bury her.'[2]

This pattern – of a male sense of menace from literary women, who felt themselves to be more threatened than threatening – was general in the nineteenth and twentieth centuries, write Sandra Gilbert and Susan Gubar in their *No Man's Land*.

Though, for the most part, nineteenth- and twentieth-century women writers have been far less confident of women's victory than their male contemporaries were, they nevertheless document the casualties of a battle of the sexes, a battle over the zone that many men experienced as a no man's land because it debilitated masculinity but that a number of women defined, if only fleetingly, as a no man's land because it seemed to herald what [the American feminist writer] Charlotte Perkins Gilman called a "Herland". That women have been less confident may seem paradoxical, in view of the resentment with which such men as . . .

1

T.S. Eliot, D.H. Lawrence, Ernest Hemingway and Norman Mailer reacted to what they perceived as unprecedented female power. Yet when we turn to works by women who were contemporaries of these men, we find that female writers have often felt even more imperiled than men did by the sexual combat in which they were obliged to engage. For, as is so frequently the case in the history of sex relations, men view the smallest female steps towards autonomy as threatening strides that will strip them of all authority, while women respond . . . with a nervous sense of guilt and a paradoxical sense of vulnerability.[3]

But Gilbert and Gubar's focus is on the turn-of-the-century period and after; Fuller died exactly at the midpoint of the century. This alone makes things much more complicated. If literary men of the late nineteenth and early twentieth centuries felt themselves to be under siege, it was by a monstrous regiment of women novelists, the most successful of whom wrote after Fuller: George Eliot was their chief of command. Male reaction was typified by Algernon Charles Swinburne, who wrote to his friend Edmund Gosse that 'George Eliot was hounding on her myrmidons to his destruction.' As I argued in my earlier *George Sand*,

> . . . men of letters in [Henry] James's generation and after were stymied by a Himalayan range of female novelists – George Eliot, the Brontës, Jane Austen, and George Sand – which now stood between them and their [eighteenth-century] forefathers. Whereas Elizabeth Barrett Browning had complained that she sought everywhere for grandmothers and found none, Lawrence, James, and other late-nineteenth- or early-twentieth-century writers looked for literary fathers and saw only 'thinking bosoms.'[4]

Initially Fuller *was* respected and successful: not only the first woman critic to earn a living by her journalism, but the premier critic of either sex – and a best-selling author with her *Woman in the Nineteenth Century* (1845).[5] Although male reaction to her work – particularly to *Woman* – was sometimes vituperative and violent, her most entrenched critics were known to change their minds on meeting her – as was true of George Sand's literary enemies. Both women, depicted as monsters of egotism by disparagers, were in fact good conversationalists who disarmed their opponents with their equable reasonability. During their lifetimes, Fuller and Sand were 'allowed' fame by the male literary establishment; the most malicious legends, the critical downgrading and the most intense misogyny only began after their deaths.

But even if men of letters felt at their most vulnerable in the late nineteenth and early twentieth centuries, as Gilbert and Gubar argue, early nineteenth-century men were suspicious enough to narrow the gates so that only one female invader at a time could pass. In her time, Fuller was that one. Norman Podhoretz, in his essay 'Making It',[6] suggested that at most only one woman of her generation and place is allowed to be the 'Dark Lady', the intellectual superstar of her sex. This female lead in the mid twentieth-century United States was acted first by Mary McCarthy, and then by Susan Sontag; perhaps the equivalent English figure might be Margaret Drabble. Clearly Sand was the Dark Lady of mid nineteenth-century France.

Elaine Showalter has identified Margaret Fuller as the Dark Lady of the American Renaissance. Showalter goes on to suggest that the Dark Lady is inevitably punished for accepting the eminence thrust upon her, citing recent harsh criticism of Sontag's previously influential work. Could this also help to explain the *volte-face* in Fuller's reputation after her death?

In fact the two explanations, drawn from Showalter and from Gilbert and Gubar, reinforce rather than contradict each other when applied to Fuller. The late nineteenth-century male critic or writer's feeling of being besieged by an occupying army of literary ladies was less pronounced in the literary men of Fuller's time, but it was there. Although it was American women, Susanna Rowson (1762–1824) and Lydia Huntley Sigourney (1791–1865), who were the first writers of either sex to earn a living by the pen, the high tide of American women's literary success came later. By midcentury 'Woman's Fiction' dominated the marketplace,[7] much to the later discomfiture of Henry James, who believed that

> women, with their free use of leisure, were the chief consumers of novels and therefore were increasingly becoming producers of them. The feminine attitude, now disengaging itself from that of men, was in point of fact coming to be all that the novel was.[8]

Women novelists were widely read, to the extent that President Lincoln introduced Harriet Beecher Stowe as 'the little lady who made this great war'. In the 1850s the combined sales of all the works of Hawthorne, Melville, Thoreau, Emerson and Whitman were less than the typical sales of any one of the popular domestic novels.[9] By the 1870s about two-fifths of the poems published in the *Atlantic Monthly* were by women, as were three-quarters of the novels on the market. The American novelist Silas Weir Mitchell griped in 1887, 'The monthly magazines are getting so lady-like that naturally they will soon menstruate.'[10] By 1896, the American poet Louise Guiney could boast, 'The women over here are regular Atalantas in the poetic race.'[11] The 'feminisation of American culture',[12] some writers argue, had sentimentalised the arts, theology, and popular attitudes and cast doubt on whether male writers could be 'real men.' By the early twentieth century, this terrible emasculation was complete, according to Harold Sterns, writing in 1922:

> Hardly any intelligent foreigner has failed to observe and com-
> ment upon the extraordinary feminization of American social life,
> and . . . the intellectual anemia or torpor that seems to accompany
> it . . . [M]en and women in America share their intellectual life
> . . . The men have been feminized.[13]

It is less than clear why sharing intellectual life should mean that men must be 'feminised,' rather than women 'masculinised' – and still less obvious why 'feminisation' produces 'anemia or torpor.' But if the dreaded 'feminisation' seemed a raging epidemic by the early twentieth century, men of the early nineteenth century were already drawing attention to its first symptoms. Although the microbes were few in number, American men feared themselves particularly vulnerable to the disease:

> Cut off not only from the long history of the English fatherland
> but also from the literary patrilineage . . . American artists felt
> simultaneously rebellious towards the British tradition and emas-
> culated by their alienation from the authority of that tradition.
> Thus they reacted to the achievements of women more quickly
> than their British contemporaries did, and reacted by beginning
> to create a myth of America as a country of aggressive women.[14]

If intellectual American men of the early part of the century were smarting under taunts of inferiority, it was primarily as Americans rather than as men. Under attack as 'provincials', however, American men of letters did choose to see themselves also under threat as men, although there was no such Himalayan range of literary women cutting them off from their forefathers as there was for late nine-teenth-century male novelists. But there was an ocean – and there-fore no hope of reinforcements against the incipient female uprising.

In 1820, for example, the editor of the *Edinburgh Review*, Sidney Smith, had jeered, 'In all the four corners of the globe, who reads an American book?'[15] The response of certain prominent American men of letters, however, was to blame women for having already begun to 'feminise' previous American culture and to vow a new heroic model of American literature which would be all man. Ralph Waldo Emerson – who occupied a pivotal position both in relation to the American Renaissance and to Fuller's work, as her posthumous editor – promised a new 'manly' Americanness in response to Smith's taunt, later writing 'Give me initiative, spermatic, prophesying, man-making words.'[16] Twentieth-century critics, male as well as female, have come to see Emerson as obsessively concerned with sexual politics in language: 'a priest and a psychologist of the combined power of language and sex.'[17] So little room for women was there in the new American literature, as Emerson proposed and composed it, that

> if an inhabitant of another planet should visit the earth, he would receive, on the whole, a truer notion of human life by attending an Italian opera than he would by reading Emerson's volumes. He would learn from the Italian opera that there are two sexes; and this, after all, is probably the fact with which the education of such a stranger ought to begin.[18]

If women were to be allowed any place in this new American pan-theon, there could at most be one Dark Lady, one solitary goddess, half muse, half mother. Later I will suggest that this is exactly the role into which Emerson pushed Fuller during her co-editorship of *The Dial* with him. I will also discuss the problems which Fuller had in breaking away from Emerson's influence. She could and did use the same language of 'manliness'; but she could never be a native of that country.

EMERSON AND THE OTHER EDITORS OF THE *MEMOIRS*

It was Emerson, too, who began the process of mythologising Fuller into obscurity after her death. As one of three editors of her posthumous *Memoirs*, together with James Freeman Clarke and William Henry Channing, friends of Fuller's youth, he rewrote the heroic epic which she had lived into a novelette. The 'best possible motives' with which he and his fellow editors were generally acknowledged to have acted[19] – saving Fuller's sexual reputation – absolved them of any blame for finishing the 'autobiography' which her premature death had stopped short. They rewrote her life, apparently with her own posthumous permission.

The three editors' names did not even appear on the title page of the *Memoirs* which re-invented Fuller in their preferred image. Nevertheless, Emerson sold more copies of Fuller's *Memoirs* than of any work of his own: his *Nature* (1836) took seven years to clear an edition of 500 copies. Fuller's *Woman in the Nineteenth Century* (1845) sold out an edition twice that size in one week. Published in two volumes by Phillips, Sampson and Company of Boston in February 1852, the *Memoirs* appeared in Britain (in three volumes) shortly thereafter, with great popular success though some personal calumny from the critics. At least forty critical notices appeared in British and American periodicals, and A.H. Clough wrote to Emerson in June 1852 that the *Memoirs* was one of the 'two most circulating books of the [British] libraries I think.'[20]

Although the surviving members of the Fuller family had co-operated with the three editors, they were so dismayed by the distortions of the *Memoirs* that they commissioned an alternative, authorised biography. The writer, Caroline W. Healey – a former student at Fuller's 'Boston Conversations' classes – wrote that the Fullers wanted to 'put an end many absurd and painful rumours which had followed the publication of the first *Memoir*.'[21] But the early death of Fuller's brother Richard Frederick – the main mover in the enterprise – put an end to the project. Healey's volume, *Margaret and her Friends*, did not appear until 1895. By then even more harm had been done.

The *Memoirs* give the impression of having been written entirely by Fuller herself, except the letters and eulogies from friends and the biographical sections on her life in Cambridge, Concord and Boston, explicitly attributed to James Freeman Clarke and Emerson. But the manuscript which went down with Fuller in the shipwreck off Fire Island in July 1850 was an eyewitness history of the Roman revolution. She had written no *Memoirs* before she died young, and indeed I shall argue later that she lacked the egotism ever to have done so, no matter how long she might have lived. Indeed, she destroyed her early diaries – hardly the action of someone preparing eventually to write memoirs. (Fuller did write semi-autobiographical fables, but how much *is* autobiography and how much critical reading-in remains open to question.) The mere act of presenting memoirs ostensibly from Fuller's own hand itself reinforced the image of a monster of unfeminine egotism which the *Memoirs* promoted. After all, she was much too young to have written her memoirs. It was this stereotype – of a bulging-eyed, bulging-ego'd, self-appointed sybil – which caused many a literary gentleman, and no doubt some women too, to remark, 'My God, how I hated her!'[22]

I do not believe that Emerson, Clarke and Channning chose the term 'memoirs' out of sheer Machiavellian cunning. Calls for a selected volume of her writings, to be accompanied by a memoir, began appearing almost immediately after Fuller's death.[23] The editors' original title for the memorial volume which they began planning at that time was *Margaret and Her Friends*. As a later chapter argues, her capacity for friendship was one of Fuller's greatest strengths, and that title would have been more true to life. However, the editors decided that such a form would be dramatically unworkable: it would require 'the queen' – as they somewhat derisively dubbed Fuller – to be on stage all the while, surrounded by an admiring chorus – in which they were rather loath to play their part.

Nor do I necessarily mean to imply that the three editors themselves hated Fuller. In a way, her reputation would have been less damaged if they had. The mushy thought and the prissy self which the editors presented as the real Margaret – in the name of respectability – killed off interest in Fuller more effectively than blatant mud-slinging could ever have done.

Again, George Sand's posthumous reputation affords an interesting comparison. The French Senate, in a wave of anti-republican legislation under the Third Empire, proposed to ban all Sand's works from public libraries. But Sand's friend, the critic Sainte-Beuve, pleaded against total censorship and succeeded in persuading the Senate to exempt two short bucolic romances, *La Petite Fadette* and *La Mare au Diable*. Since only these two novels out of her sixty or seventy were known to subsequent generations of French readers, she was slighted as a writer of rural fantasies for adolescent girls. Had Sand been totally proscribed, she might have been remembered as the socialist writer who was too subversive to be allowed a voice.

Like Sand, Fuller was vulnerable to charges of sexual impropriety as well as political radicalism, and it was against these slurs that her editors sought to 'protect' her – or legitimise their own acquaintance with her, as a cynic might prefer to put it. The nub was the question of whether and when Fuller had married Marchese Giovanni Angelo Ossoli, before or after the birth of their son Angelo Eugene Philip on 5 September, 1848. Fuller and Ossoli had kept the date and indeed the existence of their marriage secret until shortly before their return to America, fearing censure and disinheritance from his family.

In a letter to her sister Ellen, written on 11 December 1849, Fuller had predicted that Emerson would be the among the least sympathetic to Ossoli of her acquaintances, when news of the marriage did reach him. (As with Sand and Chopin, Fuller had attracted a younger man; and Ossoli was not cast in the stiff New England intellectual mould.) 'I expect that to many of my friends Mr Emerson for one, he will be nothing, and they will not understand that I should have life in common with him.'[24] Most tellingly, the reference to Emerson in this letter was crossed out by one of the editors in the *Memoirs* version.

Perhaps it would have been better for Fuller's reputation if Emerson had followed his original inclination to decline editorship of the *Memoirs* – on the grounds that Fuller wasn't important enough. Those who knew both Emerson and Fuller well, like her younger brother Richard, thought Emerson the sort of friend who puts enemies out of work. In a prescient letter of 1845 he wrote to Margaret:

> Emerson is not your true friend. I know that thoroughly, and I rejoice that you are away from him. His influence is bad, and he does not know you. I was pained by his saying of your book [*Woman in the Nineteenth Century*], that you ought not to write, you talked so well.[25]

Added to the editors' prurience about Fuller's Italian years was their fear of what might be revealed about their own idiosyncrasies when Fuller's correspondence with them was printed. Fuller had a talent for inspiring confidences. Very soon after her death, Emerson wrote in his journal: 'When I heard that a trunk of her correspondence had been found and opened, I felt what a panic would strike all her friends, for it was as if a clever reporter had got underneath a confessional and agreed to report all that transpired there in Wall street.'[26] What he had to fear appears to have been less any sort of sexual innuendo than the embarrassing revelation that Fuller could actually make the august sage of Concord laugh. He recorded of their first meeting in July 1835:

> She had a dangerous reputation for satire, in addition to her great scholarship . . . her talk was a comedy in which dramatic justice was done to everybody's foibles. I remember that she made me laugh more than I liked . . . She had an incredible variety of anecdotes, and the readiest wit to give an absurd turn to whatever passed; and the eyes, which were so plain at first, soon swam with fun and drolleries, and the very tides of joy and superabundant life.[27]

Very little of Fuller's wit survives in the *Memoirs*, which are high-minded to the point of windiness. Perhaps this pomposity represents a deliberate editorial decision to exclude anything which might be construed as gossip. James Freeman Clarke, another of Fuller's editors, admitted in his entry for the *Memoirs* that he felt a similar trepidation to Emerson's:

> The difficulty which we all feel in describing our past intercourse and friendship with Margaret Fuller is, that the intercourse was so intimate, and the friendship so personal, that it is like making a confession to the public of our most private selves. For this noble person, by her keen insight and her generous interest, entered into the depth of every soul with which she stood in any real relation.[28]

Despite their own nervousness about what might be revealed, the three editors enjoyed the co-operation of the Fuller family – except for the relatives' suppression of letters to an earlier lover, James Nathan, a German businessman whom Fuller met in New York – and of scores of friends and correspondents in both America and Europe. They had difficulty keeping the volume of material in good order; some letters vanished through carelessness. However, the editors' sins were not only of omission, but of commission as well.

> In many ways the book was a notable success, for her biographers were talented men . . . But Channing, Clarke and Emerson so bowdlerized and manipulated their evidence as to ruin a splendid book. The *Memoirs of Margaret Fuller Ossoli* is a mess . . . [T]he mid-

nineteenth century did not share our insistence on the sanctity of texts. For them, private writing was just that: private. No one saw a problem in excising paragraphs written in haste or sickness, in pique or passion; no one doubted the need to protect the reputations of surviving friends and acquaintances. The evidence, though, suggests another level of creation, an attempt to make Fuller intellectually safer and sexually acceptable, her marriage normal, her son legitimate . . . *Memoirs of Margaret Fuller Ossoli* went beyond its functions as a memorial to a dead friend: it created a mythic Margaret Fuller.[29]

Of the three editors, Emerson was actually less brutal in his mishandling of precious manuscripts than Channing, who married together separate letters and drastically altered Fuller's language. The editor of the authenticated modern version of the *Letters*, Robert Hudspeth, quoted above, calls Channing's section of the *Memoirs* 'a briar patch'. Wrong identifications are common, Hudspeth asserts, and 'capricious' transmogrifications of Fuller's language abound. Some of these changes are blue-stocking beyond twentieth-century belief: references to 'Jesus' are altered to 'a saint', for example.[30] It is ironic that Fuller's style as it was left to us – often seen as frilly, namby-pamby, prissy and florid, quintessentially a 'woman's way of writing' – was so much the product of her male editors. The *Memoirs* supposedly allowed Fuller to speak to subsequent generations, but the editors wrote the lines.

All the editors of the *Memoirs* largely ignored Fuller's work as editor of *The Dial* – the donkey work of editing which Emerson himself had refused – and her triumphs as the most successful literary critic and foreign correspondent of her generation. When they did mention her achievements rather than her foibles, they attributed them to frustrated spinsterly energy. Even Channing, whom Fuller's biographer Bell Gale Chevigny calls 'the one of the three who seems to have struggled hardest against his sexual prejudices,' trips into this snare:

> The very glow of her poetic enthusiasm was but an outflush of trustful affection; the very restlessness of her intellect was the confession that her heart had found no home . . . [H]er absorption in study [was] the natural vent of emotions which had met no object worthy of life-long attachment.[31]

Lest twentieth-century readers smile too readily at this as long-dead male condescension, Ted Hughes believes exactly the same of Emily Dickinson: '[T]he eruption of her imagination and poetry followed when she shifted her passion, with the energy of desperation, from [the] lost man onto his only possible substitute – the Universe in its Divine aspect.'[32] Literary production is clearly second-best to a husband, and the professional inevitably secondary to the personal in such male views of woman writers – even a woman who had so little personal life as Dickinson.

But Channing was freer in his praises of Fuller – for her 'directness, terseness and practicality' – than was Emerson, though Emerson was the better textual scholar. Emerson omitted the names of almost all correspondents – preserving the sanctity of the confessional, as he might have seen it. He ran together letters and journal entries and took quotations out of context, but he did not deliberately rewrite passages.

The tone of Emerson's entry on Fuller shares, however, the same malevolent superiority as his patronising dismissal of Thoreau's talents in the funeral oration which he delivered at the younger man's grave. In later life Emerson changed his mind about Fuller, finding her letters much more profound and astute on rereading them than he had while he was editing the *Memoirs*;[33] but the critical damage to her reputation had already been done by his generally unfavourable judgement there. Perhaps by his later years, Emerson no longer felt so threatened by Fuller's superior sales and worldwide reputation – having done his conscious or unconscious best to undermine them. Still, Emerson's dismissal of Thoreau does at least indicate that he bore Fuller no particular ill-will because she was a woman; his jealousy was distributed justly and evenly among both sexes.

But Emerson's damning faint praise of Fuller is additionally informed by the fact of her femaleness. During the time that he was editing the *Memoirs*, he wrote in his journal: 'The unlooked for trait in all these journals to me is the Woman, poor woman: they are all hysterical. She is bewailing her virginity and languishing for a husband'.[34]

Emerson also lays great stress on Fuller's supposed ugliness – accepted as fact by subsequent critics, though feminists have pointed out that Thoreau's horsy nose and Emerson's fishy eyes have never been held against *them*. The abiding image of Fuller has been the one

Emerson paints: bulging eyes, half-closed in perpetual sybilline contemplation; dishwater-blond locks; and a stooped posture. 'It is to be said that Margaret made a disagreeable first impression on most persons, including those who became afterwards her best friends, to such an extent that they did not wish to be in the same room with her.'[35]

Male bitchiness about Fuller's appearance has continued apace. Henry James imagined her as 'glossily ringletted and monumentally breastpinned;' Perry Miller as 'phenomenally homely,' her hair 'not quite blond, stringy and thin.'[36] But the most salacious have been her admirers:

> At thirteen her breasts were so developed that she seemed eighteen, or twenty . . . Her hair was blond, fine and softspun, reflecting light like buckwheat honey when poured from a pottery jar. Her mouth was soft and curving . . .[37]

Other contributors to the *Memoirs* thought that Fuller was inclined to exaggerate her own plainness – as she did her own lack of 'Art'. Here, subsequent generations have taken Fuller at her own over-modest word, and at Emerson's over-censorious one. The Reverend F.H. Hedge remembered her differently:

> . . . [S]he had no pretensions to beauty. Yet she was not plain. She escaped the reproach of positive plainness, by her blond and abundant hair, by her excellent teeth, by her sparkling, dancing, busy eyes which, though usually half closed from near-sightedness, shot piercing glances at those with whom she conversed, and most of all, by the very peculiar and graceful carriage of her head and neck, which all who knew her will remember as the most characteristic trait in her personal appearance.[38]

The third editor of the *Memoirs* was James Freeman Clarke, a Unitarian minister and a close friend of Fuller's youth. Halfway through the compilation of the volumes, he had taken over as co-editor from another youthful friend, Sam Ward – who had himself departed taking with him a clutch of letters which were never seen again. (Ward seems to have despaired of the project, writing to Emerson: 'How can you describe a Force? How can you write the life of Margaret?'[39]) Clarke thus had less impact on the finished manuscript than did Emerson or Channing, though even that has to be a speculation: few of the primary sources entrusted to him survive, so that comparison of his versions and the originals is usually impossible. However, the influence which he did exert was perhaps more than was healthy.

For example, in a surviving letter of 1834 expressing her doubts about Christian belief to Hedge, Fuller had written, 'My mind often burns with thoughts on these subjects and I long to pour out my soul to some person of superior calmness and strength and fortunate in more accurate knowledge.'[40] Clarke replaces Fuller's words with more grandiloquent ones and twists the sentence structure to make it *less* grammatical: 'My mind often *swells* with thoughts on these subjects, *which I long to pour out on* some person of superior calmness and strength, and fortunate in more accurate knowledge.' And Clarke strikes out altogether the impious sentence which preceded this one, Fuller's statement that 'I have no confidence in God as a Father, if I could believe in Revelation and consequently in an over-ruling Providence many things which seem dark and hateful to me now would be made clear or I could wait.'[41]

At least Clarke did his best to spread an image of a Fuller ambivalent about her own powers. In contrast to Emerson's reminiscence of her, which coined the term that stuck forever after – 'a rather mountainous me'[42] – Clarke thought Fuller arrogant only on the surface. In contrast to her underlying modesty about herself, Clarke thought, she estimated her friends too highly. She possessed, he said, 'genuine humility, which being a love of truth, underlaid her whole character, notwithstanding its seeming pride. She could not have been as great as she was, without it.'[43]

Unlike Emerson, Clarke does generously acknowledge Fuller's 'greatness', and even uses the term 'heroic' to describe her career. This, however, he views more as a foible than a virtue, accusing her of 'an idolatrous hero-worship of genius and power.'[44] (In their mutual youth Fuller had often reassured Clarke that he would achieve the fame he lusted after, so that his remark seems more than a little disingenuous.) Both Emerson and Clarke were much concerned to disallow anything so unfeminine as personal ambition in Fuller. Despite his arguably contradictory view of her 'mountainous me,' Emerson explicitly denied that Fuller was ambitious – which perhaps tells us more about Emerson than about Fuller.

A woman in our society finds her safety and happiness in exclusions and privacies. She congratulates herself when she is not called to the market, to the courts, to the polls, to the stage, or to the orchestra . . . [W]illingly she [Fuller] was confined to the usual circles and methods of female talent.[45]

Fuller could not with decorum be allowed both longing for personal fame and thirst for the abstract absolute, though male Romantics might wear both these modish Byronic garments:

> If ever she was ambitious of knowledge and talent, as a means of excelling others, and gaining fame, position, admiration, – this vanity had passed before I knew her, and was replaced by the profound desire for a full development of her whole nature, by means of a full experience of life.[46]

Some biographers have thought to make 'amends' by pointing out – as did David Watson in his 1987 study of Fuller[47] – that *both* Emerson and Fuller had Everests for egos. Yet Fuller spent the best of her youth teaching her younger siblings for five to eight hours a day, doing the household dressmaking, making soap and bread for a large family, and tending her sick mother and grandmother, while desperately trying to continue her self-education at a time when most of her male colleagues were strolling in the groves of academe. The letters as restored by Hudspeth document her continuous preoccupation with her family's wellbeing and financial support. There is frustratingly little of *her* in much of her correspondence – though quite a lot on providing coats and books for her younger brothers – and in fact precious little correspondence during the years when she was most heavily weighed down with domestic labour.

Self-abnegation combined in Fuller with self-cultivation. The most telling and poignant example of her modesty is the shipwreck itself. The boat did not go down immediately: there was time for the captain and crew to rescue other passengers' jewellery, watches, money, figs and wine. But Fuller did not like to trouble the sailors to bring up the heavy trunk containing her manuscript history of the Italian revolution. It went down with her, and, like her body, was never found.[48]

Although Fuller does sometimes sound pretentious in her early letters to Emerson, that tone reflects her own insecurity in addressing the great man, I think. This is the mode in which he would have expected an acolyte to hail him, and Fuller was willing to play that role. (Even before she met him she wrote, 'I cannot think I should be disappointed in him as I have been in others to whom I had hoped to look up.'[49] The mountainousness is almost entirely Emerson's:

> ... Emerson can say, 'Most of the persons whom I see in my own house I see across a gulf; I cannot go to them nor they come to me.' This hero is not at home engaged in intimate conversation; he appears more comfortable 'towering . . . over the culture of the United States' or, perhaps, standing on a mountaintop thundering commandments to a multitude. He is a purely male 'prophet', and, indeed, purely a prophet of maleness.[50]

Emerson's reaction to Fuller's death was to enter this comment in his journal: 'I have lost in her my audience.' Although he wrote tenderly of her in some parts of his contribution to the *Memoirs*, his affection is largely possessive, his conceit stupendous, and his compliments often backhanded:

> ... [Fuller] studied my tastes, piqued and amused me, challenged frankness by frankness, and did not conceal the good opinion of me she brought with her, nor her wish to please . . .[51]

> She drew her companions to surprising confessions. She was the wedding-guest, to whom the long-pent story must be told . . . [O]ne seemed to see his life *en beau*, and was flattered by beholding what he had found so tedious in its workaday weeds, shining in glorious costume . . . The auditor jumped for joy, and thirsted for unlimited draughts. What? is this the dame, who, I heard, was sneering and critical? this the blue-stocking, of whom I stood in terror and dislike? this wondrous woman, full of counsel, full of tenderness . . .[52]

Not only did the three editors create a 'Margaret myth' which – like this quotation – tells us more about them than about Fuller; their violation of the letters and manuscripts entrusted to them has been impossible to make fully right, despite the assiduous textual analysis of Robert Hudspeth's authenticated edition. The editors snipped out chunks of Fuller's letters and pasted them on their text. The resulting manuscript came back from the printers in a filthy condition, too illegible for any further use. Of the letters which remain, some have paragraphs blotted by purple ink, passages in Fuller's hand struck out and editorial changes written in over her words. Not only did the editors of the *Memoirs* write this woman's life for her; they made sure – by incompetence or design, it matters little which – that no one else could rewrite it. Fuller was wrecked twice over.

Some modern biographers of Fuller have excused the editors of the *Memoirs* on the grounds that they were only following Fuller's own model of criticism.[53] Factual details of the text or the author's life were less important to her than the symbolic value of the work and the spiritual character of the author, this view holds. But neither the texts nor the portrait is accurate in the *Memoirs*. I have argued that this should not be surprising. Emerson, in particular, could not afford to allow an accurate rendering.

Some of the *un*intentional inaccuracy in drawing Fuller comes from the editors' choice of pen and ink rather than oils. Almost entirely absent from the *Memoirs* is the richly coloured social and European dimension to Fuller's thought which replaced the black-and-white New England individualism. At best, the three editors could only have drawn the Fuller they knew before her European quest of 1846–50. To be fair, they were aware of their limitations, and requested contributions from the Brownings and Giuseppe Mazzini, who knew Fuller well in her last years. But they did not seek remembrances from most of the stars in the galaxy of European intellectuals and social reformers with whom Fuller was acquainted: George Sand, Thomas Carlyle, the Polish patriot Adam Mickiewicz, the exiled Italian revolutionary aristocrat Costanza Arconati Visconti, the English reformer and essayist Harriet Martineau, and many others. And the reminiscences from Mazzini and the Brownings were 'mysteriously' lost, as Fuller's biographer Bell Gale Chevigny puts it.[54]

Chevigny thinks that the editors of the *Memoirs* were actually rather jealous of the freedom which Fuller found in Europe, and that the inaccuracy of the portrait is largely deliberate. Whatever the editors' motivation, they left out the successful end in Italy of Fuller's quest to relive the tales of Roman heroism on which she had been fed as a girl. Instead, Emerson, Clarke and Channing left posterity with a myth of a thwarted spinster continually knocking against the walls of her time and place, driven into hysteria by that woman's curse, a superfluity of blood.

I think, in her case, there was something abnormal in those obscure habits and necessities which we denote by the word Temperament. In the first days of our acquaintance, I felt her to be a foreigner, – that, with her, one would always be sensible of some barrier, as if in making up a friendship with a cultivated Spaniard or Turk. She had a strong constitution, and of course its reactions were strong; and this is the reason why in all her life she has so much to say of her fate . . . I had always an impression that her energy was too much a force of blood . . . It were long to tell her peculiarities. Her childhood was full of presentiments. She was then a somnabulist. She was subject to attacks of delirium, and, later, perceived that she had spectral illusions . . .[55]

The image of Fuller which the *Memoirs* convey is preachy, smug, and sometimes seriously potty. Emerson's supposed tribute leaves the reader with the same impression of a second-rate mind that the listener was meant to imbibe from his funeral oration on Thoreau. In Fuller's case, the impression that she simply wasn't very good is reinforced by the implication that she had overstepped the bounds of sense to compensate for her inferior sensibility. It is a similar charge to Emerson's slur against Thoreau: 'In the absence of a vision, he had renounced too much.'

She paid homage to rocks, woods, flowers, rivers and the moon. She spent a good deal of time outdoors, sitting, perhaps, with a book in some sheltered recess commanding a landscape. She watched by day and night, the skies and the earth, and believed she knew all their expressions. She wrote in her journal, or in her correspondence, a series of 'moonlights', in which she seriously attempts to describe the light and scenery of successive nights of the summer moon. Of course her raptures must appear sickly and superficial to an observer, who with equal feeling, had better powers of observation.[56]

Now who might that observer be? Here Emerson claims for himself both the 'feminine' power of feeling – in which Fuller might be expected to excel – and a superior, implicitly 'masculine' power of observation. Further, Emerson associates Fuller with the pale, derivative moon, a popular nineteenth-century symbol of the inferior female in visual art. As Bram Dijkstra puts it,

For the artists the link between the moon and woman – her weakness, her imitative nature, her passivity, and her emotional waxings and wanings – was a subject with far too many attractive

symbolic possibilities to ignore . . . The moon represented woman's sterile, self-reflective identity.[57]

This is typical of the empire-building in which Emerson's section of
the *Memoirs* indulges. There was to be no room for women in this
new land. Ultimately, even one Dark Lady, one eerie Hecate, was
one too many.

Emerson's section of the *Memoirs* is not unflaggingly small-minded.
He credited Fuller with 'a broad good sense, which brought her near
to all people.'[58] He praised her industry in educating herself under
adverse circumstances, but also sought to dispel the already-
prevalent impression that she harped endlessly on her own exceptional intellect.

> This rumour was much spread abroad, that she was sneering,
> scoffing, critical, disdainful of humble people, and of all but the
> intellectual. I had heard it whenever she was named. It was a
> superficial judgment. Her satire was only the pastime and neces-
> sity of her talent, the play of superabundant animal spirits . . .
> [H]er mind presently disclosed many moods and powers, in suc-
> cessive platforms or terraces, each above each, that quite effaced
> this first impression.[59]

In Fuller's absence from New England, tongues had already begun
to wag and mud to fly. Revenging an unfavourable review of his
poetry, James Russell Lowell had published in 1848 a widely circulated satirical portrait of Fuller, 'the whole of whose being's a capital
I . . .'[60] (Lowell later repented of his satire when he learned that Fuller
was then largely penniless in Italy, but the damage was done.)
Emerson should not get all the blame for the generally unflattering
angle from which Fuller's portrait was done in the *Memoirs*; sometimes he tried to soften the lighting.

But the abiding impression left by Emerson's treatment of Fuller
is of *his* failure, of nerve. In discussing the *Memoirs* project with the
original third editor, Sam Ward, Emerson had predicted – with a
frankness which *is* admirable – that it might demand a valour he
didn't possess: 'I think it could really be done, if one would heroic-
ally devote himself, but . . . it might turn out to be a work above our
courage.'[61] A letter written by Fuller to William Henry Channing on
25 August 1842 seems to foretell Emerson's failure in a poignant and
eerie way.

After the first excitement of intimacy with him [Emerson], – when I was made so happy by his high tendency, absolute purity, the freedom and infinite graces of an intellect much beyond any I had known, – came with me the questioning season. I was greatly disappointed in my relation to him. I was, indeed, always called on to be worthy, – this benefit was sure in our friendship. But I found no intelligence of my best self; far less was it revealed to me in new modes; for not only did he seem to want the living faith which enables one to discharge his holiest office of a friend, but he absolutely distrusted me in every region of my life with which he was unacquainted . . . But now I am better acquainted with him . . . the 'I shall learn' with which he answers every accusation, is no less true. No one can feel his limitations, in fact, more than he, though he always speaks confidently from his present knowledge as all he has yet, and never qualifies or explains. He feels himself 'shut up in a crystal cell,' from which only 'a great love or a great task could release me,' and hardly expects either from what remains in this life.[62]

Had Emerson been able to break through this xenophobia about any region of Fuller's life of which he was not a native, the *Memoirs* project might have released him from his 'crystal cell.' Even dead, Fuller could have been the prince who kissed the sleeper awake. But this time Emerson's 'I shall learn' was false.

That is all the sadder in that Emerson was genuinely fond of Fuller, though on his own terms. Of her visits to Concord, he wrote that 'her arrival was a holiday'. He had described Fuller warmly in a letter of introduction to Thomas Carlyle: '[O]f all the travellers whom you have so kindly received from me, I think of none . . . whom I so much desired that you should see and like, as this dear old friend of mine.' But Emerson could not bring himself to write such a generous reference for Fuller to posterity in the *Memoirs*. Abstract and dead, she became a presence to be feared, a harbinger of the disaster of 'feminisation' in American literature and culture.

HAWTHORNE AND HIGGINSON

The same impression – an initial offering of good will and trust to Fuller, later burnt out by professional jealousy – is left by Nathaniel Hawthorne's damaging but influential depiction of Fuller. Although

in life Fuller counted Hawthorne more 'a brother to me, than ever
. . . any man before',[63] Hawthorne fulminated after her death against
'a damned mob of scribbling women'.[64] More woundingly, he created in *The Blithedale Romance* (1852) a character who was widely
assumed to be Fuller, with implications which were less than flattering. Most unpleasantly of all, he wrote in his notebooks – later
published by his son with much fanfare – that Fuller was better off
dead.

Hawthorne had many and various contacts with Fuller – through
the attendance of his wife and her family at Fuller's further education classes for women, the Boston 'Conversations' of 1839–44; the
utopian socialist community at Brook Farm; and her editorship of
the Transcendentalist journal, *The Dial*. But Fuller was only an occasional visitor at Brook Farm, and Hawthorne never a fully paid-
up Transcendentalist. They were simply friends who enjoyed each
other's company during her visits to Emerson in Concord, as
Hawthorne recounts in his notebooks for 1842, describing a golden
afternoon in an unlikely location:

> [E]ntering Sleepy Hollow [cemetery], I perceived a lady reclining
> near the path which bends along its verge. It was Margaret her-
> self. She had been there the whole afternoon, meditating or read-
> ing; for she had a book in her hand, with some strange title, which
> I did not understand, and have forgotten. She said that nobody
> had broken her solitude, and was just giving utterance to a theory
> that no inhabitant of Concord ever visited Sleepy Hollow, when
> we saw a whole group of people entering the sacred precincts.
> Most of them followed a path that led them remote from us; but
> an old man passed near us, and smiled to see Margaret lying on
> the ground, and me sitting by her side. He made some remark
> about the beauty of the afternoon and withdrew himself into the
> shadow of the wood. Then we talked about Autumn – and about
> the pleasures of getting lost in the woods – and about the crows,
> whose voices Margaret had heard – and about the experiences of
> early childhood, whose influence remains upon the character
> after the collection [sic] of them has passed away – and about the
> sight of mountains from a distance, and the view from their
> summits – and about other matters of high and low philosophy.
> In the midst of our talk we heard footsteps above us, on the high
> bank; and while the intruder was still hidden among the trees, he
> called to Margaret, of whom he had gotten a glimpse. Then he

emerged from the green shade; and, behold, it was Mr. Emerson, who, in spite of his clerical consecration, had found no better way of spending the Sabbath than to ramble among the woods. He appeared to have had a pleasant time; for he said that there were Muses in the woods to-day, and whispers to be heard in the breezes. It being now nearly six o'clock, we separated, Mr. Emerson and Margaret towards his house, and I towards mine, where my little wife was very busy getting tea.[65]

There is an droll contrast between the manly philosophical conversation which Hawthorne and Fuller enjoy and Emerson's sickly speculations on whispers and Muses. But if Hawthorne found Fuller fascinating for the stimulus of her company, in the end he returned home to his 'little wife'. A similar plot underlies A Blithedale Romance (1852), the novel widely taken at the time to portray Fuller – in a harsh glaring light. Whether or not Hawthorne intended its central character, Zenobia, really to be Fuller, the novel ends with Zenobia's drowning, and most readers took that to be more than coincidence.

Zenobia has seceded from her station and background, as her predecessor, the Syrian queen Zenobia (d. AD 274) declared her independence from Rome. A domineering advocate of the woman's rights and socialist causes, Zenobia, as her name hints, is fatally foreign to her wintry place and straightlaced time: dark, voluptuous, brilliant, akin to one of the hothouse flowers which she always wears in her hair – although her mind is 'full of weeds.' Indeed, like Beatrice Rappaccini in Hawthorne's story 'Rappaccini's Daughter', she is the sexual flower, and lives and dies with it: 'That flower in her hair is a talisman. If you were to snatch it away, she would vanish, or be transformed into something else.'[66]

Fuller, too, was constantly described as alien to her New England roots by Emerson and others: 'I felt her to be a foreigner . . . with her, one would always be sensible of some barrier, as if in making up a friendship with a cultivated Spaniard or Turk.' She herself judged that 'I grew not in the right soil', and felt Italy to be her rightful birthplace. Zenobia, born in the rich South, is continually contrasted with the retiring New England violet, her half-sister, Priscilla – the 'little wife' whom the desirable Hollingsworth prefers to Zenobia, inciting her suicide by drowning.

But there the parallels seem to end. Hawthorne, like Emerson, described Fuller as pale and plain, resembling Priscilla more than Zenobia. Although he dismissed Fuller's feelings for the handsome

Ossoli as entirely sensual, the entry in his notebooks sniffed: 'As from him towards her, there could hardly have been even this, for she had not the charm of womanhood.'[67] Yet the paintings which we have of Fuller do not bear this out. It is almost as if Hawthorne and Emerson were trying to convince themselves of Fuller's ugliness, particularly after her death, when they no longer had her brilliant eyes to look into for disproof. Did the gentlemen protest too much?

Throughout *The Blithedale Romance* the narrator, Miles Coverdale, makes openly sexual remarks about Zenobia. On first meeting her, he admits to imagining her in 'Eve's earliest garment' (448). Hastening to put *his* sexual fantasies down to *her* 'scorning the petty restraints which take the life and colour out of other women's conversation', (448) he is still panting a few pages later:

> She should have made it a point of duty, moreover, to sit endlessly to painters and sculptors, and preferably to the latter; because the cold decorum of the marble would consist with the utmost scantiness of drapery, so that the eye might chastely be gladdened with her material perfection in its entireness. I know not well how to express the native flow of colouring in her cheeks, and even the flesh-warmth over her round arms, and what was visible of her full bust, – in a word, her womanliness incarnated, – compelled me sometimes to close my eyes, as if it were not quite the privilege of modesty to gaze at her. (465)

But gaze on he does, until Zenobia complains, 'I have been exposed to a great deal of eye-shot in the few years of my mixing in the world, but never, I think, to precisely such glances as you are in the habit of favoring me with.' (466)

Yet this is Coverdale's obsession with Zenobia, not necessarily Hawthorne's with Fuller. Indeed, Hawthorne uses a device in *The Blithedale Romance* which appears to make it plain that Fuller is the one real person on whom the fictional Zenobia *couldn't* have been patterned. The only non-fictional person mentioned explicitly in the novel is Fuller – which would seem to preclude her also 'being' Zenobia. Coverdale receives a letter from Fuller, brought to him by Priscilla, who has an uncanny power of taking on the persona and mannerisms of others, even those she has never met. (In the same way, she also takes over her half-sister's suitor, Hollingsworth, and, after having been described as 'scarcely half alive' (458) at the start of the novel, takes for herself the abundant life with which Zenobia had been endowed.)

I perceived that Priscilla had a sealed letter, which she was waiting for me to take . . . [I]t forcibly struck me that her air, though
not her figure, and the expression of her face, but not its features,
had a resemblance to what I had often seen in a friend of mine,
one of the most gifted women of the age. I cannot describe it.
The points easiest to convey to the reader were, a certain curve
of the shoulders, and a partial closing of the eyes, which seemed
to look more penetratingly into my own eyes, through the nar-
rowed apertures, than if they had been open at full width. It
was a singular anomaly of likeness coexisting with perfect
dissimilitude.

'Will you give me the letter, Priscilla?' said I.

She started, put the letter into my hand, and quite lost the look
that had drawn my notice.

'Priscilla,' I inquired, 'did you ever see Miss Margaret Fuller?'

'No,' she answered.

'Because,' said I, 'you reminded me of her, just now; and it
happens, strangely enough, that this very letter is from her.'
(468–9)

Why introduce the name of a real person into a fiction? – and why
only this one person? The device is typically Hawthorne: the enig-
matic infiltration of one person's identity by another occurs also in
'Rappaccini's Daughter' and *The Scarlet Letter*. But why not simply
invent some female savant whose manner Priscilla intuits in her
sybilline way? This 'faction' style of combining fiction and reality
did not begin with Truman Capote's *In Cold Blood*; it has been called
a common device in nineteenth-century historical fiction.[68] But this
novel is not historical, and indeed Hawthorne is at pains elsewhere
to distance the narrative from any charge that real persons – the
Brook Farmers in particular – are depicted.

These characters, he [the author] feels it right to say, are entirely
fictitious. It would, indeed (considering how few amiable qualities he distributes among his imaginary progeny) be a most griev-
ous wrong to his former excellent associates, were the author to
allow it to be supposed that he had been sketching any of their
likenesses. Had he attempted it, they would at least have recognized the touches of a friendly pencil. But he has done nothing of
the kind. The self-concentrated Philanthropist; the high-spirited
Woman, bruising herself against the narrow limitations of her

sex; the weakly Maiden, whose tremulous nerves endow her with Sibylline attributes; the Minor Poet, beginning life with strenuous aspirations which die out with his youthful fervor, – all these might have been looked for at Brook Farm, but, by some accident, never made their appearance there. (439–40)

Using the real Fuller's name jars oddly: it makes us sit up and take notice. Perhaps that is exactly what it is meant to do. The device clears Hawthorne of the accusation that he is preying on Fuller's death in the loathsome description of Zenobia's drowned body. Even though pierced in the bosom by the dredgers' grappling-hook, Zenobia's corpse, continuing to resist his advances, still compels Coverdale's fascination. Now he can enjoy all the 'eye-shot' he wants. But the dream of seeing her nude body chiseled into a chaste sculpture has come horribly true: she is now 'the marble image of a death-agony'.

> Were I to describe the perfect horror of the spectacle, the reader might justly reckon it to me for a sin and a shame. For more than twelve long years I have borne it in my memory, and could not reproduce it as freshly if it were still before my eyes. Of all modes of death, methinks it is the ugliest. Her wet garments swathed limbs of terrible inflexibility. She was the marble image of a death-agony. Her arms had grown rigid in the act of struggling, and were bent before her with clenched hands; her knees, too, were bent, and – thank God for it – in the attitude of prayer. Ah, that rigidity! It is impossible to bear the terror of it. It seemed, – I must needs impart so much of my own miserable idea, – it seemed as if her body must keep the same position in the coffin, and that her skeleton would keep it in the grave, and that when Zenobia rose at the day of judgement, it would be in just the same attitude as now! (578)

Gilbert and Gubar surmise that Hawthorne was 'covertly crowing' over Fuller's death in this grisly description.

> What makes matters worse, the narrator sardonically implies, is that this egotistical woman's 'Arcadian affectation' had probably led her to believe that in her death she would appear picturesque. The ugliness of her corpse now functions, however, as a comment on the ugliness of her inflexible self-will.[69]

'The cleverer [Zenobia] is, the faster she rots,' gloated a later commentator whom Gilbert and Gubar also identify as an embattled masculinist, D.H. Lawrence.[70]

Like Fuller, Zenobia was allowed greater privileges during her lifetime than other woman: the sole Dark Lady.

> In fact, so great was her native power and influence, and such seemed the careless purity of her nature, that whatever Zenobia did was generally acknowledged as right for her to do. The world never criticized her so harshly as it does most women who transcend its rules. It almost yielded its assent, when it beheld her stepping out of the common path, and asserting the more extensive privileges of her sex, both theoretically and in her practice. The sphere of ordinary womanhood was felt to be narrower than her development required. (551)

But when she did break the unbreakable rules – among them, chaste and vestal devotion to the Muses – her account was called in. When the queen was dethroned – and both Zenobia and Fuller were referred to as queens[71] – the revolution was bloody. The literary men who had elevated her apparently felt personally betrayed by her open expression of sexuality in having a child by that very symbol of romantic virility, an Italian count.

Hawthorne may have been more angered by Fuller's disclosure of her sexuality than was Emerson, more 'disappointed' in her, because of the two men he actually shows the greater awareness of the Woman Question. In chapter fourteen of *The Blithedale Romance*, 'Eliot's Pulpit', Hawthorne demonstrates quite a sophisticated understanding of the conflicting pressures on Zenobia. Though the eloquent advocate of her sex, she can only win the orator Hollingsworth's heart by letting him monopolise her speech and belief. Hawthorne parodies Hollingsworth's tired arguments about male superiority very tellingly: woman is made to be protected by man, Hollingsworth asserts, and if she doesn't recognise that, by God, she should be beaten into it.

> She is the most admirable handiwork of God, in her true place and character. Her place is at man's side. Her office, that of the sympathizer; the unreserved, unquestioning believer . . . All the separate action of woman is, and ever has been, and always shall be, false, foolish, vain, destructive of her own best and holiest

qualities, void of every good effort, and productive of intolerable mischiefs! Man is a wretch without woman; but woman is a monster – and, thank Heaven, an almost impossible and hitherto imaginary monster – without man as her acknowledged principal! As true as I had once a mother whom I loved, were there any possible prospect of woman's taking the social stand which some of them, – poor, miserable, abortive creatures, who only dream of such things because they have missed woman's peculiar happiness, or because nature made them really neither man nor woman? – if there were a chance of their attaining the end which these petticoated monstrosities have in view, I would call upon my own sex to use its physical force, that unmistakable evidence of sovereignty, to scourge them back within their proper bounds! But it will not be needful. The heart of true womanhood knows where its own sphere is, and never seeks to stray beyond it! (511)

After this stirring conclusion Priscilla gazes adoringly at Hollingsworth, and Zenobia herself – much to Coverdale's disgust – merely replies, 'Well, let it be so . . . I, at least, have deep cause to think you right. Let man be but manly and godlike, and woman is only too ready to become to him what you say!' It is Zenobia's hypocrisy which infuriates Coverdale – but to it is again conjoined his sexual jealousy.

I smiled – somewhat bitterly, it is true – in contemplation of my own ill-luck. How little did these two women care for me, who had freely conceded all their claims, and a great deal more, out of the fullness of my heart; while Hollingsworth, by some necromancy of his horrible injustice, seemed to have brought them both to their feet!

'Women almost invariably behave thus,' thought I. 'What does the fact mean? Is it their nature? Or is it, at last, the result of ages of compelled degradation? And, in either case, will it be possible ever to redeem them?'

An intuition now appeared to possess all the party that, for this time, at least, there was no more to be said. With one accord, we arose from the ground, and made our way through the tangled undergrowth that wound among the over-arching trees. Some of the branches hung so low as partly to conceal the figures that went before from those who followed. Priscilla had leaped up more lightly than the rest of us, and ran along in advance . . .

Zenobia and Hollingsworth went next, in close contiguity, but not with arm in arm. Now, just when they had passed the impending bough of a birch-tree, I plainly saw Zenobia take the hand of Hollingsworth in both her own, press it to her bosom, and let it fall again! (512)

Why such overt sexual jealousy? and such a blatantly voluptuous action? One disturbing explanation, offered by Fuller's nephew Frederick T. Fuller in 1885, was that Hollingsworth represents Emerson, Zenobia does indeed stand for Fuller, and Hawthorne (Coverdale) was incensed by Fuller's preference for Emerson as more manly than himself. Coverdale thinks Hollingsworth a bumptious charlatan; Hawthorne considered that Emerson was 'stretching his hand out of cloud-land in vain search for something real'.[72] But Zenobia enjoins Coverdale to benefit from Hollingsworth's superior wisdom. Did Hawthorne likewise resent Fuller's Emerson-worship, waning though his star was in her pantheon? Zenobia's action in pressing Hollingsworth's hand to her heart is modelled on Margaret's leave-taking from Waldo as recorded in her 1844 journal, claims Frederick Fuller: 'At parting I rose. He stil sate [sic] with his eyes cast down. His hand I pressed to my heart; it was a gentle vow. He looked like the youngest child.'[73]

Hawthorne wrote from pique as well as sexual jealousy, Frederick Fuller surmises. Free with her exhortations to those whom she considered worthy and capable of improvement, Fuller, he thinks, may have offended the prickly Hawthorne with some presumptuous but well-intentioned remark.

Again, when Zenobia reproaches Coverdale with 'a cold-blooded criticism, founded on a shallow interpretation of half-perceptions; a monstrous skepticism in regard to any conscience or any wisdom except his own,' those who know the bent of Hawthorne's mind [realise he may have been offended by a remark of Fuller's], bereft of its asperity by the kindly purpose of a friend . . . 'Faithful are the wounds of a friend,' but when the reproof is felt to be just, and yet rejected, few rankle more sorely.[74]

Whether or not Hawthorne felt personally betrayed by Fuller, his response to her is shot through with a sense of ideological apostasy, another interpreter has argued. Charles Swann has suggested that the ending of *The Scarlet Letter* can only be understood in terms of

Fuller's *Woman in the Nineteenth Century.*[75] Swann views as crucial this passage from the novel's conclusion:

> Women . . . in the continually recurring trials of wounded, wasted, wronged, misplaced, or erring and sinful passion, – or with the dreary burden of a heart unyielded, because unvalued and unsought, – came to Hester's cottage demanding why they were so wretched, and what the remedy . . . She assured them of her firm belief, that, at some brighter period, when the world should have grown ripe for it, in Heaven's own time, a new truth would be revealed, in order to establish the whole relation between man and woman on a surer ground of mutual happiness. Earlier in life, Hester had vainly imagined that she herself might be the destined prophetess, but had long since recognized the impossibility that any mission of divine and mysterious truth should be confided to a woman stained with sin, bowed down with shame, or even burdened with a life-long sorrow. The angel and apostle of the coming revelation must be a woman, indeed, but lofty, pure and beautiful; and wise, moreover, not through dusky grief, but the ethereal medium of joy; and showing how sacred love should make us happy, by the truest test of a life successful to such an end![76]

Swann locates the source of this credo in what has elsewhere been called the 'apocalyptic feminism' of *Woman in the Nineteenth Century.*[77] In *Woman* Fuller appears to share Hawthorne's belief that the female Messiah must herself be pure – though not his extraneous assumption that she must also be beautiful. There Fuller remarks: 'Those who would reform the world must show that they do not speak in the heat of wild impulse; their lives must be unstained by passionate error; they must be severe lawgivers to themselves.'[78] Before Fuller met George Sand, whom this passage concerns, she was sometimes inclined to condemn her for the hypocrisy of living one life and preaching another in such idealistic works as *Spiridion:* 'Would indeed the surgeon had come with quite clean hands! A woman of Sand's genius, as free, as bold, and pure from even the suspicion of error, might have filled an apostolic station among her people.'[79]

Perhaps it might seem fair enough of Hawthorne to do the same to Fuller. A charitable reading of Hawthorne's denunciation of Fuller after her death would dwell on his disappointment that she had failed to materialise into the awaited female saviour. The problem is that Hawthorne was himself so rabidly uncharitable in his remarks, to the effect that Fuller was better off dead. (Emerson put the same sentiment in more tactful terms, writing that 'she died in happy hour for herself.') Even before she met Sand – after which she wrote 'M[m]e. Sand personally inspired me with warm admiration and esteem; she would have done so, if I had read no word of hers'[80] – Fuller was ultimately able to distinguish between the woman and the work. The passage bemoaning the surgeon's dirty hands is prefaced by a call for American readers to be more generous and – ironically – manly, in their judgement of Sand:

> To the weak or unthinking the reading of such books [as Sand's] may not be desirable, for only those who take exercise as men can digest strong meat. But to anyone able to understand the position and circumstances, we believe this reading cannot fail of bringing good impulses, valuable suggestions, and it is quite free from that subtle miasma which taints so large a portion of French literature, not less since the Revolution than before. This we say to the foreign [non-French] reader. To her own country Sand is a boon precious and prized both as a warning and a leader, for which none there can be ungrateful. She has dared to probe its festering wounds, and if they be not past all surgery, she is one who, most of any, helps toward a cure.[81]

Consuelo, the first Sand novel to be translated in America, seemed to Fuller not a plea for free love, but a proof of 'how inward purity and honor may preserve a woman from bewilderment and danger, and secure for her a genuine independence.'[82] While American literary society branded Sand with a scarlet A, Fuller credited her with

> the same high morality of one who had tried the liberty of circumstance, only to appreciate the liberty of law, to know that licence is the foe of freedom. And, though the sophistry of passion in these books [*André*, *Jacques* and *Les sept cordes de la lyre*] disgusted me, flowers of purest hue seemed to grow upon the dank and dirty ground.[83]

By contrast, Hawthorne knew Fuller intimately, but was unable or disinclined to give his old friend the benefit of the slightest doubt. In

Fuller's lifetime Hawthorne had expressed his loyalty to her in such sentiments as these:

> There is nobody to whom I would more willingly speak my mind, because I can be certain of being thoroughly understood. (Hawthorne to Fuller, 28 August 1842[84])

> How strange [that he must refuse to do something Fuller had asked] when I should be so glad to do anything that you had the slightest wish for me to do, and when you are so incapable of wishing anything that ought not to be. (Hawthorne to Fuller, 1 February 1843[85])

Hawthorne's wife Sophia, a student in Fuller's classes for women, the Boston Conversations, thought so highly of Margaret that she made Fuller the first confidante of the news about her engagement. In this letter she assured Fuller that Hawthorne approved sharing the secret with this special friend, out of 'our love and profound regard for you'.[86] Fuller sometimes looked after the first fruit of the marriage, the Hawthornes' daughter Una, while they went out walking, during her Concord stay with them in 1844.

The betrayal, then, was Hawthorne's. In a passage in his notebooks of 1858, eight years after Fuller's death, he records as gospel truth the gossip of one Joseph Mozier, a merchant and amateur sculptor who lived in Rome at the same time as Fuller but knew her only superficially. Hawthorne adds to Mozier's scurrilous remarks his own considered view that Fuller deserved her drowning: 'of all the modes of death the ugliest', as he had written in *The Blithedale Romance*. (Hawthorne was unpleasantly fascinated by drowned women: his diary includes a long morbid description of a drowned Concord girl's precise physical appearance, presumably in 'Eve's earliest garment'.[87])

About the only excuse which can be made for Hawthorne's comments is that he kept them confined to his notebooks. But after his widow's death they were published by his son, Julian, in his biography, *Nathaniel Hawthorne and His Wife*. In reply to outrage from the dying band of Fuller's friends and admirers, Julian gloated, 'The majority of readers will, I think, not be inconsolable that poor Margaret Fuller has at last taken her place with the numberless other dismal frauds who fill the limbo of human pretension and failure.' As Chevigny says, 'He was right about the majority, and the image

Hawthorne sketched here has endured and spawned scores of apocryphal tales as no image of Fuller's defenders has done.'[88]

[Mr Mozier] called to see us last night, and talked for about two hours in a very amusing and interesting style; his topics being taken from his own personal experience, and shrewdly treated . . . [He] passed to Margaret Fuller, whom he knew well, she having been an intimate of his during a part of her residence in Italy. His developments about poor Margaret were very curious. He says that Ossoli's family, though technically noble, is really of no rank whatever; the elder brother, with the title of marquis, being at this very time a working bricklayer, and the sisters walking the streets without bonnets – that is, being in the station of peasant girls, in the female populace of Rome. Ossoli himself, to the best of his belief, was Margaret's servant, or had something to do with the care of her apartments. He was the handsomest man whom Mr Mozier ever saw, but entirely ignorant even of his own language, scarcely able to read at all, destitute of manners; in short, half an idiot, and without any pretensions to be a gentleman . . . He could not possibly have had the least appreciation of Margaret, and the wonder is, what attraction she found in this boor, this man without the intellectual spark – she that had always shown such a cruel and bitter scorn of intellectual delinquency. As from her towards him, I do not understand what feeling there could have been, except it were purely sensual; as from him towards her, there could hardly have been even this, for she had not the charm of womanhood. But she was a woman anxious to try all things, and fill up her experience in all directions; she had a strong and coarse nature, too, which she had done her utmost to refine, with infinite pains, but which of course could only be superficially changed. The solution of the riddle lies in this direction; nor does one's conscience revolt at the idea of thus solving it; for – at least, this is my own experience – Margaret has not left, in the heart and minds of those who knew her, any deep witness of her integrity and purity. She was a great humbug; of course with much talent, and much moral reality, or else she could not have been so great a humbug. But she had stuck herself full of borrowed qualities, which she chose to provide herself with, but which had no root in her.

Mr Mozier added, that Margaret had quite lost all power of literary production, before she left Rome, though occasionally the charm and power of her conversation would reappear. To his certain knowledge, she had no important manuscripts with her when she sailed (she having shown him all she had, with a view to his securing their publication in America); and the History of the Roman Revolution, about which there was so much lamentation, in the belief that it had been lost with her, never had existence. Thus there appears to have been a total collapse in poor Margaret, morally and intellectually; and tragic as her catastrophe was, Providence was, after all, kind in putting her, and her clownish husband, and their child, on board that fated ship. There never was such a tragedy as her whole story; the sadder and sterner, because so much of the ridiculous was mixed up with it, and because she could bear anything better than to be ridiculous. It was such an awful joke, that she should have resolved – in all sincerity, no doubt – to make herself the greatest, wisest, best woman of the age; and, to that end, she set to work on her strange, heavy, unpliable, and, in many respets, defective and evil nature, and adorned it with a mosaic of admirable qualities, such as she chose to possess; putting in here a splendid talent, and there a moral excellence, and polishing each separate piece, and the whole together, till it seemed to shine afar and dazzle all who saw it. She took credit to herself for having been her own Redeemer, if not her own Creator; and, indeed, she was far more a work of art than any of Mr Mozier's statues. But she was not working on an inanimate substance, like marble or clay; there was something within her that she could not possibly come at, to re-create and refine it; and, by and by, this rude old potency bestirred itself, and undid all her labor in the twinkling of an eye. On the whole, I do not know but I like her the better for it, – the better, because she proved herself a very woman, after all, and fell as the weakest of her sisters might.

In this verdict and sentence Hawthorne's own personality has been infiltrated by another: that of his ancestor, Judge Hathorne of the Salem witchcraft trials. This fifth-hand gossip and first-rate libel was widely believed by those who didn't want to know better. Reviewing Julian Hawthorne's biography, the *Boston Evening Transcript* wrote:

Of all Margaret Fuller's contemporaries none has shown so much insight into character in general as Hawthorne, and his judgment of her, severe as it is, wonderfully reconciles all the others which, conflicting in many ways, have puzzled those who never saw her, and who, when declaring that they found little in her works, have been silenced with 'You should have heard her! You could only know Margaret through her conversation.' He said, 'She was a great humbug; of course with much talent, or else she could never have been so great a humbug . . .' This explains everything; the admiration of certain really great but humble-minded men; the awe of the hangers-on of transcendentalism; the repulsion of the hard-headed and keen-witted, and the instinctive dislike of thousands who, with less intellect, had infinitely more delicacy and refinement. It is not a pleasant solution of the riddle, but it is better to know precisely what sort of an Isis is behind the veil.[89]

In a particularly toadying review, the *New York Times* reproduced the full nastiness of Hawthorne's private fixations and then grovelled, 'Hawthorne, we may be sure, never wrote these lines for publication. But how worthy of his powers of insight they are!'[90] 'That the judgment must be just, because it is Hawthorne's, I find to be a somewhat common sentiment in some quarters where a suspension of judgment until both sides were heard might have been looked for,' remarked Frederick T. Fuller drily.[91]

Despite corrections of Mozier's 'facts' by those who actually *did* know Fuller well[92] – as Mozier did not – the mud stuck. Fuller's friend Christopher Cranch shook his head dolefully: 'The aforesaid extract seems to going the rounds in several newspapers, and not only not censured, but applauded as a masterly portrait.'[93] 'Another ageing friend, James Freeman Clarke, philosophised that 'As there are always those who enjoy such cynical remarks, and are pleased to see any great reputation diminished, these censures of Margaret Fuller have already been widely copied, and will probably have a still larger circulation.'[94]

These widely publicised 'revelations' about Fuller from Hawthorne eclipsed the good work of Fuller's stoutest male defender: Thomas Wentworth Higginson, who had published a biography of her in the same year, 1884. Exactly how damaging Julian Hawthorne's grapeshot was to Higginson's defences can be measured by this review:

The new life of Hawthorne sounds a discordant note in regard to Margaret Fuller, and discloses more truth about her than her friends and biographers have seemed willing to have told . . . [I]n his Roman journal facts are set down against her and opinions expressed which materially change the heretofore generous and sympathetic estimate of her character ... This is a view of Margaret Fuller's career which anyone might have read between the lines of her biography as a possibility, and which Mr Higginson has not at all covered up, though he is at no pains to magnify it.[95]

A man of letters who had penned a satirical reply to opponents of further education for women, 'Ought Women to Learn the Alphabet?', Higginson was later to co-edit Emily Dickinson's poems. Although he gave Dickinson a voice and a name – she had published only seven poems in her lifetime, all anonymously – he made judicious improvements in her 'spasmodic' and 'uncontrolled' metres, presented her poems as unrevised effusions, and tacked on irrelevant titles, preferably of the pretentious French variety.[96] For her own good, Higginson rewrote Dickinson's work into vapidity, much as the editors of the *Memoirs* did with Fuller. Yet he was quietly incensed at the false currency about Fuller which the *Memoirs* had passed off as legal tender – even before the publication of Julian Hawthorne's gossip. Armed with what material remained in decent condition despite the efforts of the *Memoirs'* editors, as well as some newly released letters and diaries casting light on the period after Fuller left New England, Higginson had mounted a valiant rearguard action.

With every disposition to defer to the authors of the *Memoirs*, all of whom have been in one way or another my friends and teachers, I am compelled in some cases to go with what seems the preponderance of written evidence against their view ... In their analysis, these biographers seem to me to have given an inevitable prominence to her desire for self-culture, perhaps because it was on this side that she encountered them; but I think that anyone who will patiently study her in her own unreserved moments will now admit that what she always most desired was not merely self-culture, but a career of mingled thought and action, such as she finally found ... I cannot resist the opinion that the prevalent tone of the *Memoirs* leaves her a little too much in the clouds, and gives us too little of that vigorous executive side which was always prominent in her aspirations for herself, and which was visible to all after she reached Italy ... [T]his life [of the mind] was only preliminary, and . . . she would not have wanted to be judged by it after she had once entered on the life of action.[97]

Higginson was not Fuller's literary rival, but the playmate of her younger brothers, and the brother-in-law of her younger sister Ellen's ne'er-do-well husband, Ellery Channing. After Margaret's death Ellen and her children came under his protection for a time, as they had sometimes done with Margaret during her life. He remembered Fuller not as a 'mountainous me,' but as the dedicated eldest sister of a large family – and he was advanced enough to think her unwillingness to sacrifice in silence healthy.

> Margaret Fuller made great sacrifices for her own household . . . and showed a self-devotion that undoubtedly told severely on her health. She not only had the courage to do this, but the courage to let it be known by those for whom it was done, when it was best that they should know it. Feminine self-sacrifice is a very common fruit on every soil, and certainly on that of New England; but it often spoils its object by leading to selfishness and then dying unrevealed, all from a mistaken sense of duty.[98]

Higginson did his best to dispel the continuing effect of Lowell's and Emerson's disparaging comments about Fuller's egotism and arrogance. He re-examined the evidence for the prosecution, a famous letter to Emerson of 1 March 1838 in which Fuller says, 'I see no divine person. I myself am more divine then any I see.' Locating this sentence in textual and biographical context – Fuller was then isolated in Providence, teaching long humdrum hours in a girl's school and offering $300 of her annual $1000 salary to help establish her brother Eugene in his career – Higginson goes back to what precedes it: 'At present I am . . . very sombre and sullen . . . I must kindle my torch again . . . I feel very humble just now . . . There are noble books but one wants the breath of life sometimes.'[99]

> She was sometimes said to despise her fellow-creatures . . . Yet behind it, if I understand it rightly, is a profound and even self-torturing humility. Always dissatisfied with herself, she finds to her dismay that other people share the same condition, or worse. 'I see no divine person; I myself am more divine than any one I see. I think that is enough to say about them.' To a lower depth,

that is, she can scarcely assign them than to say that they seem to be accomplishing even less than she does. The woman who wrote this was but 27, poor, a martyr to ill-health, and with a desperate hungering of the soul to do her appointed work in the world, and make full use of the talents confided to her. When we consider that she was writing to her father-confessor, in absolute freedom and in an almost fantastic mood of depression, – with her supposed profession of teaching crumbling beneath her feet, and nothing before her but an intellectual career, which in a worldly way was then no career; her plans uncertain, her aims thwarted, her destiny a conundrum, – what man of intellectual pursuits, looking back at the struggles of his own early years, can throw a stone at Margaret Fuller?[100]

Fuller's 'father-confessor' Emerson had cast his share, of course, and Higginson quietly lets it be known in this extract what he thinks of Emerson. Thinking of Fuller as neither a 'force', a sexual turncoat, nor a threat, Higginson attempted to restore both the heroic and the humorous to the prevailing Fuller myth. The tone of his biography is iconoclastic and pleasantly acidic. Of Fuller's father and uncles, for example, he writes: 'They were in general men of great energy, pushing, successful, of immense and varied information, of great self-esteem, and without a particle of tact.'[101] He reminds his readers that Fuller had a quick sense of humour herself, and a talent for mimicry. He is wry about why she was so often hated: '. . . [H]er exceptional attainments brought on her some of those criticisms from which educated men are not exempt, and which are quite sure to visit highly-educated women.'[102]

Higginson is not entirely free of sexual politics: he is eager to assure his readers that Fuller was a 'true woman.'[103] (As I shall argue in Chapters 4 and 5, Fuller herself was imbued with the Cult of the True Woman, and Higginson's concern to locate her in this context would probably not have been unwelcome.) Nor does he feel any need to refrain from comments about Fuller's appearance, which he agrees was plain. (This is, after all, the man who replied to Emily Dickinson's 1862 letter asking his literary advice with a request for a photograph.) But Higginson did not bifurcate womankind into virgin devotees of the muses and maternal bosoms; unlike Emerson and Hawthorne, he was not troubled that Fuller had in her time played both parts. Celibacy was not part of her Faustian bargain for fame as the Dark Lady, in Higginson's view, and there was no reason to censor her sexuality. Indeed, Higginson takes a certain *épater-les-bourgeois* pleasure in publicising it: 'It is abundantly evident that her young husband discharged all the obligations of his relation to her *con amore*.'[104]

The metaphor which Higginson uses to summarise Fuller's life is the heroic quest, and the victory is genuine, not Pyrrhic:

> [H]er life seems to me, on the whole, a triumphant rather than a sad one, in spite of the prolonged struggle with illness, with poverty, with the shortcomings of others and with her own. In later years she had the fulfillment of her dreams; she had what Elizabeth Barrett, writing at the time of her marriage to Robert Browning, named as the three great desiderata of existence, 'life and love and Italy'. She shared in great deeds, she was the counselor of great men, she had a husband who was a lover, and she had a child. They loved each other in their lives, and in their death they were not divided. Was not that enough?[105]

But Higginson wrote at the very period when men were reclaiming the heroic romance entirely for themselves, after the death of George Eliot and the subsidence of realism. 'Now that Queen Realism was dead, King Romance might recover his virility and power.'[106] The narrative of adventure, as developed by Rider Haggard, Stevenson, Conrad and Kipling, was a Boy's Own Tale. The quest plot was claimed by and for men: it was, after all, an escape from the 'feminisation' of culture. And its sexual aspect also excluded women.

> The literary genre which these writers created is called the male quest romance. In various ways, these stories represent a yearning for escape from a confining society . . . to a mythologized place elsewhere where men can be freed from the constraints of Victorian morality. In the caves, or jungles, or mountains of this other place, the heroes of romance explore their secret selves in an anarchic space which can be safely called the 'primitive.' Quest narratives all involve a penetration into the imagined center of an exotic civilization, the core, Kor, *coeur*, or heart of darkness . . .[107]

Together with the damaging 'true stories' about Fuller circulated in the same year by Julian Hawthorne, the rise of the quest novel dashed Higginson's hopes of presenting Fuller as heroine rather than harridan. As the rest of this book argues, Fuller was writing an epic by living it. The narrative she constructed was a quest plot; but quests were defined, with increasing vehemence, as all-male expeditions. An adventure narrative that ended in marriage, as hers did, was even less conventional: the quest is a male flight from marriage, and, Showalter suggests, from compulsory heterosexuality. Fuller was a trespasser on masculine terrain, and prosecuted for it.

HENRY JAMES: THE MARGARET-GHOST

Higginson was far less influential than the next contributor to the 'Margaret myth', Henry James. In place of the tragic but triumphant heroine depicted by Higginson, James resurrects the sickly Fuller of the *Memoirs*, turning her into the even less substantial Margaret-wraith.

Like Hawthorne, Henry James found in Fuller a bountiful source of inspiration for uppity women characters,[108] particularly in the novel which Gilbert and Gubar think best illustrates his sense of literary women as threat, *The Bostonians*. The Fuller myth informs the characters of both the sickly bluestocking Olive Chancellor and her protegée, the loquacious prodigy Verena Tarrant. The novel's hero, Basil Ransom, upholds masculine values against those of 'a feminine, a nervous, hysterical, chattering, canting age'[109] – in terms which directly recall the *Memoirs'* characterisation of Fuller. The plot of the novel is Olive's defeat in love and sexual war: she loses Verena to Ransom. In just the same way, Zenobia was beaten by Priscilla in a love triangle and willingly outgunned by Hollingsworth's superiority in argument. Gilbert and Gubar see in both *The Bostonians* and *The Blithedale Romance* the rout of the female sex, as strategised by two male novelists who pictured themselves as intrepid scouts riding out against monstrous regiments of women. *The Bostonians*, they argue, is a revision of *The Blithedale Romance* to incorporate a hero who is even more openly contemptuous about women's advancement than is Hollingsworth.[110]

This picture is deliberately sketched in black-and-white. Elaine Showalter thinks that James is rather ambivalent about Basil Ransom as a hero – more so than the 1984 film of *The Bostonians*, which cast Superman Christopher Reeve in the role.[111] This may be true, but the theme of sexual Armageddon runs throughout James's work – whatever the merits of the various combatants. It is this sense of menace from literary women which Gilbert and Gubar document – in stories such as 'Greville Fane,' contrasting a male writer whose failure is 'admirably absolute' with a gallingly successful woman novelist 'who could invent stories by the yard but couldn't write a page of English,' or 'The Next Time', which pits high male literature against female writers' 'trash triumphant'. And it is this sense of imminent threat that informed James's response to Fuller, I argue.

Like his ambivalence about Basil Ransom, James's feeling for Fuller is not straightforward. As an expatriate New England intellectual, James was curious about and sympathetic to Fuller, one of the first of that ilk. In James's life of William Wetmore Story, Fuller figures as one of the most prominent members of the American community in Rome, and a close friend of Mrs Story. But she is both more and less than a character in the Story story: she is not a person, but 'the unquestionably haunting Margaret-ghost'.

> What comes up is the wonderment of *why* she may, to any such degree, be felt as haunting; together with other wonderments that brush us unless we give them the go-by. It is not for this latter end that we are thus engaged at all; so that, making the most of it, we ask ourselves how, possibly, in our own luminous age, she would have affected us on the stage of the 'world,' or as a candidate, if so we may put it, for the cosmopolite crown. It matters only for the amusement of evocation – since she left nothing behind her, her written utterance being naught; but to what would she have corresponded, have 'rhymed,' under categories actually known to us? Would she, in other words, with her appetite for ideas and her genius for conversation, have struck us but as a somewhat formidable bore, one of the worst kind, a culture-seeker without a sense of proportion, or, on the contrary, have affected us as a really attaching, a possibly picturesque New England Corinne?
>
> Such speculations are, however, perhaps too idle; the *facts* of the appearance of this singular woman, who would, though conceit was imputed to her, doubtless have been surprised to know that talk may be still, after more than half a century, made about her – the facts have in themselves quite sufficient colour, and the fact in particular of her having achieved, so unaided, and so ungraced, a sharp identity. This identity was that of the talker, the moral *improvisatrice*, or at least had been in her Boston days, when, young herself, she had been as a sparkling fountain to

other thirsty young. In the Rome of many waters there were doubtless fountains that quenched, collectively, any individual gush; so that it would have been, naturally, for her plentiful life, her active courage and company, that the little set of friends with whom we are concerned valued her. She had bitten deeply into Rome, or, rather, *been*, like so many others, by the wolf of the Capitol, incurably bitten; she met the whole case with New England arts that show even yet, at our distance, as honest and touching; there might be ways for her of being vivid that were not as the ways of Boston . . . The 'underplot' was precisely another of the personal facts by which the lady could interest – the fact, that is, that her marriage, should *be* an underplot, and that her husband . . . should make explanation difficult. These things, let alone the final catastrophe, in short, were not talk, but life, and life dealing with the somewhat angular Boston sibyl on its own free lines. All of which, the free lines overscoring the unlikely material, is doubtless partly why the Margaret-ghost, as I have ventured to all it, still unmistakably walks the old passages . . .[112]

On the whole this portrait is not unflattering, but it is unimaginative. With 'the extreme conventionality of the other sex,'[113] James recognises Fuller's courage and honesty but cannot help harping on her appearance and sexuality. Most tellingly, however, James presents a Fuller who is no threat, a bloodless phantom whom the male writer can evoke at will, to frighten himself a little, for his own 'amusement of evocation'. He dismisses her work: 'she left nothing behind her, her written utterance being naught'. Her only real identity was 'that of the talker, the moral *improvisatrice*'. And of course, conversation leaves no trace. Fuller's name was written on the annihilating waves.

Everyone agrees that Fuller's conversation was superb, but that too has been used against her. Contemporary male critics only praised Fuller's style as a reflection of her conversation. Even her obituary in the paper for which she had been a principal domestic and foreign correspondent, the *New York Daily Tribune,* failed to present her as a writer rather than a 'force'. Her writing ability and facility were already being played down:

> Passages of rare beauty as well as signal elevation of sentiment may be gleaned from her works, but as a whole they must commend themselves mainly by their vigor of thought and habitual fearlessness rather than freedom of utterance.[114]

During Fuller's lifetime, Thoreau had prefigured James's depiction of Fuller as an *improvisatrice*, calling 'The Great Lawsuit' 'rich extempore writing, talking with pen in hand'. Poe said he knew of no style superior to Fuller's. 'It is singularly piquant, vivid, terse, bold, luminous, leaving details out of sight, it is everything that a style should be.'[115] This was generous, considering Poe's advice to aspiring women writers in his journal, the *Southern Literary Messenger*: 'Dear Aunts . . . If you have nothing to say, do not write "Poetry". No: knit stockings – knit stockings in all such cases'.[116]

But Poe tempered his unwonted praise for a female writer with the remark that a [male] poet's work is truer to his highest self than is his life. Fuller is the exception, the Dark Lady: with her the personal and the professional are identical[117], Poe says, and this implies that the professional is less valuable than it is in the man's case.

> What poet, in especial, but must feel at least the better portion of himself more fairly represented in even his commonest sonnet (earnestly written) than in his most elaborate or most intimate personalities [*sic*]?
>
> I put all this as a general proposition, to which Miss Fuller affords a marked exception – to this extent, that her personal character and her printed book are merely one and the same thing . . . Her acts are bookish, and her books are less thoughts than acts. Her literary and her conversational manner are identical.[118]

Once the personal and the political have been shown to be the same for women writers, it becomes perfectly legitimate to dwell on personal details about appearance. This is not just 'eye-shot,' to the male critic like Poe, but serious literary criticism – since to know the authoress we must know the woman.

> To get the conversational woman in the mind's eye, all that is needed is to imagine her reciting the paragraph just quoted [a paragraph reproduced from Fuller's *Summer on the Lakes*, 1844]; but first let us have the personal woman. She is of the medium height; nothing remarkable about the figure; a profusion of lustrous light hair; eyes a bluish gray, full of fire; capacious forehead; the mouth when in repose indicates profound sensibility, capacity for affection, for love – when moved by a slight smile, it becomes even beautiful in the intensity of this expression; but the upper lip, as if impelled by the action of involuntary muscles, habitually

uplifts itself, conveying the expression of a sneer. Imagine now, a person of this description looking you at one moment earnestly in the face, at the next seeming to look only within her own spirit or at the wall; moving nervously every now and then in her chair; speaking in a high key, but musically, deliberately (not hurriedly or loudly), with a delicious distinctness of enunciation – speaking, I say, the paragraph in question, and emphasizing the words which I have italicized, not by impulsion of the breath (as is usual) but by drawing them out as long as possible, nearly closing her eyes the while – imagine all this, and we have both the woman and the authoress before us.[119]

This is a more flattering portrait than James's picture of the 'somewhat angular Boston sibyl,' and certainly more complimentary than Emerson's remark that some people couldn't bear to be in the same room with the twitchy bundle of ugly grimaces which constituted Margaret Fuller. But it is still a sort of sexual harrassment. It denies professional standing to the female writer, as does the claim that she merely improvises. Real writers write, and real writers are men; women, being women, can only talk in print.

It seems more than a little suspicious that James pronounced George Sand, too, an *'improvisatrice'*. Since Sand left behind over one hundred volumes of fiction, travel narrative, political and literary essays, plays and autobiography, it was harder for James to assert that *she* 'left nothing behind her, her written utterance being naught'. But he shrugged off this threateningly potent production as a mere feminine grace: 'She was pressed to write because she had the greatest *instinct* of expression ever conferred on a woman.'[120]

Nevertheless Fuller published five books in her short life, along with the trunk-filling history of the Italian revolution which went down in the shipwreck. She produced three essays a week for the *New York Tribune* – 250 in all, despite those problems with 'freedom of utterance' with which the newspaper charged her in her obituary – and left six volumes of her correspondence with the great intellects of her time – Mazzini, Mickiewicz, Sand, Elizabeth Barrett and Robert Browning, Emerson, Thoreau, Hawthorne – aside from those lost forever by Ward and her other editors. She achieved the sort of sales enjoyed in James's time – much to his discomfort – by another woman, Edith Wharton. James was eager to pronounce Sand 'a fictionist too superannuated and rococo at the present time',[121] even when she was still widely read. Is there something of the same intentionally self-fulfilling prophecy in his assertion that Fuller 'left nothing behind her'? This would be consistent with his fear of women writers' vitality, copious production and popular success. True, James was not the first to write off the importance of Fuller's writing: by 1884 the *Sunday Herald* was pronouncing, 'In all that she has written there is not a line that will live', in the same review which welcomed Julian Hawthorne's juicy titbits.[122] But to charge that Fuller 'left nothing behind her', as James did, implies that she actually wrote nothing – not even anything worth forgetting.

Emerson, Hawthorne and James were *all* haunted by the Margaret-ghost. They found different ways to exorcise her unruly spirit: re-writing her words, fictionalising her actuality, and prescribing a lesser ambition for her, the suitably feminine vocation of chattering. Fuller is the first and foremost example of male writers' victimisa-tion of successful women of letters because she was the most pro-minent literary woman of her time. That she is still so little known now, after two decades of feminist evocation of her spirit in bio-graphy and study,[123] shows how successful those tactics were. Gilbert and Gubar identify that strategy as a general one for winning the literary war of the sexes, in which, I argue, the Fuller campaign was a first and critical engagement.

> [B]oth men of letters and women of letters devised a variety of strategies for defusing anxiety about the literary combat in which they often felt engaged. Among male writers, such strategies included mythologizing women to align them with dread proto-types; fictionalizing them to dramatize their destructive influ-ence; slandering them in essays, memoirs, and poems; prescribing alternative ambitions for them; appropriating their words in or-der to usurp or trivalize their language; and ignoring or evading their achievements in critical texts.[124]

The 'Margaret myth' removed Fuller from the list of flesh and blood writers. Zenobia, Olive Chancellor, and Verena Tarrant fictionalised her into defeated acceptability. Sexual and personal slanders in the *Memoirs* and Hawthorne's notebooks laid her low. James, Emerson and other male writers prescribed for her the alternative ambition of being a friend, a conversationalist, an *improvisatrice*. The editors of the *Memoirs* rewrote her words and trivialised her language. Fuller's consolidation of the Trancendentalist movement as first editor of *The Dial* was largely ignored, as is her position as the foremost literary critic of her times, who helped to establish the reputations of such canonical writers as Poe and Thoreau, while her own has slid downward.

But Gilbert and Gubar also mention the strategies used by *women* of letters. Did no literary women of her time or after come to Fuller's defence?

WOMEN AUTHORS' RESPONSES TO FULLER

The editors of the *Memoirs* solicited a contribution from Elizabeth Barrett Browning, but it was lost in transmission. The Brownings came to know the Ossolis intimately after the republican couple fled from fallen Rome to Florence. The two women had in common not only their intense and constricted childhoods but also their romances in middle age. They were also drawn together by having an infant son each. But although Elizabeth Barrett Browning counted herself Fuller's friend in life, she ran with the male hounds in dismissing Fuller's work after the shipwreck: 'Her written works are just naught . . . Never read what she has written.'[125] Though Barrett Browning knew Fuller during the time when Margaret was working on her history of the Italian revolution, she dismissed that, too, not least for its political radicalism.

> The work she was preparing upon Italy would probably have been more equal to her faculty than anything previously produced by her pen (her other writings being curiously inferior to the impressions her conversation gave you); indeed, she told me it was the only production to which she had given time and labour. But, if rescued, the manuscript would be nothing but the raw material. I believe nothing was finished; nor, if finished, could the work have been otherwise than deeply coloured by those blood colours of Socialistic views, which would have drawn the wolves on her, with a still more howling enmity, both in England and America. Therefore it was better for her to go. Only God and a few friends can be expected to distinguish between the pure personality of a woman and her professed opinions.[126]

Elizabeth Barrett Browning knew Fuller at the time when her political feelings were at their most intensely socialist and radical. But Barrett Browning held socialism to be 'the most desecrating and dishonouring to humanity of all creeds. I would rather (for me) live under the absolutism of Nicholas of Russia than in a Fourier machine, with my individuality sucked out of me by a social air-pump'.[127] However, her dismissal of Fuller to the oblivion of the deep also exemplifies what Gilbert and Gubar call women authors' 'nervous sense of guilt and . . . paradoxical sense of vulnerability'.

Perhaps her personal association with the Ossolis, whose marriage still smacked of the improper to some, made the Englishwoman feel *more* nervous and vulnerable: would she be tarred with the same brush? Over ten years after Fuller's death, on the publication of *Aurora Leigh* (1861), Barrett Browning drew down the 'howling enmity' of many critics, unable to 'distinguish between the pure personality of a woman and her professed opinions', for the Sandian frankness with which she discussed sexual passion. Perhaps her nervousness on Fuller's behalf was justified, though it is grim to find yet another 'friend' thinking Fuller was better off dead. Or perhaps Barrett Browning, who 'looked everywhere for grandmothers and found none', was not all that unhappy to lose a contemporary and a possible rival. After all, there can only be one Dark Lady.

By contrast, George Eliot swam against the critical tide of her time and place by reviewing the *Memoirs* favourably in 1852 and by writing a sympathetic essay comparing Fuller with Mary Wollstonecraft in 1855. (Eliot may have been well disposed towards Fuller because of the favourable impression Fuller made on Eliot's partner George Henry Lewes during her 1846 stay in London; he pronounced her conversation superior to Carlyle's and his own.[128]) The really nasty slurs on Fuller only began in America with Julian Hawthorne's publication of his father's notebooks, but in England Fuller-bashing got off to a much prompter start. The most virulent review of the *Memoirs* came from the *New Quarterly:*

Margaret Fuller was one of those he-women, who, thank Heaven! for the most part figure and flourish, and have their fame on the other side of the Atlantic. She was an intellectual Bloomer of the largest calibre. She understood Socrates better than Plato did, Faust better than Goethe did, Kant Philosophy [*sic*] better than Kant did . . . but alack the difference between a encyclopaedia bound in calf and an encyclopaedia moving in blue stockings. Every fact, word, thought, idea, theory, notion, line, verse, that crowded in the cranium of Margaret Fuller was a weapon. The shot from her like pellets from a steam gun. She bristled all over

with transcendentalism, assaulted you with metaphysics, suffoc-
ated you with mythology, peppered you with ethics, and struck
you down with heavy history . . . We need hardly say that we do
not recommend this book to English family reading . . . [W]e think
it is not a nice book for English ladies, and not an entertaining
book for English gentlemen.[129]

Male critics are often tempted by metaphors of war in condemning
Fuller. It is their vocabulary, not hers, and bears out Gilbert and
Gubar's contention that literary men were fighting a military campaign – in which they were the aggressors. Eliot's praise of Fuller in
her *Westminster Review* article on the *Memoirs* is a good deal more
battle-shy: 'From the time she became a mother till the final tragedy
. . . [Fuller] was an altered woman, and evinced a greatness of soul
and heroism of character so grand and subduing, that we feel disposed to extend to her whole career the admiration and sympathy
inspired by the closing scenes.'[130] Eliot awards Fuller the Victoria
Cross for heroism, but as Paula Blanchard has pointed out in her
biography of Fuller, the medal is somewhat tarnished.

> This is meant to be complimentary, and the rest of the review is
> generous. But the inference that before she had a child Margaret
> was not capable of 'greatness of soul' and so on, is unfair, and
> more than a little incongruous considering its source.[131]

In her 1855 essay, 'Margaret Fuller and Mary Wollstonecraft',[132] Eliot
does try more valiantly to stem the critical assaults. But even here
her sympathy was lukewarm. Against the English critical consensus
that Fuller was a hysterical harpy, Eliot pronounced *Woman in
the Nineteenth Century* moderate, calm and wise. She agreed with
Fuller's proposals for women's education and for a broader choice
of careers. Like Mary Wollstonecraft. Eliot argued, Fuller proved
the cost to both men and society of women's enforced leisure. Although men fear educated women, Eliot surmised, they are really
put at a disadvantage by women's obligatory ignorance – an argument also made by Fuller. In Eliot's words,

> There is a notion commonly entertained among men that an in-
> structed woman, capable of having opinions, is likely to prove an
> impracticable yoke-fellow, always pulling one way when her hus-

band wants to go the other, oracular in tone, and prone to give certain lectures on metaphysics. But surely, so far as obstinacy is concerned, your unreasoning animal is the most unmanageable of creatures . . . So far as we see, there is no indissoluble connexion between infirmity of logic and infirmity of will, and a woman quite innocent of an opinion in philosophy, is as likely as not to have an indomitable opinion about the kitchen.[133]

But showing her common nationality with the condescending reviewer of the *New Quarterly*, Eliot bemoaned in Fuller 'certain defects of taste and a sort of vague spiritualism and grandiloquence which belong to all but the very best American writers'.[134] Although in her private correspondence Eliot wrote that she found passages of the *Memoirs* 'inexpressibly touching,' she somewhat circumscribed her expressions of sympathy with Fuller in public. Her compassion was most pronounced in private writings, such as the letter of 1852 in which Eliot wrote:

It is a help to read such a life as Margaret Fuller's. How inexpressibly touching that passage from her journal – 'I shall always reign through the intellect, but the life! the life! O my God! shall that never be sweet?' I am thankful, as if for myself, that it was sweet at last.[135]

The best of Fuller's female defenders lacked all conviction, while the worst of her attackers – male and female alike – were full of a passionate intensity. Matthew Arnold, broad-minded on the subject of George Sand, sent Fuller's essays packing with the comment: 'My G-d, what rot did she and the other female dogs of Boston talk about Greek mythology!'[136] Of Harriet Martineau he said, 'What an unpleasant life and unpleasant nature!' One might therefore expect to find Martineau hastening to defend Fuller against similar male slanders – particularly because Martineau was an old acquaintance of Fuller's youth.

But Martineau was one of Fuller's sharpest and most influential critics, eager perhaps to set herself apart from any purges against female intellectuals which the *Memoirs* might provoke. Her snide account (1877) of Fuller's Boston Conversations, college-level lectures for women (who were at that time almost entirely denied university education), probably represents a delayed revenge for

Fuller's mixed review of Martineau's *Society in America* in a letter written at the time of the book's American publication in 1837. Fuller had lamented the haste with which Martineau had written, producing, she felt, 'a degree of presumptuousness, irreverence, inaccuracy, hasty generalization, and ultraism on many points. . . .'[137] But her criticisms were tempered with praise for Martineau's 'high ideal standard, genuine independence, noble tone of sentiment, vigor of mind and powers of picturesque description'.[138] However, nearly forty years had not dimmed Martineau's resentment.

> The difference between us was that while she was living and moving in an ideal world, talking in private and discoursing in public about the most fanciful and shallow conceits which the transcendentalists of Boston took for philosophy, she looked down upon persons who acted instead of talking finely, and devoted their fortunes, their peace, their repose, and their very lives to the preservation of the principles of the republic. While Margaret Fuller and her adult pupils sat 'gorgeously dressed,' talking about Mars and Venus, Plato and Goethe, and fancying themselves the elect of the earth in intellect and refinement, the liberties of the republic were running out as fast as they could go, at a breach which another sort of elect persons were devoting themselves to repair; and my complaint against the 'gorgeous' pedants was that they regarded their preservers as hewers of wood and drawers of water, and their work as a less vital one than the pedantic orations which were spoiling a set of well-meaning women in a pitiable way. All that is settled now. It was over years before Margaret died. I mentioned it now to show . . . what the difference was between me and her . . .
>
> She was not only completely spoiled in conversation and manners: she made false estimates of the objects and interests of human life. She was not content with pursuing, and inducing others to pursue, a metaphysical idealism destructive of all genuine feeling and sound activity; she mocked at objects and efforts of a high order than her own, and despised those who, like myself, could not adopt her scale of valuation. All this might have been spared, a world of mischief saved, and a world of good effected, if she had found her heart a dozen years sooner, and in America instead of Italy. It is the most grievous loss I have ever known in private history – the deferring of Margaret Fuller's married life so long.[139]

Martineau's cattiness was all the more damaging to Fuller because it came from a one-time friend. Fuller and Martineau had first met during the English author's visit to America in 1835. Then at the nadir of her intellectual life, isolated on her father's farm as unpaid tutor to her younger siblings and general household factotum, Fuller pinned high hopes on the older woman as her liberator:

> I sigh for an intellectual guide. Nothing but the sense of what God has done for me, in bringing me nearer to himself, saves me from despair . . . I have hoped some friend would do, – what none has ever yet done, – comprehend me wholly, mentally, and morally, and enable me to comprehend myself. I have had some hope that Miss Martineau might be this friend, but cannot yet tell. She has what I want, – vigorous reasoning powers, invention, clear views of her objects, – and she has been trained to the best means of execution. Add to this, that there are no strong intellectual sympathies between us, such as would blind her to my defects.[140]

Fuller need hardly have feared that Martineau would be insensible to her faults. The inaccuracy of Martineau's account is exceeded only by its self-serving smugness. Fuller set up the Boston Conversations in order to earn the money to support herself, her widowed mother, and her younger siblings with less all-consuming drudgery than being a teacher or governess entailed. (Martineau had herself crusaded against the lowly station of governesses.) Emerson and other male writers could lecture publicly to supplement an income from the professions which barred women; but women were also banned from the lecturing circuit in the 1830s, often heckled and assaulted if, like the abolitionist Grimké sisters, they spoke anywhere but in a private forum. Martineau might have been expected to sympathise, having earned her own way all her life; but she disparaged her own financial need and ignored Fuller's.

> Authorship has never been with me a matter of choice. I have not done it for amusement, or for money, or for fame, or for any reason but because I could not help it. Things were pressing to be said; and there was more or less evidence that I was the person to say them.[141]

There was nothing self-indulgent about the Conversations, and everything practical about Fuller's theory of education. Indeed, in her

Summer on the Lakes (1844), Fuller had condemned the practice of sending frontier girls back East to learn useless refinements. This is precisely the position which Martineau took in condemning the education of middle-class English girls whose parents had pretensions to gentility.[142] Martineau also ignored Fuller's later activity in the Roman revolution, where she ran a hospital for republican soldiers. For her 'socialism' and revolutionary activity, Elizabeth Barrett Browning had condemned Fuller; Martineau pilloried her for lacking political commitment.

In the requisite final peroration to motherhood, in the picture of Fuller as a spoilt lady of leisure, in the portrayal of her mind as full of weeds, Martineau conforms to every requirement laid down by male critics for discussions of Fuller. Deirdre David suggests that Martineau had little choice but to collude with patriarchal literary culture in order to win acceptance[143] – to be allowed the status of 'Dark Lady' for her own society. Having herself been attacked as shameless when, as a single women, she dared to utter Malthusian warnings against excessive childbearing, she had to be very careful about being associated with any but the purest of female messiahs. As a marginal man, she had to condemn less successful male impersonators more loudly than any member of the first sex.

> . . . Mary Wollstonecraft was, with all her powers, a poor victim of passion, with no control over her own peace, and no calmness or content except when the needs of her individual nature were satisfied . . . Nobody can be further than I am from being satisfied with the condition of [my] own sex, under the law and custom of my own country; but I decline all fellowship and co-operation with women of genius or otherwise favourable position, who injure the cause by their personal tendencies . . . The best friends of that cause are women who are morally as well as intellectually competent to the most serious business of life, and who must be clearly seen to speak from conviction of the truth, and not from personal unhappiness . . . [W]omen, like men, can obtain whatever they show themselves fit for.[144]

David asserts that 'Martineau's feminist programme is dictated by a dualistic perspective on the sexes that unassailably values male over female.'[145] That is, 'why can't a woman be more like a man?' This outlook was not necessarily conscious or face-serving, David claims: merely the price of Martineau's admission to a hall of fame crammed from ceiling to floor with male busts. Martineau both complied with and subverted patriarchal values, David believes.

As I will argue in a later chapter, Fuller's perspective on the Woman Question was of an entirely different stripe to Martineau's: she sought a positive female identity, refusing to define feminine as the mere negative of masculine. Although also a marginal man, a Dark Lady, she did not condemn women in order to gain acceptance in the male literary world. Martineau's accusation that Fuller looked down on other women with lesser intellects is exactly back-to-front, but it stuck.

But Martineau's ill-will was not only personal: her disagreement with Fuller was also philosophical and political. Together with Barrett Browning and Eliot, Martineau set out to refute in life and work precisely this idea of a permanently separate female intellectual personality, whether defined as equal, superior or lesser to male identity.[146] Barrett Browning played with androgyny in invoking George Sand as 'large brained woman and large hearted man'. Eliot created her own androgynous self. Inferior education accounted for much of the difference between men and women, Martineau thought, and equal opportunities would eradicate most gender differences. For those which remained – such as 'the natural desire and the natural faculty for housewifery, which I think I see in every girl I meet'[147] – Martineau argued 'educated acceptance rather than angry refutation'.[148] Oddly, then, Martineau was more sceptical about any idea of a separate female nature than was Fuller, but also more quietist. The claim that women are simply different from men is usually used to reinforce the status quo, though not in Fuller. Martineau, in contrast, had little patience with movements for equality:

If there was anything more distasteful to Martineau than subjugated and debased womanhood, it was women who whined about their wrongs and rights: she wanted women to be more like herself, or at least as she imagined herself – rational, confident, the intellectual equal of any man, or certainly equal enough to sanction his ideas.[149]

All three Englishwomen could therefore be expected to find Fuller's approach to the Woman Question uncongenial. 'Separate' may not entail 'lesser', but male writers have often used the notion of a separate female identity to justify inequality. Emerson's bromides on women's modest lack of ambition reflect this all-too-convenient dualism. Yet in actuality Fuller's proposals – though founded on the idea of a separate female nature, 'electrical in function' – were uncomfortably extreme for Barrett Browning and Martineau in particular.

Eliot – 'Queen George'[150] of English letters – could afford to be more generous towards 'Queen Margaret' than could Martineau or Barrett Browning. But even Eliot, 'the most thoroughly self-made of the three women writers . . . *the* woman intellectual of the Victorian period',[151] was less than a firm ally. The stoutest defender Fuller ever had was a man, Thomas Wentworth Higginson.

This exception tests but does not disprove Gilbert and Gubar's rule. Not all literary men lived in fear and trembling of raiding parties of Amazon authoresses, but the majority of Fuller's male contemporaries and successors felt threatened by her. Higginson was perhaps unique because he could accept her as an older sister – a role which gives some rightful authority in addition to its obligations. Literary women – Martineau, Eliot and Barrett Browning – were ambivalent about Fuller, the pattern which Gilbert and Gubar identify as typical. They sought to distance themselves from the pernicious aspects of her myth.

Mother, sister, friend, virginal devotee – these were the ambitions dictated for Fuller by male writers after her death. But what ambitions did she prescribe for herself in life?

2

Father's Language, Mother's Name

[T]here is a memorable interval between the spoken and the written language, the language heard and the language read. The one is commonly transitory, a sound, a tongue, a dialect merely, almost brutish, and we learn it unconsciously, like the brutes, of our mothers. The other is the maturity and experience of that; if that is our mother tongue, this is our father tongue, a reserved and select expression, too significant to be heard by the ear, which we must be born again in order to speak.

Henry David Thoreau[1]

Margaret Fuller learned from her father the 'reserved and select expression' of Latin – generally reserved for boys' education. Her early immersion in Latin epics left her with a longing to be 'born again' as a Roman hero, and informed the quest narrative which she lived. But for Fuller to imbibe such an education and name her destiny in a masculine language was not the same as for John Stuart Mill or Thoreau to do so. The language of her mother was not 'transitory' for her: indeed, against her father's will, she chose also to be 'born again' by taking on her mother's Christian name for the rest of her life.

In this chapter, on Fuller's childhood and early education, from her birth in 1810 to her departure for a girl's boarding school in 1824, I will contrast the law and language of the father with the lore and name of the mother. Drawing on parallels from the childhood of other women writers, particular Emily Dickinson, I will argue that the role of the mother is typically underestimated. Only women who model themselves exclusively on their fathers can become great, in the conventional view – because they make themselves surrogate men. But in order to define themselves as women who do not fit the conventional female role, women writers must *both* reproduce and reject their mothers, I argue. Fuller composed an autobiographical fantasy in which her mother died during her childhood; Emily Dickinson wrote 'I never had a mother.' Why this should be so will be examined in terms of modern psychoanalytic theories about female development and identity differentiation, particularly the work of Nancy Chodorow and Carol Gilligan.[2]

Throughout I will draw extensively on the authenticated Fuller correspondence, letting Fuller speak for herself in whichever of the languages she chooses – father's or mother's. The Fuller family preserved most of Margaret's early letters, and the editors of the *Memoirs* made fewer depredations onto this territory: there were no embarrassing references to any of them *here*.

Sarah Margaret was the eldest of the surviving Fuller children by five years; a sister two years younger, Julia Adelaide, died at eighteen months. The death was Fuller's first memory; there is a terrible symmetry between that and her last moments, when her not-quite-two-year-old son was taken from her in the shipwreck by the steward, who vainly hoped to get the boy to shore. The *Memoirs* describe Julia Adelaide's death in these terms:

> I remember coming home and meeting our nursery-maid, her face streaming with tears. That strange sight of tears made an indelible impression . . . She took me by the hand and led me into a still and dark chamber, – then drew aside the curtain and showed me my sister. I see yet that beauty of death! The highest achievements of sculpture are only the reminder of its severe sweetness. Then I remember the house all still and dark, – the people in their black clothes and dreary faces, – the scent of the newly-made coffin, – my being set up in a chair and detained by a gentle hand to hear the clergyman, – the carriages slowly going, the procession slowly doling out their steps to the grave. But I have no remembrance of what I have since been told I did, – insisting, with loud cries, that they should not put the body in the ground.[3]

There was no son in the family until the birth of Eugene in 1815. Fuller's ambitious and energetic lawyer father, Timothy, had no boys on whom to try out his theories of education, but luckily Sarah Margaret was promising. As Blanchard says, 'for the next two years [after Julia Adelaide's death] there would be no other child in the family to shade her occasionally from the full glare of her father's attention'.[4] Nor would there be another sister born until Ellen, ten years younger than Margaret. With a total of six brothers in the family, of whom five survived, female companionship would be in short supply, except for Fuller's mother. Most biographers have asserted that Fuller had little sense of sisterhood, and this literal lack of sisters might account for that, if it were true. (Later I will examine that assertion more critically.)

This pattern of standing in for not-yet-existent or dead men and boys occurs among other successful women. George Sand's father died when she was four, her younger brother having died eight days before and another boy two years earlier. (Being made to put on 'death's legs' – black stockings – was one of Sand's formative memories.) The family's resources were all concentrated on this girl survivor, their expectations of her – and hers of herself – heightened by her physical resemblance to the dead father. A modern study of nearly 300 women whose fathers died before they were eighteen suggests that this pattern is typical. Fatherless girls often view themselves as standing in for the absent male, protecting the mother, particularly if there are no brothers. They 'approach life with an earnestness of purpose and a resistance to self-indulgence' which often means that they are 'most impressively represented among women who have gained worldwide recognition, women in whom the elements of mother's dependency and/or a beloved father's absence created an urgent need for compensation, independence, and applause'.[5]

Although many biographers have presented Margaret Fuller's father as domineering, he, too, was actually absent for much of her childhood – away in Washington half the year after Margaret was seven. After standing in for brothers not yet born in her early childhood, Fuller had to substitute for her absent father: her mother was frequently pregnant and often ill, in need of her 'protection'. Fuller, too, resembled her father in energy and intelligence; nor did Timothy regard this girl as a mere second-best. A son of the Enlightenment who had been demoted to second position in his Harvard graduating class for having led a student revolt against saying grace before meals, he had read Mary Wollstonecraft's *Vindication of the Rights of Woman* (1792) and resented his own father's indifference to his sisters' education. The experiences of tutoring his younger brother Elisha, working during his college terms as an assistant schoolmaster, and serving as an English preceptor at Leicester Academy for girls, near Princeton, Massachusetts, gave him further opportunities to develop his own philosophy of education.

The content of the training which he gave his precocious daughter had little to do with Wollstonecraft's prescriptions, which he thought 'sensible and just' but quite unsuitable for young ladies. Like Emily Dickinson's father Edward, the young Timothy Fuller – whom Margaret called 'more than half a Jacobin' – hardened into more conservative opinions in later life. (He did retain some revolutionary enthusiasms, praising Simon Bolivar in an 1826 speech.) But the Jacobins had forbidden women to join political clubs and shouted down proposals that they should be given the vote in the 1793 constitution. Revolutionary 'radicalism' only went so far in relation to women,[6] although American exceptionalism combined with the absence of restrictive precedents and the Calvinist emphasis on self-improvement to create more educational opportunities for women in the New World. Puritanism emphasised the importance of cultivating a girl's mind: 'a woman was dependent on no one but herself for her own spiritual well-being, and it was by an intense spiritual striving that she was to gain her own salvation.'[7]

'The female mind, so sensitive, so capable of improvement, should not be neglected . . . God hath designed nothing in vain.'[8] This sentiment, typical of the time, was voiced by Edward Dickinson's father Samuel Fowler Dickinson, who founded Amherst Academy for the education of both sexes. Both Edward Dickinson and Timothy Fuller valued daughters' education, but not to the extreme of creating bluestockings. In a letter written in 1826 to his future wife, Emily Norcross, Edward Dickinson asserted his pride in meeting a native New England authoress but warned his fiancée against taking on any such intellectual airs. Similarly, Timothy Fuller wrote condescendingly of the condescension which he experienced from a Boston bluestocking:

> [She is] about thirty, rather plain, has read considerable, which makes her both pedantic and dogmatical; by frequenting Boston company she has contracted a kind of politeness which shews itself in all she says and does; it consists in her conviction of her own superior sense and breeding, and she deems it condescension to be civil.[9]

Timothy Fuller's position on female advancement was typical of moderately progressive American thought at the turn of the nineteenth century. What Jane Rendall calls 'the rhetoric of republican motherhood' elevated educational aspirations for women without challenging their confinement to the domestic sphere. In that realm – through boycotting tea, producing cloth for the revolutionary army's uniforms, and bearing the burden of billeting troops – American women had shown themselves worthy. The popular heroines 'Molly Pitcher' (Mary Hays), who carried water to American troops at the Battle of Monmouth, and Betsy Ross, who sewed the revolutionary flag, epitomised this combination of patriotism and domesticity.

Some women, like the poet and playwright Mercy Otis Warren (1728–1824), had also used their pens to denounce the corruption of the old order and proclaim the glories of the new republic.[10] These women writers of the late eighteenth and early nineteenth centuries saw no contradiction between female independence of spirit and domestic harmony. The successful novelist and poet Susanna Rowson (1762–1824) urged husbands to treat their wives as intelligent and free beings if they wanted peace at home. Her patriotic comedy *The Slaves in Algiers, or, a Struggle for Freedom* centres on a group of American women held for ransom by Barbary Coast pirates. A parable of liberty from the former colonial oppressor whose privateers still ravaged American shipping on the seas, Rowson's text has one of the women say, 'I feel that I was born free, and while I have life, I will struggle to remain so.'[11]

In an essay, 'On the Equality of the Sexes,' written in 1779 and published in 1790 in the *Massachusetts Magazine*, Judith Sargent Murray urged her fellow Americans to instil republican virtues into new generations of women. (Coincidentally Murray's essay described the education given to a girl called 'Margaretta' by 'Mrs Vigilius'.[12]) Timothy Fuller chose to indoctrinate his daughter in the republican virtues of Rome as well as those of America. Margaret's first extant essay, written at the age of about twelve for her father, showed the cult had a new convert.

> Resolved, united hearts freed America . . . [I]t is not in the power of circumstance to prevent the earnest will from shaping round itself the character of a great, a wise, or a good man.[13]

But when Margaret took his teaching *too* much to heart, Timothy reverted to more conventional models of graceful womanhood. Although Fuller enjoyed normal female activities such as dancing, she was aware at the time of the gaping contradictions in her father's programme for her education when he substituted deportment lessons for Greek. It was to be her first occasion for resisting what the French psychoanalyst Jacques Lacan calls 'the Law of the Father.'[14] Timothy Fuller's word was largely law, and he issued laws about what words, what discourses, what narratives, what ways of thought were suitable. He intended his yoke to be easy and his burden light: he was not a tyrant. But Margaret later attributed to the rigour of her father's training most of the symptoms which the *Memoirs* editors took to be the weakness of her woman's nature: mood-swings, paralysing headaches, dispiriting gloom.

From an early age Margaret learned Latin, French, logic, rhetoric, and a little Greek. One of her first letters to her father, written at seven, shows that she was being fed on a diet of warrior kings:

> I have been reviewing Valpy's Chronology [of ancient and English history]. We have not been able to procure any books [on] either Charles 12th of Sweden or Philip IId of Spain but Mama intends to send to Uncle Henry. I hope to make greater proficuncy [*sic*] in my Studies I have learned all the rules of Musick but one.[15]

By nine she was writing letters to Timothy in Latin and working her way through the fifth book of Virgil, whom she had begun memorising at six, along with passages from Plutarch and Ovid. She had ingested not only the language but also its agonistic spirit, smarting inwardly because one Mary Elliot had finished *her* Virgil in thirty days. The ambitiousness which she expressed openly all her life – *pace* Emerson – was already alive in a letter to her father of 3 February 1820. There she reiterated her determination to best Mary Elliot's record and sealed her resolve with the Lord's Prayer in Latin. In reply, Timothy wrote, 'I would not discourage you, my girl, by being too critical and yet I am anxious to have you admit to one *fault*, which you will remember I have often mentioned, as the source, the very fountain of others – carelessness.'[16]

In later life Fuller resented the strictness of her father's strictures:

> Trained to great dexterity in artificial methods, accurate, ready, with entire command of his resources, he had no belief in minds that listen, wait, and receive. He had no conception of the subtle and indirect motions of imagination and feeling. His influence on me was great, and opposed to the natural unfolding of my character, which was fervent, of strong grasp, and disposed to infatuation, and self-forgetfulness.[17]

Like John Stuart Mill, she was put under additional pressure by having her father as schoolmaster. With the additional duties of an eldest sister to fulfil, there was little free time. Evenings were filled with recitations, and nights with sleepwalking, convulsions and bad dreams – pools of blood which reached her lips, horses trampling her in the galloping rhythm of the *Aeneid*, eyes springing out of their sockets and attaching themselves to her like limpets, trees dripping gore. Like Mill, who attributed his nervous breakdown at twenty to similarly forced mental feeding, Fuller suffered from the insensitivity of her father's educational demands. Before Timothy was elected to Congress when Margaret was seven, he was busy in his law practice and in the state legislature well into the evening. Her recitations had to be put off until his anxiety-inducing return.

> Thus frequently, I was sent to bed several hours too late, with nerves unnaturally stimulated. The consequence was a premature development of the brain, that made me a 'youthful prodigy' by day, and by night a victim of spectral illusions, nightmare and somnabulism, which at the time prevented the harmonious development of my bodily powers and checked my growth, while later, they induced continued headache, weakness and nervous affections, of all kinds . . . Poor child! Far remote in time, in thought, from that period, I look back on these glooms and terrors, wherein I was enveloped, and perceive that I had no natural childhood.[18]

Mill's traumatic education could at least secure him entry to the professions: Fuller's led only into a dead end.

But there is little trace of resentment in the letters which Margaret wrote to Timothy at the time. Even later in life she recognised the benefit of having been judged by the standards applied to boys. And the Language of the Father was as rigorous as the Law. Although as a young man the most favourable epithet which Timothy applied to the girls he favoured was 'modest,' he discouraged feminine modesty of expression in his daughter:

> You must not speak, unless you can make your meaning perfectly intelligible to the person addressed; must not express a thought, unless you can give a reason for it, if required; must not make statements, unless sure of all particulars – such were his rules. 'But', 'if', 'unless', 'I am mistaken', and 'it may be so,' were words and phrases excluded from the provinces where he held sway.[19]

Fuller was taught to talk like a man. This alone would account for why so many men found her insufferable.

The dominant theory of education before 1830 favoured competition and discipline, the Law of the Father; it was only later that there was a reaction towards what might be called the Rule of the Mother, methods emphasising gentle persuasion.[20] But if they could bear the discipline, girls were sometimes admitted to the patriarchal sanctum of classics study. The essayist and reformer Harriet Martineau and the suffragist Julia Ward Howe, author of an 1883 biography of Fuller, received a similar grounding in classics and modern languages. At the school which Fuller attended between the ages of ten and twelve, Dr Park's establishment in Boston, Cicero and Horace were standard fare, and the curriculum also included French, Italian, ancient and modern history, geometry, trigonometry, natural history, geography and English composition. Harriet Beecher Stowe was also educated as a prodigy by her father, who fed her on Plutarch's *Lives*.

This seems to contradict Walter Ong's argument[21] that education in the classics was intended to demarcate girls' training from boys' – and that the classics were valued *precisely* because they were only studied by males. As with the deliberately useless education instilled in the Chinese mandarins, the mark of male privilege was education in dead languages. In addition, classical education glorified martial values – in the books read – and oral competition – in the teaching methods employed. (Fuller wrote later that her studies had inculcated in her 'a gladiatorial disposition'[22].) Classical education represented 'a puberty rite that further developed male identity. These men and boys . . . had access to a privileged priestly language . . . a *"patrius sermo"* (a "father speech") as opposed to the *"materna lingua"* (or "mother tongue")'.[23] They studied tales of male valour in battle and adventure – even more exclusively male in Latin than Greek, which would have offered Fuller the compensatory bravery of Antigone, the alternative wisdom of Diotema in Plato's *Symposium (Banquet)*, the rebellion of Lysistrata.

Fuller could and did learn to speak this man's language, Latin, but to her needs, as a girl, it really *was* dead. Yet she felt herself to be as fluent as a native in this discourse:

In accordance with [my father's] discipline in heroic common sense, was the influence of those great Romans, whose thoughts and lives were my daily food during those plastic years . . . Who that has lived with these men, but admires the plain force of fact, of thought passed into action? They take things up with their naked hands. There is just the man, and the block he casts before you, – no divinity, no demon, no unfulfilled aim, but just the man and Rome, and what he did for Rome. Everything turns your attention to what a man can become, not by yielding himself freely to impressions, not by letting nature play freely through him, but by a single thought, an earnest purpose, an indomitable will, by hardihood, self-command, and force of expression; man present in nature, commanding nature too sternly to be inspired by it . . . There is something indefinite, somewhat yet unfulfilled in the thought of Greece, of Spain of modern Italy, but ROME! it stands by itself, a clear word. The power of will, the dignity of a fixed purpose is what it utters. Every Roman was an emperor . . . [E]very thought put on . . . its toga virilis.[24]

Fuller underwent the initiation rite of memorising Virgil, but would never wear the *toga virilis*. Nevertheless, the themes of heroism and action identified in this passage helped her to construct her own narrative. But for a girl the manly classical values were hard taskmasters, like Fuller's father. They could not substitute for the female virtues, only contradict them. In Greek thought there is only one virtue for women: *sophrosyne*, self-restraint.[25]

The Roman constancy of will and purpose which Fuller so much admired played no part in the growing early nineteenth-century American cult of the True Woman, which celebrated submissiveness, piety, and passivity as the 'genius' of the female.[26] The Cult of Republican Motherhood had allowed women a sturdy independence: but that of True Womanhood saw her as fully absorbed in her vocation, purifying and restoring fallen Man.[27] Selfishness of any kind was the prime sin for women, and independence was a kind of selfishness. In return for abjuring all autonomy of thought and action, the true woman – the epitaph on Margarett Crane Fuller's tombstone – could expect worship. As an article of 1830 in the *Ladies' Magazine* put it:

A halo of glory encircles her, and illumines her whole orbit. With her, man not only feels safe, but is actually renovated. For he approaches her with an awe, a reverence, and an affection which before he knew not that he possessed.[28]

This conservative backlash against the model of 'republican mother-hood' began at the turn of the nineteenth century – with the victory of the Federalist government and the puritanical American reaction to the publication of the frank *Memoirs of Mary Wollstonecraft* by her husband, William Godwin, after her death in 1797. (The damage done to Wollstonecraft by Godwin – who was more than a little rivalrous – neatly parallels that done to Fuller by Emerson and the other editors.) Although conservative reaction to women's advance-ment was less pronounced in America than in England or France, it combined with the rise of religious evangelicalism, the narrowing of female employment opportunities outside the home, and concern for family cohesion on the frontier to prescribe a different ideal, that of Ruth.

> [A]s men were drawn away from the home to sell commodities or their labor, women were thrust more decisively into it . . . [A]s the home lost its productive function in the economy, its 'moral' functions took on added weight. For as men learned to scant moral, religious and emotional values in an increasingly competi-tive industrial society, women were expected to embody and enact these values for their men; hence the helpmeet was trans-formed into the 'better' – and wholly other – half.[29]

True Womanhood was largely incompatible with the virtues of self-reliance and critical thought. Over-indulgence in intellectual activity would be a girl's undoing:

> As for training young ladies through a long intellectual course, as we do young men, it can never be done. They will die in the process . . . She must be on the strain all the school hours, study in the evening until her eyes ache, her brain whirls, her spine yields and gives way, and she comes through the process of education, enervated, feeble, without courage or vigor, elasticity or strength. Alas! must we crowd education on our daughters, and for the sake of having them 'intellectual', make them puny, nervous, and their whole earthly existence a struggle between life and death?[30]

As the cult of True Womanhood rose and the star of Republican Motherhood fell, as predictions of dire trauma to over-educated girls appeared to come true in the form of Sarah Margaret's nightmares and migraines, as he acquired sons to train her place, Timothy Fuller stopped trying quite so hard to teach his daughter his language. Although the letters home from his Congressional post in Washington enquired how she was progressing in her formal studies, they showed an increasing concern about her awkward social deportment. Against her wheedling protest, 'I hope you are not quite so anxious to get rid of your *little* daughter',[31] he admonished her that going to boarding school would mean 'You have a fair opportunity to *begin the world anew*, to avoid the mistakes and faults, which have deprived you of *some esteem*, among your present acquaintances.'[32] At the age of thirteen she was sent against her will not to the Boston academy run by Ralph Waldo Emerson and his brother, but to Miss Prescott's School for Young Ladies in forty-miles-distant Groton – little better than a finishing school, in her initial opinion: 'I feel myself rather degraded from Cicero's Oratory to One and two are how many. It *is* rather a change is it not?'[33]

In this letter Fuller protests only by inflecting the 'is,' and by using the greeting 'Dear Sir' rather than her usual 'My dear father.' Throughout her childhood, and increasingly in adolescence, she combined a feline reserve with puppyish eagerness to please her father on the terms he set – 'My love to the little Sarah Margarett. I love her if she is a good girl and learns to read', he wrote to his wife when the girl was three. Her earliest letters to him in Washington are full of pleas that he write more often. At ten she is still importunate and humble: 'Has your affection decreased? I fear it has; I have often pained you but I hope you still love me.'[34] By thirteen she is outwardly correct but inwardly resentful: 'I had not intended to have written to you again, till I had received an answer to my last letter, as I consider regularity proper in all things, but in consideration of the pleasure my very interesting letters must give you, I h[ave] altered my resolution.'[35] At fourteen she was adding to her repertoire of ways for resisting her father the trick of mock humility: 'Indeed, I cannot make myself interesting to you; to your strictures on my conduct manners &c however valuable to me I can return nothing but thanks . . .'[36]

This ambivalence shows that she did not model herself solely and slavishly on her strong father, as many biographers have asserted. And nowhere was her rebellion more pronounced than over the issue of whether she should be allowed access to what was defined as the epitome of *women's* literature: the novel. At eight she had defied Timothy's edict that Shakespeare was unsuitable reading on Sundays, returning to her *Romeo and Juliet* in open disobedience to his reprimand when she was caught the first time. Reflecting on this incident in later life, Fuller pitied her ageing father's narrowness of spirit but condemned his dictatorship as less than benevolent:

> Often since have I seen the same misunderstanding between parent and child, – the parent thrusting the morale, the discipline, of life upon the child, when just engrossed by some game of real importance and great leadings to it . . . None but poets remember their youth; but the father who does not retain poetical apprehension of the world, free and splendid as it stretches out before the child, who cannot read his natural history, and follow out its intimations with reverence, must be a tyrant in his home . . .[37]

On any day but the Sabbath, she *was* free to read Shakespeare, as well as Smollett, Fielding, Molière and Cervantes, and the poetry of Goldsmith, Cowper, Thompson and Gray. But Timothy Fuller disliked narrative which was not didactic: he denied her request to read a translation of Wieland's *Oberon* because the story line might interest her more than the niceties of prosody. Too compelling a plot was outlawed. So it was primarily over the novel that Margaret staked her claim to her own discourse.

It was women's exclusion from training in the classics which impelled them to develop alternative literary forms to the classically-inspired epic and lyric. The novel developed from the less prestigious forms in which women were allowed to excel, correspondence and diaries.[38] But Timothy Fuller forbade his daughter to find out about her literary ancestors on this maternal side. The price of admission to the male priesthood of classicists was renunciation of the sin of novel-reading.

Writing on Christmas Day, 1819 – no rest for the virtuous – Fuller dutifully enclosed a Latin composition – 'I assure you I wrote the former off much better and made *almost* as many corrections as your critical self would were you at home' – and a progress report on her translation into Latin of Oliver Goldsmith's poem 'The Deserted Village.' But she also informed her father – perhaps relying on seasonal good will – that she had been reading a novel called *Hesitation*.[39] There was no hesitation in her mind about reading it without waiting for his permission, Nor was she diffident in its defence, though she argued in Timothy's language: 'Do not let the name novel make you think it is either trifling or silly. A great deal of sentiment, a great deal of reasoning is contained in it. In other words it is a moral-novel.'[40]

She was still pursuing the issue, with different tactics, in a letter of 16 January 1820. Although in this letter and the previous one she asked for his approval – none too humbly – before she embarked on John Moore's proto-Byronic novel *Zeluco: Various Views of Human Nature taken from Life and Manners, Foreign and Domestic* (1789), she was still unrepentant about having presented him with a *fait accompli* in reading *Hesitation* without his leave. To make matters worse, she was writing stories herself, and unabashed about it.

> You will let me read Zeluco? will you not and no conditions . . . I am writing a new tale called The young satirist. You must expect the remainder of this page to be filled with a series of unconnected intelligence . . . Have you read Hesitation yet. I knew you would (though you are no novel reader) to see if they [the characters] were rightly delineated for I am possessed of the greatest blessing of life a good and kind father. Oh I can never repay you for all the love you have shown me. But I will do all I can.[41]

At the end she issued another challenge: 'P.S. I do not like Sarah, call me Margaret alone, pray do!'[42] Timothy's mother was called Sarah; his daughter must have known that her request would appear disrespectful.

In his answer written a month later, on 25 January 1820, Timothy brooked little challenge to the Law of the Father. He addressed the envelope and the heading to Sarah Margarett, although he slipped slightly in the text of the letter by calling her 'my dear Margaret' in passing. (Later, writing to his wife about his daughter's request to change her name, he played the lawyer as well as the heavy father: 'That cannot be done without an act of General Court – is she willing to petition for the alteration?') And he replied that she should 'acquire a taste for books of higher order than tales and novels'. She ignored his disapproval of *Hesitation* in her reply, pointedly thanking him only for his permission to read *Zeluco* – and for sending her a pen. (Pens, apparently in Timothy's gift alone, were a constant request: the means of written expression depended on the will of the father.) A letter written later that year was still sharper:

> Mr Waldo was here the other evening and protested as vehemently against novels and such trash as you do papa and he is not

even so moderate as you for he will not even except historical novels. Well I dare say he as silly [*sic*] I when arrived at the same age, shall be as wise, at present though you tell me I am foolish, you are angry at me for being so. I wish I could be wiser, but that person *is* illiberal who condemns Scotts and Edgeworths novels.[43]

It might seem pompous to make so much of Fuller's insistence on reading novels: every girl of her time did the same, though not always against the opposition of a father so formidable as Timothy. But not only did Fuller defy her father's law in claiming the right to read women's literature; in her letters to women, she practised a consciously female style. In her correspondence with her father Fuller was soberly analytical, though she occasionally indulged in wistful humour: 'I expect sir that when you come home you will bring me home a complete case of jewels or something equal to it . . .'[44] But in writing to women of the right age to be the older sisters she never had, Fuller dared to be more blatantly comic – and more insolent about the name her father had given her. To her friend Mary Vose, twelve years older, she wrote:

> If you ever write to me leave out that name Sarah. Out upon it I will not be content to be called by it till I am sixty years old Then I will take it for it is a proper, good, old maidish name. I will be willing to sit down and knit stockings look cross and be called Miss Sarah Fuller for the rest of my life. But for the present time I will be addressed by the name of Margarette . . .[45]

At the beginning of this letter, the ten-year-old Fuller flirted with the high style of the novel:

> As I am in a fair way to be very idle very dull and very cross this afternoon if I do not write to somebody I will give the preference to employment and to you I do not imagine you will thank me but it is not because I have any thing pretty or new or even remarkable to tell you but to rid myself of the burden of an insupportable idleness.
>
>   Ah my poor Mary I fear that the die is cast and that you have lost the generous independant [*sic*] noble highminded and spirited Redmond.[46] What a pity that a man of such elegant manners should throw himself away upon Susan Messinger. You were the

only person fit for him. You alone could equal his fine talents
uncommon genius and superior understanding.[47]

But Fuller consciously parodied the usual happy ending prescribed
for the novel's heroine. She went on:

> How happy would you have been with him . . . How I should
> admire to see my sweet cool Mary in the midst of a parcel of
> children vexed with one scolding another and whipping a third.
> It wou'd do my heart good.[48]

The editors of the *Memoirs* were po-faced about Fuller, but she was
full of banter from the beginning, despite the severity of her childhood. Writing at the age of nine to her English friend Ellen Kilshaw,
she proposed making arrangements for her two-year-old brother's
betrothal to Kilshaw's little niece. She joked in an oddly prescient
way ('I as you well know am a queen'):

> How old is Miss Elisa K. Green now – her betrothed lover is in his
> 3d year. Do you think it would do any harm to let them be
> married at 13 . . . I doubt not if Wm Henry were to see her he
> would be charmed with her. As to nobility of blood our family
> needs no ennobling I as you well know am a queen William
> Henry unites a prince and king in his single person and Eugene is
> prince of Savoy I am beside being a queen the duchess of
> Marlborough.[49]

Not having to censor her wit or her style for her father, Fuller could
practice her vivid powers of expression in this letter to her woman
friend. Ellen Kilshaw spoke a different dialect, not merely because
she was English: 'She did not say much to me – not much to anyone.
She spoke in her whole being rather than by chosen words. Indeed,
her proper speech was dance or song . . .'[50] This was not the language
of the father; it was the enabling silence of the female friend. With
Kilshaw the nine-year-old Fuller could try to dance in words:

> As the slow messenger Mercury [the name of the mail packet
> ship] will soon bend his course toward England I sit down to the
> pleasant duty of writing you a letter . . . I do not write often
> enough to write as easy as some persons who seem to have so
> much to say that they cannot write fast enough and they have not

paper enough to hold all they have to say. When I have some event to talk about I think will be interesting to the person to whom I am writing, then indeed I can talk fast enough.

Friday night the ropewalk [ropeworks] in Boston was burnt ... Some new machinery had been bought which sparing a good deal of labor several workmen were dismissed . . . They were Irishmen of a fierce vindictive spirit. As they departed they declared they would be revenged and told the proprietor of the ropewalk he should not enjoy it long ... The fire was a most awful spectacle which if I attempted to describe I should not be able to give you an adequate idea of its grandeur.

On the same night the Aurora Borealis or Northern Light shone out in splendor. We had walked out to have a nearer view of the fire. When we were returning papa observed some streaks of it but it was not till we had entered the house we saw it in full splendour. At last I grew weary even of grandeur and went to bed or to express it more elegantly retired to rest. I shall expect when our faithful Hermes returns (whether he is faithful I know not but I know he is not nearly as swift as his namesake the messenger of the gods) I shall expect a long letter from you.

This letter is signed 'Margaret Fuller', at the time when she was still abbreviating her preferred name to an initial in her signature for Timothy, 'Sarah M. Fuller'. To the older woman, Fuller could call herself by her own name. Ellen Kilshaw was the first adult who agreed to address her as she chose to be called. Later Fuller was to write 'When shall I be given to myself?' She had made a start by giving herself a name.

But her chosen name was also her mother's name. This is itself means little – giving the eldest girl the combination of grandmother's and mother's Christian names was not uncommon – but it does have a symbolic value. Margaret Fuller both reproduced and rejected her mother, although most biographers have only concentrated on the rejection. Margarett Crane Fuller is generally a mere shadow, Timothy the burning sun. This is the implicit metaphor behind Paula Blanchard's remark that during her first five years Margaret had no other child to shield her from the full glare of her father's scrutiny. David Watson merely remarks that 'Margaret's mother . . . sank into the background of family decision-making . . .'.[51] Bell Gale Chevigny, who thinks that acceptance of male and female stereotypes hampered Fuller's development as a writer on the Woman Question, nevertheless subscribes to those stereotypes herself in judging the Fuller parents:

> Since the notions of 'masculine' and 'feminine' were bound to cultural norms, it is clear that as long as she cast her problem in these terms, she was unwittingly conspiring to delay her progress toward freedom . . . But it was virtually impossible for her to think beyond these formulations. By their natures, her parents reinforced the sexual stereotypes and by their method of rearing her they contributed to her sense of being hopelessly divided between these stereotypes . . . [Margarett Crane Fuller] seems to have submitted serenely as a wife to her husband's domination . . . (It is tempting to read between the lines the mother's conditioned passivity and disengagement from her children's lives in the world beyond home.) Individuality, even idiosyncratic behaviour, and strong opinion seem to have been all on the father's side.[52]

Chevigny does at least allow that Margaret Fuller identified with both parents, though she rather wishes that Fuller *had* unequivocally rejected her mother. Freudian accounts, such as that by Katherine Anthony, present the whole of Fuller's career as propelled by rivalry with her mother for her father.[53] Fuller's own eulogy of her mother – that of all the people she knew, Margarett Crane Fuller 'had in her most of the angelic' – might be mere grist to this Oedipal mill. Not only did Margaret Fuller reject her mother, this argument might run; she wanted to kill her off in any available fashion, and gagging her on syrupy praise would do nicely.

But less doctrinaire observers would have to recognise the unmistakable and unbreakable tenderness between mother and daughter. (They should also beware of an oddly sexist tendency to accept that Mrs Fuller was always the Angel in the House. She was something of a demon for grudges, still resenting her sister-in-law's coldness at the time of Timothy's death in a letter written seven years later.[54]) Margaret's warmth about her mother is returned in the entry which Margarett Crane Fuller wrote on the leaf of her daughter's 1844 journal, as Margaret was preparing to depart for New York:

> . . . [A]s all separations are solemn things for the infirm, I give my blessings on this last page of the journal, as if it were my last, with many acknowledgements for the love and tender care I have experienced at the hands of my dear daughter . . .[55]

Mrs Fuller's flower garden was her sanctum; the library was Timothy's domain. In her semi-autobiographical romance, Fuller wrote movingly of the refuge which the mother's garden offered:

> Here I felt at home. A gate opened thence into the fields, – a wooden gate made of boards, in a high, unpainted board wall, and embowered in the clematis creeper. This gate I used to open to see the sunset heaven; beyond this black frame I did not step, for I liked to look at the deep gold behind it. How exquisitely happy I was in its beauty, and how I loved the silvery wreaths of my protecting vine! . . . it stands in nature to my mind as the emblem of domestic love. Of late I have thankfully felt what I owe to that garden, where the best hours of my lonely childhood were spent . . . I loved to gaze on the roses, the violets, the lilies, the pinks; my mother's hand had planted them, and they bloomed for me.[56]

But she also found this little private space literally and symbolically constricting. In contrast to the frequently quoted passage from this autobiographical fantasy – which may or may not be literal truth – Fuller remembered her childhood reactions as much more restless in the purely non-fictional travel journal which she kept for her brother Richard:

> Merely gentle and winning scenes are not enough for me; I wish my lot had been cast amid the sources of the streams, where the voice of the hidden torrent is heard by night; where the eagle soars, and the thunder resounds in long peals from side to side; where the grasp of a more powerful emotion has rent asunder the rocks, and the long purple shadows fall like a broad wing upon the valley . . . I feel this all the more for having passed my childhood in such a place as Cambridgeport. There I had nothing except the little flower-garden behind the house, and the elms before the door. I used to long and pine for beautiful places such as I read of. There was not one walk for me except over the bridge; I liked that very much, the river, and the city glittering in the sunset, and the lovely undulating line all around, and the light smoke seen in some weathers.[57]

Our mother's gardens, in Alice Walker's phrase, not only shelter us; they hem us in. The same is true of our mothers' expectations: in trying to reconcile us to expected norms of female beauty and behaviour, Judith Arcana has argued, they hurt us all too literally.[58] Fuller blamed her mother's insistence on tight-lacing her young daughter's waist for many subsequent physical ailments, as much as she did the whalebone stays in which her father corseted her mind: 'I can't help mourning sometimes, that my bodily life should have been so destroyed by the ignorance of *both* my parents.'[59]

Yet when Margaret had a choice of parents to write to – in December 1821, when her mother was in Washington with her father – she chose her mother. In a letter of the 2nd, she wrote, 'Tell my dear father that I have not cried once since *he* went away. I am as happy here as I can be separated from *you*.'[60] Following the pattern of modestly unveiling her novelistic attractions only to female correspondents, in the next letter to her mother she let her pen run florid in this description of a melodrama of which Timothy could never have approved.:

> The performance was Blue Beard, in which we had the pleasure of seeing fire, smoke, battles, death, blood, skeletons and all the ghostly preparations. But there were many beautiful horses and some of the performances really wonderful. One of the little ponies being ordered to jump through a balloon went and stuck his nose through the paper and then not liking the sport ran back.[61]

In this letter Fuller sounds years younger than in her august performances for Timothy; she can be a child with her mother – without having to wheedle, 'I hope you are not quite so anxious to get rid of your *little* daughter.' She can also be a sister to other girls – despite the stereotype, even in feminist biographies, that her sense of sisterhood was not powerful.[62]

> Yesterday, Miss Heard, Miss Cunningham, Miss Hart, and Miss Greenleaf, Dr Parks oldest sholars [sic] left school having made and received very elegant presents to and from the scholars. The Dr addressed them in a very pathetic manner no one could restrain her tears and he was so much affected, that he could hardly speak as he bid [sic] them farewell. The four ladies shed abundance of tears and could not prevail on themselves to go, until the last minute. Then kissing us all round they went, but still it

seemed to give them great pain. I think that we are all sisters, it is hard for me to stand unconnected; and all girls who have no intimate friends are not so much beloved.[63]

If Margaret Fuller learned the dissecting language of parsing and conjugating from her father, from her mother and female schoolmates she learned the idiom of connection. To focus only on her father's influence is to accept an implicitly male-centred view of children's development. A boy would not have to learn the vocabulary of connection: only that of independence.

According to the psychologist Nancy Chodorow,[64] boys' and girls' different experiences in childhood produce radically disparate ways of naming the self. Because mothers do most of the child-rearing in our culture, it is primarily against the mother that the growing boy must define himself as an individual. His experience of growing up is one of asserting himself and standing apart. Girls can learn proper behaviour for their sex by directly imitating the mother, who is present more frequently than the father. (This was particularly true in Fuller's case: how her father could be the only important influence in her life when he wasn't even there half the year has never been explained.) Boys, in contrast, absorb abstract rules of proper male behaviour through social conditioning.

> Thus, not only do girls learn roles with more interpersonal and relational skills, but the process of role learning itself is embodied in the concrete relation with the mother . . . This early experience forms an important ground for the female sense of self as connected to the world and the male sense of self as separate, distinct, and even disconnected.[65]

On the other hand, argues the psychoanalyst Maureen Murdock,[66] the girl must learn to separate herself from the mother, who represents the devalued feminine. While boys are expected to reject the feminine, a girl who wants to be a heroine – like Fuller – cannot remain in the mother's domain. But this rejection is likely to be experienced as more hurtful than the boy's.

When Margaret was twenty-three, her father decided to sell their Cambridge house and retire to the countryside at Groton, near his boyhood home – and the scene of her schoolgirl miseries. During Fuller's first year in this paternal prison, she tried to lay plans for escape to the West, where she hoped that her friend James Freeman

Clarke would help her set up a school. Clarke himself had set out to find his clerical fortune in Kentucky, and Fuller's brothers Eugene, William Henry and Arthur were all to light out for the frontier. But when Margaret broached her plans to her mother, she was hurt and frightened at the prospect of tending her large household with no other daughterly aid than that of fourteen-year-old Ellen. Margaret abandoned her plans for her mother's sake: 'Unless her health should improve I ought not to leave her and assume such a responsibility that I could not return if she wanted me. – I have spoken to her (though not to my Father) of the plan and observe she regards it with great aversion.'[67] It does not take the heavy hand of the father to hem the daughter in: compassion for the mother does just as well.

A letter of apology written when Margaret was supporting and living with her mother, while simultaneously trying to write, shows that resolution of this quandary – independence versus caring – continued to elude Fuller:

> I was and am quite grieved, dearest Mother, to give you pain tonight. I am too well aware that a momentary ebullition of impatience may give more pain than many days of tenderness can atone for . . . But all I feel is that you do not sympathize entirely with my great desire to have a clear space round me for a time. It is very natural that you should not; the purposes for which I would free my thoughts are not the same as those that act on your beneficent life. Believe me I will not again for a long time be thus ungentle . . .[68]

In adulthood, the psychologist Carol Gilligan argues,[69] the business of asserting and defining individual rights is central to men's worldviews. But it is not an everyday concern for most women, who are more likely to think in terms of caring and responsibilities. Ethical behaviour is defined, for women, as paying proper attention to the web of relationships in which individuals are caught up. In Fuller's letters to her mother, she gossips happily about an acquaintance's child who is cutting a tooth, buying a doll for her younger brother, an uncle's 'paralytic shock', a friend's 'shivering fits'. This discourse has been ignored in most works on Fuller, which have mainly dealt with the 'serious' matters of scholarship and learning in her childhood – serious as defined by the father. But the mother's language of relationships was also a subject for the daughter's serious study.

Further, according to Chodorow and Gilligan, male identity depends on escaping from the mother and therefore from the household. The duality of public and private realms is created by this masculine psychological need, some feminist writers argue. 'Masculinity must be attained by means of opposition to the concrete world of daily life, by escaping from contact with the female world of the household into the masculine world of public life.'[70] Timothy Fuller was pre-eminently a man of the public realm, Margarett Crane Fuller a denizen of the private world. But Sarah Margaret could not simply be one or the other. Throughout her adult life her letters concern coats and careers for younger brothers as much as they do the condition of prostitutes in Sing Sing. The *Memoirs* omitted such domestic concerns as trivial – and so they might be for Emerson, who was allowed by the gender laws of his society to ignore them. To dismiss them in Fuller's case succumbs to a male ethic of what counts, leaves out the attractive caring element of her personality, and underrates her achievement. 'I could do well enough if free from anxiety about the family,' Fuller wrote in 1841 to her mother.[71] She did well enough, though never free from that disquiet.

Margarett Crane Fuller taught her daughter both the maternal and the paternal languages. When Timothy was away, she enforced the Law of the Father in relation to Margaret's studies. Even when Timothy had given Margaret permission to read *Zeluco*, her mother would not let her have it until she had done her recitation for Uncle Elisha. But the mother was also the point of connection for the father and the daughter; through her Timothy's diffident but powerful affection for Margaret could be expressed without loss of paternal authority. When Margaret was seven, she developed an inflamed gum from a broken baby-tooth whose root remained embedded in the jaw. Timothy, newly arrived in Washington on his Congressional duties, did not hear from the family for three weeks. To Margaret he wrote a hortatory epistle commending Roman fortitude in bearing pain. But to his wife he unburdened himself: 'Now listen a moment to my fears – You are sick – or Sarah Margarett, dear child of mine, has been in some peril and some pain, and very much anxiety with her tooth.'[72]

But if Margaret had learned the maternal language of connection, why did she apparently reject her mother? Although her letters to her mother in later life are deeply affectionate, she also wrote a semi-autobiographical romance which pictures her mother dying of grief after her younger sister's death. As a child Margaret had a recurrent dream of following her mother's coffin, a nightmare which persisted until she left New England. This fantasy may be nothing more than a way of exorcising that demon. But Bell Gale Chevigny thinks it symbolised Fuller's rejection of her mother's unfulfilled life as a True Woman.[73] I think this is probably a twentieth-century projection. There is little indication in Fuller's correspondence that she looked down on her mother's devotion to the family; indeed, she emulated it.

How then to explain Fuller's fantasy? We may get some help from Emily Dickinson's fabrication in a letter to Thomas Wentworth Higginson: 'I never had a mother. I suppose a mother is one to whom you hurry when you are troubled.' Dickinson, like Fuller but even more explicitly, seems to be saying that her forbidding father took her mother's place: 'I always ran Home to Awe when a child, if anything befell me. He was an awful Mother, but I liked him better than none.'[74]

One explanation of this letter, suggested by Barbara Mossberg, is that Dickinson had to reject her normal, nurturing mother in order to allay her own guilt at choosing the abnormal role of female poet.[75] Male critics have claimed that both Dickinson and Fuller only became writers because they suffered loss. As Chapter 1 discusses, Ted Hughes explains Dickinson's vocation as a form of blighted love, and Emerson similarly put Fuller's writing down to frustrated spinsterdom. Does a woman writer subconsciously need to produce a loss for herself, in order to justify her calling in the eyes of the world? But even if so, why choose the loss of a mother? After all, it is only the loss of a *man* which matters, in the world's opinion.

Carolyn Heilbrun's analysis of a number of autobiographical essays by women writers suggests that casting off the father's spell is pivotal in female authors' lives, but comparatively straightforward. The relationship with the mother is more complex for any woman, Heilbrun thinks: rebellious and loving at the same time. When a writer is a daughter – the title of Mossberg's book on Dickinson – the daughter must both reproduce and reject the mother. A domesticated mother may be loved tenderly, but she cannot legitimise the quest towards a more heroic life through her own example.

One can generalize from these essays with minor, if any, exaggeration that fathers, as representatives of the patriarchy, are the pivot on which, usually in memory, the new awareness turns . . .

Mothers may come to be recognized with a new, loving perception, but it is not mothers who free women from their fathers. They leave their daughters as yet unawakened.[76]

The language of bewitchment is suggestive. In *Woman in the Nineteenth Century* Fuller uses an authorial stand-in called Miranda. Elaine Showalter thinks that the reference to *The Tempest* is deliberate. This was a play with great resonance for a gifted woman who had learned what wizardry of knowledge she possessed largely from her father. (Harriet Beecher Stowe recorded her enchantment when, as a child force-fed on Plutarch, she came across a tattered copy of the play in the family attic. Here was a woman's life, isolated and cramped though it was; in Plutarch there were none.)

Like Prospero, Timothy Fuller isolated his daughter on an island of anomaly, making her a fish out of water, a learned lady. Miranda speaks the language her father taught her and has no conversation with other women; she does not even remember her mother. Showalter calls Fuller 'a motherless Miranda trying to give birth to herself.'[77] I think the case is a little more complicated. To accept that Fuller viewed herself as motherless would be to confirm a patriarchal view of who mattered in her life, whose language was her native tongue. Fuller was not literally motherless, and indeed her mother was her preferred parent, I think – much more of a presence in her life than her frequently absent father.

But Fuller may have had to *make* herself motherless – at least in the safe house of fiction, this semi-autobiographical romance – to make herself a writer. In *The Tempest* only Ariel frees himself from Prospero: as Showalter says, Miranda is confined to the marriage plot, but Ariel's plot is liberty. When Fuller was in her teens, her father recast the production, giving principal roles to the sons he now possessed. Previously Margaret had thought hers was the liberty plot: instead her role was now to walk on gracefully. Between the eighteenth century and the 1930s, Ariel was always played by a woman. Perhaps Fuller wanted to be one woman who in her time played many parts, Ariel and Miranda both.

Shipwrecked on an uncharted island: the sea metaphor holds good for the next period of Fuller's life, the twenty years from 1824 to 1843. In her young womanhood she was becalmed in an unproductive period – what Heilbrun calls the 'moratorium' which affects many women writers. It was only when she became her own navigator that she could sail out of this wide Sargasso Sea.

3

'Where Can I Hide till I am Given to Myself?'[1]

I feel the power of industry growing every day, and besides, the all-powerful motive of ambition, and a new stimulus lately given through a friend. I have learned to believe that nothing, no! not perfection is unattainable. I am determined on distinction, which formerly I thought to win at an easy rate; but now I see that long years of labor must be given to secure even the 'succès de société,' – which, however, shall never content me . . . I know the obstacles in my way . . . Yet all such hindrances may be overcome by an ardent spirit. If I fail, my consolation shall be found in active employment.

Margaret Fuller at 15, 11 July 1825

Circumstances have decided that I must not go to Europe, and shut upon me the door, as I think, forever, to the scenes I could have loved. Let me now try to forget myself, and act for others' sakes. What I can do with my pen, I know not. At present, I feel no confidence or hope. The expectations so many have been led to cherish by my conversational powers, I am disposed to deem ill-founded . . . I do not think I can produce a valuable work. I do not feel in my bosom that confidence necessary to sustain me in such undertakings, – the confidence of genius.

Margaret Fuller on her 26th birthday, 23 May 1836

Although Emerson gives the impression that Fuller was a monster of vanity who lacked all ambition, this pair of letters indicates that the reverse was true: she *was* ambitious but wanted faith in herself. Both pairs of characteristics might seem internally inconsistent, but Emerson's is more so, I think. What Fuller was striving for in the first letter above was not particularly monstrous by the standards of the cult of True Womanhood: spiritual perfection. The self-improvement manuals which attempted to reconcile the reality of women's drudgery with an ideal of high-minded devotion to cultivating inner beauty enjoined just such a quest.[2]

But Fuller did not think these virtues should be confined to the domestic hearth, as the cult prescribed: she was ambitious for a success beyond that of shining in the limited sphere of conventional society. The True Woman should keep her light under a bushel, but Fuller took that doctrine with a grain of ironic salt:

> I hate glare, thou knowest, and have hitherto successfully screened my virtues therefrom . . . So well have I played my part, that in the self-same night I was styled by two several persons 'a sprightly young lady', and 'a Syren!!' Oh rapturous sound! I have reached the goal of my ambition: Earth has nothing fairer or brighter to offer.[3]

To William Henry Channing, a less flippant Margaret had 'laid bare her secret hope of what Woman might be and do, as an author in our Republic'.[4] For a woman to desire literary distinction, and work industriously for it, is perfectly consistent with doubting whether she will attain it. There are plenty of reasons why not. As Carolyn Heilbrun puts it:

> . . . [A] time of hope [is] a phrase, significantly, that was used by C.P. Snow to characterize a man's youth, when all seems possible and his destiny awaits him if he will but set his feet upon the path. For the young woman, however, for whom the female destiny of flirtation, wedding, and motherhood is insufficient or even unattractive, youth is less a time of hope than a time of uncertainty, at worst a time of depression and some wild experimentation among the passions: as though in watching male passions turned upon oneself, one could distract one's attention from the blunted female destiny.[5]

Heilbrun suggests that 'for women who wish to live a quest plot, as men's stories allow, indeed encourage, them to do, some event must be invented to transform their lives, all unconsciously, apparently "accidentally," from a conventional to an eccentric story'.[6] This is 'a phenomenon evident in the lives of accomplished women who live in a storyless time and are either trapped in, or have wasted energy opposing, the only narrative available to them: the conventional marriage or erotic plot'.[7] As examples, Heilbrun cites George Eliot's lifting herself 'abruptly out of the conventional plot' by living with George Henry Lewes out of wedlock, and Dorothy L. Sayers's pregnancy as an unmarried woman. George Sand's decision to leave her miserable conventional marriage for an ill-paid journalist's life in Paris with her infant daughter was the equivalent break for her, I suggest.

The liberating life-crises occurred at a later period in these women writers' lives than often happens with men, Heilbrun thinks. Women are doubly disadvantaged, I suggest: the penalties for breaking with a conventional lifestyle are greater for them, yet they need that separation more than men do – in order to transform their lives into something out of the ordinary. And by definition a woman writer is something out of the ordinary, a Dark Lady.

Heilbrun refers to the period before this decisive rupture with convention as the 'moratorium', a concept borrowed from Erik Erikson and applied by him primarily to men. Heilbrun agrees that the lives of George Bernard Shaw and Henry James also demonstrate the period of the moratorium: 'a time when the individual appears, before the age of thirty, to be getting nowhere, accomplishing none of his aims, or altogether unclear as to what those aims might be. Such a person is, of course, actually preparing for the task that, all unrecognized, awaits.'[8] In women she thinks the moratorium typically lasts longer. The break required is more decisive, the tasks awaiting women in their youth – marriage, childrearing, household duties – more time-consuming, the quest plot lacking a script.

Margaret Fuller 'had to create a way of life not yet possible, and a self whose nature was without local example'.[9] An American woman who wanted to write a heroic life in the public world for herself would find no models: no Joan of Arc, no Queen Elizabeth, no Cleopatra.[10] Even an American *man* would find few exemplars of the life of action *and* the life of the mind. Eighteenth-century New England Puritanism had put up a barrier between action and scholarship, though Fuller wanted both.

For women Jacksonian America was not the land of opportunity: rather of *shrinking* opportunities. It gave her nowhere to hide until she could be given to herself. The decline of the ideal of republican motherhood and the relegation of women to the private sphere were not yet counterbalanced by the rise of female educational institutions which provided intellectual women with a base.[11] Many of these establishments, such as Mount Holyoke Seminary, founded in 1837, had a religious purpose – and Fuller was not particularly godly, though she tried to remake herself in a devout image during this blank time of the 'moratorium'.[12] In any case, female seminaries, teacher training schools, and degree-awarding courses for women arrived on the scene too late for Fuller to make use of them. Co-educational Oberlin College, for example, was founded when Fuller was 23; only when she was 27 did it offer to women the same course it gave its male students. Most boys of her acquaintance went to Harvard at 13 or 14 and were ensconced in careers by their late teens.

In this chapter I want to ague that Fuller's moratorium lasted a very long time indeed: for all of her life in New England, until she left for the Great Lakes in 1843, New York in 1844 and Europe in 1846. It was the decision to abandon New England which provided the rupture with what was expected of her – the parallel with Eliot's, Sayers's and Sand's decisions to opt for the unconventional. Only then could she live the quest plot and write herself a life.

The decision to leave was only partly a deliberate plan for improvement, despite Fuller's ambition – bearing out Heilbrun's contention that the decisive moment is half-accidental. Julia Ward Howe explained Fuller's departure not as the fulfilment of her ambition, but as the withering away of her duties towards her family.[13] By 1843 all her younger brothers except Lloyd, who had learning difficulties and behavioural disturbances, had finished college and established themselves more or less securely in business and the professions. Her sister Ellen was married and could now provide a home for her mother.

Nevertheless, most of Fuller's New England friends urged her to stay put. Among them were Emerson, Clarke and Channing. The editors of the *Memoirs* only knew Fuller during her time in New England: therefore they thought of what was actually her fallow period as the period of her greatest achievements. Hawthorne complained that his three hours a day in the Customs House at Salem blocked his creative force. Before 1843, Fuller was at various periods tutoring her four younger siblings and running a household of eight people; teaching up to twelve hours a day to support her family after her father's death; caring for her mother and mentally handicapped brother; and editing *The Dial* for no pay. That she wrote anything at all in this period is a marvel, though much of the writing is of her worst.

But although Fuller had had a bad time in those years, the *Memoirs'* editors thought it was the best time she had. Although their version of her life was the one which gained currency, they actually knew very little about her *life*: only her period of waiting. Their sense that she was forever flailing about for direction, that her life was always blocked at every turn, reflects their limited knowledge of her life after New England – although the frustration of her Massachusetts years was not primarily sexual, *pace* Emerson.

Nor should we fall into the trap of saying that Fuller only really came alive once she became a mother. This sort of Mariolatry set the tone for even the more favourable reviews of the *Memoirs*, such as George Eliot's. But having a child was not actually part of the script Fuller wrote when she set out for Europe in 1846. I do not deny that the birth of her son Nino in 1848, and the short childhood she was allowed to share with him, represented a peak in her life. But it was not a mountain she had intended to climb on her trek: it was off the map, *terra incognita*.

I do not think that Fuller was waiting for either marriage or motherhood in her stale years. The fact of not marrying may have either helped or hindered her. Heilbrun believes that in Sayers's case we need to recognise 'the possibility that it is precisely not having been sexually attractive in youth that enables women to develop the ego-strength to be creative . . .'.[14] In Fuller's case I think we need to leave the question open, not least because she was nothing like as ugly as her 'friends' made her out to be. To make the woman writer's chance of finding a vocation hang on being unattractive is as deterministic in its feminist way as Emerson's statement that all Fuller was really expressing in her journals and her letters was spinsterly malaise. George Sand was not conventionally beautiful, but no one has ever denied that men found her attractive. Yet this does not seem to have impeded her development of 'the ego-strength to be creative.'

When Margaret Fuller finally solved the problem of what script to follow by writing her own, through living it, she was still stymied by the lack of available words in which to write it down. This, combined with her lack of confidence in herself, is the reason why Fuller would never have written *Memoirs*, I argue. As Gilbert and Gubar put it, 'Margaret Fuller solved the problem of . . . "the anxiety of authorship" by living an ambitious life that she could not write about because it could not be contained within traditional literary genres.'[15] Fuller was right to doubt that her ambitions for her writing could be realised. Luckily her life became 'real' in the end.

Fuller's 'real' life was thus even shorter than her chronological life: the seven years between 1843 and 1850. When she finally reached Europe in 1846, she wrote to her long-time friend Caroline Sturgis:

> Had I only come ten years earlier; now my life must ever be a failure, so much strength has been wasted on obstructions, which only came because I was not in the soil most fitted to my nature, however, though a failure, it is less so than with most others and the matter not worth thinking about. Heaven has room enough, and good chances enough in store, no doubt, and I can live a great deal in the years that remain.[16]

The 'years that remain' were four in number.

Even though the period 1824–43 includes her years at *The Dial* and the Boston Conversations – the latter considered more fully in Chapter 4, on Fuller and the Woman Question – it was still a period of waiting to be given to herself. This is not to downgrade Fuller's professional achievement in those twenty years – two published translations from the German, an unpublished translation of Goethe's *Tasso*, a number of magazine articles and reviews, and the book *Summer on the Lakes* (1844) – nor her enormous influence on and contribution to Transcendentalism. (Susan Phinney Conrad calls her the greatest of the Transcendentalists, outranking Emerson and Thoreau.) Nor is it to underrate her steady professional-minded discipline in the most adverse circumstances. The first letter quoted at the beginning of this chapter begins with details of her Stakhanovite daily schedule after she returned from school in Groton to home in Cambridge. Her formal education had almost entirely finished, when her male contemporaries were just entering university, but she determined to give her education to herself:

> I rise a little before five, walk an hour, and then practise on the piano, till seven, when we breakfast. Next I read French . . . till eight, then two or three lectures in Brown's Philosophy. About half-past nine I go to Mr. Perkins's school and study Greek till twelve, when, the school being dismissed, I recite, go home, and practise again till dinner, at two. Sometimes, if the conversation is very agreeable, I lounge for half an hour over the dessert, though rarely so lavish of time. Then, when I can, I read two hours in Italian, but I am often interrupted. At six I walk, or take a drive. Before going to bed, I play or sing, for half an hour or so, to make

all sleepy, and, about eleven, retire to write a little while in my journal, exercises on what I have read, or a series of characteristics which I am filling up according to advice.[17]

During these years back in Cambridge, 1826–33, she read Milton, Racine, Rousseau, Epictetus, Petrarch, Alfieri, Locke, Byron, Tasso, and Schiller – having taught herself German. It was Carlyle whose writing inspired her with a lasting love of the German authors, and she went on to read Goethe, Novalis, Korner and Fichte at this time, as well as more of Carlyle himself. She returned over and over to the German romantics, but also to the French, particularly Sand and de Staël. Of the latter she wrote:

> She is a natural person – a most rare thing in this age of cant and pretension. Her conversation is charming; she brings all her powers to bear upon it; her style is varied, and she has a very pleasant and spirited way of thinking. I should judge, too, that she possesses peculiar purity of mind.[18]

For Fuller to have written that, at a time when New Englanders ranked de Staël with the Painted Whore of Babylon, indicated that she herself possessed peculiar purity of mind. Although Fuller's wide reading helped her to make the best of her period of enforced waiting – and, as Heilbrun suggests is common, to prepare her for what she was waiting *for* – it must have engendered further frustration, her reading of Mme de Staël in particular. Here was a woman who *had* written herself a life. Did the example suggest to Fuller that a woman's life could only be written successfully in Europe?

European commentators of Fuller's time denounced the 'land of the free' as the land of servitude – not only for black men, but also for all women. Alexis de Tocqueville identified a paradox: American girls – like Fuller – were more highly educated than their European counterparts, but with the exception of pioneers, the adult American woman's life was more circumscribed. 'It may be said that she has learned by the use of her independence to surrender it without a struggle.'[19] It was the cult of the True Woman which effected this sea-change. By teaching women that the culmination of their moral and intellectual education was to take over responsibility for their husbands' and children's virtue, it left American women with no independent purpose.

But de Tocqueville accepted that American wives had freely chosen marriage as their destiny. American women, he wrote, 'attach a sort of pride to the voluntary surrender of their own will, and make it their boast to bend themselves to the yoke, not to shake it off'.[20] Harriet Martineau was more trenchant: there were no economic alternatives, except the ill-paid occupations of governess and teacher. The myth of free choice was the worst tyranny of all. 'While woman's intellect is confined, her morals crushed, her health ruined, her weakness encouraged, and her strength punished, she is told her lot is cast in the paradise of women.'[21]

The example of the foremost European woman of intellect and action, Mme de Staël, could have inspired Fuller in the absence of American models. But de Staël's own self-constructed life must have both simultaneously excited and defeated Fuller, as would the example of her heroine Corinne. (Later, however, Fuller was called 'a New England Corinne'.) The restlessness which she was suffering at home in Cambridge, while all her male contemporaries were at university, was writ large in Corinne. The Byronic quest of *Corinne* is nothing extraordinary – but the fact that it is undertaken by a woman is unique.[22]

That this pursuit of the ideal ends in Italy may also have influenced Fuller, as it did the Italian nationalist movement for which she would later work. Italy becomes in *Corinne* the promised land of radiance: 'through *Corinne* it had become transformed into the essential spiritual patrimony of all those who aspired to culture and civilization'.[23] *Patri*mony indeed: Italy was the land of the Father, presented to Fuller as her spiritual homeland in her father's Latin lessons. That a woman could make it her own best home, and make her own life there, free of censure, was de Staël's potent instruction to Fuller.

By seeing a creative artist's suffering in a gifted woman's dissatisfaction, *Corinne* legitimised Fuller's unwillingness to settle for the conventional woman's plot. This example of a woman of genius influenced many other nineteenth-century female writers, including Elizabeth Barrett Browning, George Eliot and Harriet Beecher Stowe. But by depicting Corinne eventually crowned at the Capitol in Rome, dressed like a Sibyl in Indian silks, 'a goddess surrounded by clouds,' the novel ultimately left any other plot but the conventional one still out of Fuller's reach. This was too obviously fantasy for Fuller's incisive New England mind; but even in fantasy, a successful woman must be modest and humble, according to de Staël:

Her pose on the chariot was noble and modest: one could tell that she was pleased to be admired; but a feeling of timidity mingled with her joy, and seemed to ask forgiveness for her triumph . . .[24]

Corinne is barred from living the conventional marriage plot: her retiring and shadowy half-sister Lucile – the Priscilla to Corinne's Zenobia – gets the man instead. Lucile survives Corinne, as Priscilla does Zenobia. The message of the novel is ambiguous, even threatening, to an ambitious woman. Although the dying Corinne tells Lucile, 'You must be both yourself and myself at the same time', she herself cannot live both roles, or indeed live at all.

When the young Fuller wrote a quest plot, it was a 'commission' for James Freeman Clarke, with a male protagonist, not a Corinne. In a letter replying to Clarke's doubts about his own potential, she wrote in the best supportive female manner:

I have greatly wished to see among us such a person of genius as the nineteenth century can afford – i.e. one who has tasted in the morning of existence the extremes of good and ill, both imaginative and real. I had imagined a person endowed by nature with that acute sense of Beauty, (i.e., Harmony or Truth,) and that vast capacity of desire which give soul to love and ambition. I had wished this person might grow up to manhood alone (but not alone in crowds); I would have placed him in a situation so retired, so obscure, that he would quietly, but without bitter sense of isolation, stand apart from all surrounding him. I would have had him go on steadily, feeding his mind with congenial love, hopefully confident that if he only nourished his existence into pefect life, Fate would, at fitting season, furnish an atmosphere and orbit meet for his breathing and exercise. I wished that he might adore, not fever for, the bright phantoms of his mind's creation, and believe them but the shadows of external things to be met with hereafter. After this steady intellectual growth had brought his powers to manhood, so far as the ideal can do it, I wished this being might be launched into the world of realities . . . ; I wished he might collect into one burning point those withering, palsying convictions, which, in the ordinary routine of things, so gradually pervade the soul; that he might suffer, in brief space, agonies of disappointment commensurate with his unpreparedness and confidence . . . [S]uch a man would suddenly dilate into a form of Pride, Power, and Glory, – a centre, round which

asking, aimless hearts might rally, – a man fitted to act as interpreter to the one tale of many-languaged eyes![25]

The Roman emphasis on action as superior to thinking, the aching
for 'an atmosphere and orbit meet for . . . breathing and exercise' –
these are components of Fuller's own quest plot. But here she only
plays the role of the 'asking, aimless heart,' orbiting around the sun
of this male hero.To 'dilate into a form of Pride, Power, and Glory':
was this too unwomanly an ambition, then as now? To endure at
most only a brief, compressed period of waiting and disillusionment, and perhaps none at all, is a man's prerogative, Heilbrun
suggests.

> A few years ago, after having read many exciting new bio-
> graphies of women, I had a shocking experience in going through
> Peter Ackroyd's biography of T.S. Eliot . . . [T]he old sense rushed
> over me of the ease of male lives . . . Here was a life for which
> there was indeed not only *the* narrative, but so many possible
> narratives. Despite Eliot's egregious sexual and personal failures,
> despite professional uncertainties, writing blocks, and frightening
> social judgments, despite his confused national, religious, and
> marital loyalties, his story reads as easily, as inevitably, as those
> of the Hardy boys . . . I have read many moving lives of women,
> but they are painful, the price is high, the anxiety is intense,
> because there is no script to follow, no story portraying how one
> is to act, let alone any alternative stories.[26]

Even men writers who *do* undergo a restless, roaming period are
only speaking somebody else's lines: the life-scripts written by
Byron, Dylan Thomas, Thomas Wolfe.[27] An intense but concentrated
period of disillusionment was not to be Fuller's privilege, although
her disillusionment was to become yet more intense.

At the age of twenty-three, Thomas Wolfe had just completed
three years of a playwriting workshop at Harvard and was about to
seek his fortune in Europe and New York. With the aggressive
masculine confidence which Gilbert and Gubar contrast with women's ambivalence about their own powers – such as that demonstrated in Fuller's second letter, at the start of this chapter – he wrote:

> No one in this country is writing plays like mine. I don't know yet
> what I am capable of doing, but by God, I have genius, . . . and I

shall yet force the inescapable fact down the throats of the rats
and vermin who wait the proof.[28]

When *Fuller* was twenty-three, her father moved the family willy-
nilly to a farm in Groton, where she had spent her less-than-blissful
school days. Margaret wrote that 'My time has been much broken
up' with heavy housework – but added that she had set herself the
task of reading all of Goethe.[29] In the moments between cooking on
the wood stove for a family of eight, scouring rusty iron utensils,
rubbing brass pots with flannel and rum, sewing, washing and
ironing the children's clothes, making soap, and nursing her brother
Arthur through the threatened loss of an eye, she pursued a programme of self-education as extensive as Gibbon's.[30] The next year
found her even more weighed down with doing jobs for other
people – educating her younger brothers and sister to save her father
expense:

> Five days in the week I have given daily lessons in three lan-
> guages, in geography and history besides many other exercises on
> alternate days – This has consumed often eight, always five hours
> of my day – There has been a great deal of needle-work to do, and
> is now nearly finished and I shall not be obliged to pass my time
> about it when every-thing looks beautiful as I did las[t] summer –
> We have had very poor servants and for [some time past,] only
> one – My mother has been often [ill. My grand]mother (who
> passed the winter with [us) has been ill. Thus] you may imagine
> as I am the *only* [grown-up daughter, that] my time has been
> considerably [taxed.)
>
> [But as, sad or merry, I must always be learning, I laid down a
> course of study at the beginning of winter, comprising certain]
> things about which I had always [felt deficient. These] were – The
> history and [Geography of] modern Europe, beginning the former
> in the fourteenth century. The elements of Architecture – the
> works of Alfieri with his opinions on them – the hist and critical
> works of Goethe and Schiller and an outline of hist of our own
> country.
>
> All this . . . is might dry . . . I have nearly completed this course
> in the style I proposed (not minute or thorough, I confess) though
> I have had only three evenings in the week and chance hours in
> the day for it . . . I occasionally try my hand at composition but
> have not completed any thing to my satisfaction – I have sketched

a number of plans, if ever accomplished they must be so in a
season of more joyful energy, when my mind has been renovated
and refreshed by change of scene or circumstance.[31]

Later, on a New Year's eve when she had little to expect of the next
day, month or year, Fuller wrote to her brother Arthur:

> Three precious years at the best period of life I gave all my best
> hours to your children – let me not see you idle away time which
> I have always valued so, let me not find you unworthy of the love
> I felt for you. Those three years would have enabled me to make
> great attainments which now I never may. Do you make them in
> my stead that I may not remember that time with sadness.[32]

Within her twenty-year moratorium period – from being sent to her
girls' boarding school in 1824 to leaving for the West in 1843 and
obtaining a correspondent's position on the *New York Tribune* in 1844
– Fuller was stranded highest and driest during the years 1833–36, as
this last letter indicates. The second letter at the start of the chapter
also reflects the despair of that period. When she arrived in Groton,
she wrote, 'I confess I greeted my new home with a flood of bitter
tears.'[33] On the Fourth of July she had little to celebrate: 'I think I
cannot commemorate the anniversary of our independence better
than by writing to you, since all of freedom that has fallen to my lot,
is that of thought and unrestrained intercourse with my friends.'[34]
Isolation from her Cambridge intellectual acquaintances was the
worst handicap to a would-be writer. André Malraux has written
that the mainspring of art is the imitation of other art.[35] Even reclu-
sive Emily Dickinson had her sister-in-law Susan Gilbert Dickinson
as an audience, and benefited from her suggestions in revising
'Safe in their Alabaster Chambers' and other poems. Without someone to strike sparks off, with whom she could compare styles and
discuss forthcoming projects, Fuller was stymied.' . . . [T]o me the
expression of thought and feeling is to the mind what respiration
is to the lungs . . .'.[36] As a verse written in her journal during 1834
shows, she could not progress through print alone:

> Uncheered by friendly voice, oppressed/ By doubt, and fear, and
> bitter introspection,/ Performing duties, or pursuing studies/
> With cold reluctance . . . /Might but the years of childhood,/
> Which a precocious growth of mind stole from me,/ Come to me

now! Some years of mere sensation;/ I cannot *feel* this thing . . . /
My mind too early filled, – the outward sense neglected,/ I know
each object having seen its picture;/ Feelings, from the description I have read.[37]

Fuller tried to comfort herself partly with religion – she had a mystical experience in November 1831 – and partly with the Goethean
philosophy that doing the 'nearest duty' would suffice until she
could be given to herself.[38] Goethe appealed to her because he emphasised the life of action in a rather Roman way:

> How often have I thought, if I could see Goethe, and tell him my
> state of mind, he would support and guide me! He would be able
> to understand; he would show me how to rule circumstances,
> instead of being ruled by them; and, above all, he would not have
> been so sure that all would be for the best, without our making an
> effort to act out the oracles; he would have wished to see me what
> Nature intended . . . I do not wish to *reflect* always . . . I wish to
> arrive at that point where I can trust myself, and leave off saying,
> 'It seems to me,' and boldly feel, It *is* so to me.[39]

Fuller wanted to return to the certainties her father had promised
her: she had been taught never to say 'It seems so to me,' but always,
with masculine force, 'It is.' In the circumstances of a woman's life,
speaking the language of the father was worse than useless. And the
consolations of Goethean philosophy were limited:

> I shut the book [Goethe's *Second Residence in Rome*] each time with
> an earnest desire to live as he did – always to have some engross-
> ing object of pursuit. I sympathise deeply with a mind in that
> state. While mine is being used up by ounces, I wish pailfuls
> might be poured into it. I am dejected and uneasy when I see no
> results from my daily existence, but I am suffocated and lost
> when I have not the bright feeling of progression.[40]

What she was given after her father's death in October 1835 was not
her self, but even more responsibility for others. Thereafter she was
simultaneously accountable for her family's maintenance and helpless to achieve it. Fuller's early life had been largely determined by
'the Will it is that situates', in Emily Dickinson's phrase[41]: in her case
the Law of the Father. Yet her father, lawyer though he was, died

without leaving a will. 'On the evening of the 30th of September 1835, my father was seized with cholera, and on the 2nd of October was a corpse.'[42] Shortly before Margaret herself had been seriously ill, with a nine-day fever taken to be typhoid:

> You know that I looked upon Death very near, nor at the time should I have grieved to go. I thought there never could come a time when my departure would be easier to myself, or less painful to others.[43]

During this illness Timothy, whose strictures about her failings she had so intensely resented as a girl, gave her the highest praise she was ever to receive from him: 'My dear, I have been thinking of you in the night, and I cannot remember that you have any *faults*. You have defects, of course, as all mortals have, but I do not know that you have a single fault.'[44] This was the nearest she would come to a final benediction from her father.

Later, in going through her father's personal papers when the family sold the Groton house, Fuller was to return the compliment:

> How well he was prepared to meet the fiat which went forth so suddenly, I find abundant evidence in these papers. Well as I knew my father, I know him hourly better and respect him more, as I look more closely into those secrets of his life which the sudden event left open in a way he never foresaw.[45]

In business affairs, however, Timothy was ill-prepared to meet his end. The suddenness of the death threw the family into financial disarray, though Fuller had found her financial dependence on her father burdensome before his death. In February of the year he died, she wrote: 'This money this money it has fettered me always and is like to more and more.'[46] Timothy was not ungenerous: he had paid for a trip up the Hudson as a reward for her labours with her younger siblings' education. But she had had to grovel for it:

> Oh do sympathize with me – do feel about it as I do – The positive expences [sic] of the journey we have computed at forty seven dollars – I shall want ten more for spending money – but you will not think of the money – *will* you?[47]

Margaret had no financial independence, nor as a daughter at home was she likely ever to have any. To undertake the life of Goethe which she was formulating in her mind as a possible vocation, she would need to travel to Europe, but she would have had to depend on her father's largesse.

However, she was no freer now. Timothy's death put paid to the European project in Margaret's mind, although her family were willing to make sacrifices for her sake and let her go. But with the two oldest boys not yet established in careers, Mrs Fuller distraught, and Timothy's financial assets almost entirely tied up in the purchase of the farm and other unproductive real estate, Timothy's brother Abraham took upon himself the role of financial saviour, having been appointed executor. His proposals over the years before the estate was finally settled included curtailing the younger children's education, sending Ellen out to work as a governess, and putting up one of the boys for adoption. Margaret determined to stay and fight her uncle, 'that sordid man':[48]

> My father left no will . . . I have often had reason to regret being of the softer sex, and never more than now. If I were an eldest son, I could be guardian to my brothers and sister, administer the estate, and really become the head of my family. As it is, I am very ignorant of the management and value of property, and of practical details . . . But I am now full of desire to learn them, that I may be able to advise and act, where it is necessary. The same mind which has made other attainments can, in time, compass these, however uncongenial to its nature and habits.[49]

At first Fuller thought that she might earn a small living through journalism and translation. In November 1834 her name had appeared in print for the first time – a reply to the historian George Bancroft which appeared in the *North American Review*, the staid publication which Emerson called 'the snore of the Muses'. Margaret was as sarcastic about this first success as about her previous 'success' in screening her authorial virtues from the world:

> [My father requested me to write a little piece in answer to Mr B[ancroft] . . . It was responded to (I flatter myself by some bigwig as we say in Groton) from Salem. He detected some ignorance in me nevertheless as he remarked that I wrote with 'ability'

and seemed to *consider me* as an elderly gentleman I *considered* the affair as highly flattering and beg you will keep it in mind and furnish it for my memoirs as such after I am dead.[50]

Fuller had also written articles on Hannah More, Edward Bulwer-Lytton, George Crabbe, and Henry Taylor, along with her translation of Goethe's verse-play *Tasso*. Although none of these had been accepted for publication, she still had hopes. With intense discipline – always her strong point – she might just be able to keep a shred of her ambition:

> All hopes of travelling I have dismissed – All youthful hopes of every kind I have pushed from my thoughts – I will not, if I can help it, lose an hour in castle-building and repining – Too much of that already! . . . Oh! keep me steady in an honorable ambition . . . Thou art my only Friend, thou has not seen fit to interpose one feeling, understanding breast between me and a rude, woful [sic] world. Vouchsafe then thy protection that I may 'hold on in courage of soul'.[51]

It became more and more obvious, however, that Fuller would have to go into teaching, which she dreaded – perhaps because of her years at boarding school. In *Summer on the Lakes* (1844) Fuller describes an episode which the editors of the *Memoirs* took to be her own experience at Miss Prescott's school, confessed with 'touching truthfulness':[52] But Fuller's brother Arthur denied that this 'Mariana' story was true to life, and in this century Perry Miller judged it 'more revealing as a psychological disclosure than as a piece of autobiography. It is one among several efforts of plain Margaret to act out the role of a beautiful and foredoomed heroine'.[53] (Of course this is more revealing as a psychological disclosure about Perry Miller than about Margaret Fuller.)

Mariana is the Dark Lady of the school: black-haired, rebellious, dramatic, moody. She queens it over lesser dramatic lights in school plays and enjoys fancy costumes and theatrical paint. Her envious schoolmates decide to humiliate her: when she arrives, habitually late, at the dinner table, she finds that all the other girls have rouged prominent red circles on their cheeks. Although she shows no emotion at dinner, she falls into convulsions afterwards in her own room, and then vows revenge, manipulating her schoolmates through rumour-mongering, fits and suicidal impulses. When the headmistress upbraids her, she dashes her head against the hearth. Surviving, to her consternation, she goes on hunger strike. Finally a sympathetic teacher tells her about overcoming similarly embarrassing incidents in her own youth. Mariana leaves the school reformed, cured of histrionics, unable to play false any longer. (A similar inability to deceive, a penchant for awkward truth-telling, was used against Fuller as much as her supposed talent for self-dramatisation.)

Whether this story really was autobiographical is debatable. Fuller suggested playfully in a letter written after the publication of 'The Great Lawsuit' that the world should consider that the character of Miranda in that work might be no more or less the real Margaret than that of Mariana, and that different characters might represent different aspects of her own character. But the story of 'Mariana' is told in the first person, by another girl, with Mariana in the third person, at a double remove. The narrator is much more like Margaret in appearance, background and manner than is the Spanish Creole Mariana. Mariana was educated by an aunt; Margaret most certainly by a man. The rest of the Mariana narrative, after her school days, is clearly fictional – a standard romance in which Mariana dies of blighted love. Before her death Mariana writes a mawkish poem about the Law of the Father: 'Father, they will not take me home./ To the poor child no heart is free;/ In sleet and snow all night I roam;/ Father – was this decreed by thee?'[54] Fuller appends the following meditation of her own to 'Mariana's' poem:

> It marks the defect in the position of women that one like Mariana should have found reason to write thus. To a man of equal power, equal sincerity, no more! – many resources would have presented themselves. He would not have needed to seek, he would have been called by life, and not be permitted to be quite wrecked through the affections only.[55]

In this passage Fuller herself identifies the many narratives open to men, as against the sole – tragic – plot for women, the love story. If the plot of Mariana is not necessarily to be taken literally, Fuller's point about the single female plot should still be taken. The moral is more revealing than the melodrama.

Whether or not the Mariana incident actually occurred is probably also less important in explaining Fuller's abhorrence of teaching than her professionalism: she knew she would have little time for her own writing. Thomas Wolfe likewise resented the demands which college teaching made on his time, and did his best to be shot of it as quickly as he could find a female protector, Aline Bernstein. However, his university teaching also provided him with intellectual stimulation – and a student who typed the manuscript of *Look Homeward, Angel* for him. Fuller's decision to return to Boston and teach reopened the world of thought to her after her mental exile in Groton. Unlike Wolfe, however, Fuller was not to find an amenuensis in her pupils; indeed, she was to spend much of her precious free time acting as an unpaid assistant and translator to the influential Unitarian clergyman, Dr William Ellery Channing.

Fuller's labours in Bronson Alcott's Temple Street School, the post she took up in 1836, also gained her little money in the end. Alcott, whom Thomas Carlyle called 'the potato Quixote,' was a Connecticut Yankee of atypically impractical stripe. His 'Orphic sayings', later published in *The Dial* under Fuller's editorship, gained him the reputation of a head-in-the-clouds philosopher. Indeed, his daughter, Louisa May Alcott, took a leaf from Aristophanes' play *The Clouds* by describing her father as 'a man up in a balloon, with his family and friends holding the ropes which confine him to earth and trying to haul him down'. Alcott's family suffered the brunt of his impracticality: Louisa May began earning her living as a dolls' dressmaker, teacher, and occasional servant from an early age, before gaining the means to support the family as the author of *Little Women*.

But this was all in the future at the time when Fuller met Alcott; nor could she have foreseen that he would exploit her as much as he did his own family. At the time when she made her difficult choice to teach, she looked forward to the financial independence which it promised her at last. As things turned out, Alcott's controversial methods aroused such hostility – even before he dared to admit a mulatto girl, in 1839 – that by spring of 1837 the school's income was halved, and Margaret dismissed without pay.

Alcott's educational principles were the opposite of Timothy Fuller's: he did have patience with minds that 'listen, wait and receive', believing in Socratic dialogue even with young children. His credo, as Fuller characterised it, was 'that those who would reform the world should begin with the beginning of life'.[56] Like Plato in the *Meno*, which shows an uneducated slave boy's innate ability to grasp the emblematic truths of geometry; like Wordsworth's conviction that children stand closest to God, having come most recently from their previous celestial existence; Alcott's philosophy concentrated on drawing out what his pupils already knew. Although Margaret shone at conversation, both here and at her next post, the Greene Street school in Providence, she too put by overtly didactic teaching in order to listen to the children. As one of her Providence pupils wrote:

> She said it must not be our object to come and hear her talk. We might think it a delightful thing to her to talk to so many interesting auditors, but that was not the thing; she could not teach us so, *we* must talk and let her understand our minds.[57]

This enabling role allowed many of Fuller's virtues full play: her concern with individual students' welfare, her sympathy with minds dissimilar to her own, her humour. Another of her Providence pupils wrote, 'I love her more than words can tell. She is so funny – she makes me laugh half the time – we had such a glorious time Wednesday . . . when we did not recite half the time.'[58] As Chapter 1 discussed, Fuller had a talent for inspiring confidences: Emerson called her 'the wedding guest, to whom the long-pent story must be told'. He added, 'She sympathizes so fast with all forms of life, that she talks never narrowly or hostilely, nor betrays, like all the rest, under a thin garb of new words, the old droning cast-iron opinions or notions of many years' standing.'[59]

But Fuller did not want to limit herself to this part, The Mentor, any more than to that of 'The Friend,' as the *Memoirs* capitalised it – and capitalised on it, as the recipients of her friendship had done during her life. To the extent that the role of friend *was* her choice, it was always of the Hobson's variety. In a letter of 1830 to James F. Clarke, Fuller sees friendship as yet another duty, a vocation of desperation:

> [T]hose who professed to seek my friendship, and whom, indeed, I have often truly loved, have always learned to content themselves with that inequality in the connection which I have never striven to veil. Indeed, I have thought myself more valued and better beloved, because the sympathy, the interest, were all on my side. True! such regard could never flatter my pride, nor gratify my affections, since it was paid not to myself, but to the need they

had of me; still, it was dear and pleasing, as it has given me an opportunity for knowing ánd serving many lovely characters; and I cannot see that there is anything else for me to do on earth.[60]

Fuller's long period of waiting, her moratorium, was undeniably brightened by her power to both give and receive intimacy. The first letter at the start of this chapter mentions 'a new stimulus lately given through a friend' – probably Lydia Francis (Child), later to gain prominence as an abolitionist and educator. The years spent teaching in Boston and Providence were filled with satisfying relationships, sometimes modelled less on equality than on older sisterhood – and also, androgynously, older brotherhood. 'A sister I have truly been to many, – a brother to more . . . ,' she wrote.[61] With her father dead, Fuller sometimes took on the paternal role as well. Her letters to her younger siblings Ellen, Arthur and Richard often sound as if they had been dictated in his absence by Timothy's ghost:

> My dear Arthur: I was glad to get a few lines from you, but I wish you to study the art of saying more in your epistles and saying it well. Nothing [but] practice is necessary for this I know, as you have plenty of thoughts in your mind. Many boys in our school of ten or eleven, inferior to you in natural capacity, write better.[62]

Of her friends, too, she demanded high standards, the first being utter openness. James Clarke's sister Sarah wrote:

> Her eye pierced through your disguises. Your outworks fell before her first assault, and you were at her mercy. And then began the delight of true intercourse. Though she spoke rudely searching words, and told you startling truths, though she broke down your little shams and defenses, you felt exhilarated by the compliment of being found out, and even that she cared to find you out . . . No woman ever had more true lovers among those of her own sex, and as many men she also numbered among her friends.[63]

As Bell Gale Chevigny points out, the cult of True Womanhood unleashed rather more powerful sentiments between women than its founders had bargained for.[64] If women alone possessed selfless purity, why should they waste themselves on self-absorbed, worldly men? Female friendship was legitimised, even to the extent of amorous attraction such as Fuller and Caroline Sturgis seem to have experienced, at least in the early stages of their long relationship. (Later Fuller wrote that their friendship had finally 'been redeemed from the search after Eros'.[65]) The European Romantic movement primarily offered examples of male friendship, but it, too, legitimised female amity, as through the example of Mme de Staël and her companion Mme Récamier, the model for Corinne.

So did its infant American cousin, Transcendentalism: even Emerson conceded that his male and female friends were 'incomparably the richest informations of the power and order that lie at the heart of things'.[66] Of Fuller's friendship Emerson – despite his professed adherence to 'self-reliance' – wrote with warmth:

> Her arrival was a holiday . . . All tasks that could be suspended were put aside to catch the favourable hour, in walking, riding, or boating, to talk with this joyful guest, who brought wit, anecdotes, love-stories, tragedies, oracles with her, and with her broad web of relations to so many fine friends, seemed like the queen of some parliament of love, who carried the key to all confidences . . . She drew her companions to surprising confessions. She was the wedding-guest, to whom the long-pent story must be told . . . [Her conversations] interested me in every manner – talent, memory, wit, stern introspection, poetic play, religion, the finest personal feeling, the aspects of the future, each followed each in full activity, and left me, I remember, enriched and sometimes astonished by the gifts of my guest.[67]

Fuller was an intensely social being who could not satisfy herself even in the abstract with Emersonian self-reliance: 'she had an immense appetite for social intercourse', Sarah Clarke judged.[68] Withdrawing altogether from society would have been intensely lonely, and a confirmation of every prejudice among her acquaintanceship about intellectual women:

> As a bluestocking she faced a double challenge, of usurping a man's role in the face of strong opposition, and of doing so without actually becoming that asexual being which the very term bluestocking suggests. Emerson, her conscience and alter ego in this as in many things, thought her social life was frivolous and warned her against becoming 'the servant of a visiting-card-box'. But Emerson, in addition to being the uniquely self-sufficient being he was, had the advantage of simply being a man doing a

man's job. And he had his Lidian to help him keep his life in order, as Alcott had his Abby, Hawthorne his Sophia, and Carlyle his Jane. Many of the literary women of the last century – the Brontës, Emily Dickinson, George Eliot, and Elizabeth Barrett Browning, to name a few – did not work alone in the midst of society, but succeeded either by withdrawing from it altogether and living virtually as hermits, or by being fortunate enough to find men who would fulfill for them the protective and supportive role usually assigned to literary men's wives.[69]

Emerson, by contrast, believed that 'Every man is an infinitely repellent orb, and holds his individual being on that condition' – but as Paula Blanchard points out in the quotation above, he could afford to think that because he had his attendant satellites.[70] The contrast between Fuller's need for society and Emerson's view that friendship is at most an instrument by means of which the individual perfects himself bears out Gilligan's contention that girls learn to define their identity primarily in terms of forming and maintaining relationships, boys in terms of differentiation from others. Yet Fuller also wanted to name herself as a writer, and for this she wanted solitude. This tension troubled her:

> Two days in Boston; how the time flies there and bears no perfume on its wings, – I am always most happy to return to my solitude, yet willing to bear the contact of society, with all its low views and rash blame, for I see how the purest ideal natures need it to temper them and keep them large and sure. I will never do as Waldo does, though I marvel not at him.[71]

Her styles of both teaching and friendship required intense activity from her, energy that could have gone into the life of Goethe or the translations for which publishers were waiting. That friendship was no consolation for neglecting her real vocation comes out in letter after letter, full of that ambivalence about her creative powers which Gilbert and Gubar call typical of women writers:

> My book of translations is but a sorry sight; and I never rise from it without a strong desire to wash its witness from my hand and indeed, to wash my incompetent hands of the whole affair . . . I am altogether dispirited by the result and cannot, at present, summon courage to on.[72]

I pray you, amid all your duties, to keep some hours for yourself. Do not let my example lead you into excessive exertions. I pay dear for extravagance of this sort. Five years ago, I had no idea of the languor and want of animal spirits which torment me now.[73]

I believe the true cause of my not writing has been that I have not wished to write. For I have been in an irreligious state of mind, a little misanthropic and sceptical about the existence of any real communication between human beings.[74]

It is no longer in my power to write or study much. I cannot bear it and do not attempt it. Heaven, I believe, had no will that I should accomplish any-thing great or beautiful. Yet I do not dispair [*sic*], daily I do a little and leave the result to a higher power . . . Nothing disagrees with me so much as writing [letters], and I avoid it when possible. Letters from those in whom I am most interested . . . have been lying for many weeks unanswered in my desk.[75]

This is the first time I have really felt so utterly incompetent to do any thing. I do wish I could yield entirely to this languor. I wish I could lean on some friendly arm for a while. It cannot be. I cannot even neglect my friends with impunity, for , if I do, they will not write to me.[76]

I hate every-thing that is reasonable just now, 'wise limitations' and all. I have behaved much too well for some time past; it has spoiled my peace. What grieves me too is to find or fear my theory a cheat – I cannot serve two masters, and I fear all the hope of being a worldling and a literary existence also must be resigned. – Isolation is necessary to me as to others. Yet I keep on 'fulfilling all my duties' as the technical phrase is except to myself.[77]

Thoreau, too, wrote, 'If I repent of anything, it is very likely to be my good behavior. What demon possessed me that I behaved so well?'[78] But Thoreau's solution at the same age – twenty-eight – was drastically individualist: to throw over all duties, living in solitude and simplicity at Walden Pond. Gilligan's research has suggested that boys as young as eleven have an individualistic, rights-orientated view of the moral universe.[79] For example, when asked how much he owed to himself and how much to other people, Jake, one boy of that age, quickly replied, 'You go about three-fourths to yourself and one-quarter to everybody else'. A girl of the same age, Amy, could not give such a precise answer, noting instead that it would have to depend on the situation, who the others were, and many other variables. A radically isolationist solution such as Thoreau's was not natural to Fuller as a woman, particularly not as an eldest sister. And unlike Jake, she never expected to give anything like three-fourths to herself.

The calling of The Friend – which the editors of the *Memoirs* forced on Fuller after her death – turned out not to be enough for her in life. When Margaret asked her friend Caroline Sturgis to come and live in Providence for a time, she also made it clear that writing, not friendship, was her vocation: 'I do not intend to sacrifice my writing to you; my teaching, I cannot, of course.'[80] Sturgis refused, perhaps unsurprisingly, and this shows the inadequacy of friendship: it had to be worked at, in conflict with all the other things which also required Fuller's energy. To be The Friend, she would have to give four-fourths to everyone else.

What ambitious man would have been content with being remembered as 'The Friend'? It is particularly ironic that Emerson consigned Fuller to this fate: in so doing he consigned her to nothingness, in his own terms. 'O my friends, there is no friend,' Emerson opined.[81] Boswell may be known to posterity as the friend of Dr Johnson, but he also wrote his biography – and it is by virtue of the written work that the friendship is remembered and valued. Writing a name for herself only as a friend would indeed have meant that Fuller's name was written on water.

Carol Gilligan's suggestion that male development proceeds by identity differentiation[82] makes it seem unlikely that any man would be content to identify himself solely in terms of his relation to others. But he might well hive off the duty of making friendships and keeping relationships going onto a member of the female sex. By making Fuller responsible for being primarily 'the Friend', Channing and the other editors of the *Memoirs* delegated this emotional maintenance work to her, and convinced the world that this was her own choice. Further, they gave her an identity as dependent on men's as Simone de Beauvoir's has been said in this century to have been on Sartre's:

> [De Beauvoir] was the permanent personal factor in [Sartre's] life . . . Without her Sartre would have been a different person. But as has often been said, Sartre would always have been Sartre all the same. His life followed its own trail and its own logic. Simone de

Beauvoir without Sartre is difficult to imagine . . . Whatever her skills as a writer or her own role as courageous supporter of many causes, she can only be assessed in relation to the Sartrean universe.[83]

The Friend does not need a script of her own; she exists to allow others to tell their narratives. Emerson's analogy, the Wedding-Guest in Coleridge's 'Rime of the Ancient Mariner', is instructive. The Friend, like the Wedding-Guest, is a device to allow the narrative to unfold, not a person.

Teaching and friendship gave Fuller to others, and others to themselves through her – like James Freeman Clarke, who wrote to Margaret:

What should I ever have been but for you? I am not much now, but what I am, I owe in a large degree to your influence. You roused my heart with high hopes, you raised my aims from paltry amusements to those which tasked the head and fed the soul. You inspired me with a great ambition to distinguish myself above my fellows, and made me see the worth and meaning of life. Whatever we owe to those who give us confidence in ourselves, who make us believe we *are* something distinct and can do something special, who arouse our individual consciousness by an intelligent sympathy with tendencies and feelings we ourselves only half understand – all this I owe to you. You gave me to myself.[84]

But teaching and friendship could not give Fuller to herself. 'Only the woman who is Self-created can be an original woman, not fabricated by man, and a friend to other women.'[85] Until she could be given to herself, Fuller could not be fully a friend, either: or at least her friendship would continue to have that ravening quality which sometimes distressed its recipients. Friendship advanced her on her quest narrative, but it was not the narrative itself. Yet insofar as Fuller taught friendship as 'a philosophy of female affection',[86] and lived that ideal herself, she wrote an important plot for much twentieth-century feminist thought.[87]

The role of editor – a variation of The Friend, or The Muse – appeared at first to offer Fuller a more lasting compromise between her literary vocation and her avocation for friendship. This talent for nurturing others was put to use during Fuller's two years as (again unpaid) editor of *The Dial*. (Emerson subsidised the American pub-

lication of Carlyle's loss-making works, but felt he could not pay
Fuller the $200 annual salary agreed at the start of the enterprise.)
However, *The Dial* did not feed Fuller's needs and nurture her
talents; in many ways it starved them.

Editorship of *The Dial* was Fuller's first public achievement: what
the eminent textual scholar Robert Hudspeth calls 'the forum she
wanted, where she could say what she wanted about literature and
art'.[88] Most biographers present this as the end of her moratorium –
to the extent that they use that concept. It *is* important to give due
credit, as the *Memoirs* did not – only devoting two pages to Fuller's
entire *Dial* editorship, 1839–42 (counting the year of preparation).
Higginson tried to rectify this imbalance in his 1884 biography:
Emerson, who had died in 1882, no longer needed to be placated as
the journal's founding father. *The Dial*, Higginson judged, successfully challenged Americans' lingering colonial mentality, prodding
the American public to support a literature of their own. And it was
Fuller, as editor of the first issue, who set this new tone from the
start:

> After fifty years of national life, the skylark and nightingale were
> at last dethroned from our literature, and in the very first volume
> of the 'Dial' the blue-bird and the wood-thrush took their place
> ... Americans still go to England to hear the skylark, but English-
> men also come to America to hear the bobolink.[89]

But I want to argue that Fuller did not see *The Dial* period as breaking the logjam of her life; it is only in retrospect – now that we know
The Dial's influence in setting the canon of nineteenth-century American literature – that it has been elevated to the level of her first major
achievement. (Critics such as Perry Miller who ignore her feminist
and socialist writings and politics present it as her *only* real achievement, and her life as one of auxiliary usefulness to the great male
writers whom *The Dial* published, often for the first time, as in the
case of Thoreau.) Her letters reveal that Fuller was ambivalent about
The Dial from the start, and miserable with worry most of the time
she edited it. Before the first number was published in July 1840,
Fuller wrote to William Henry Channing: 'I am not sanguine as to
the amount of talent which will be brought to bear on this publication. I find all concerned rather indifferent, and see no great promise
for the present'.[90]

Even after she had successfully brought out the first edition, she wrote to Emerson: 'I am glad that you are not quite dissatisfied with the first no. I feel myself how far it is from that eaglet motion I wanted. I suffered in looking it over now'.[91]

Even after she had brought out three successful issues, Fuller was still less than enthusiastic:

> Write to me what ever you think about the Dial. I wish very much to get interested in it, and I can only do so by finding that those I love and prize are so. It is very difficult to me to resolve on publishing any of my own writing; it never seems worth it, but the topmost bubble on my life . . .'[92]

This last quotation suggests that Fuller's 'me' was less of a mountain than a crater.

At best, I suggest, *The Dial* was an apprenticeship: because the promised contributions often failed to arrive, Fuller wrote most of the copy for the first few issues herself. But contrary to the established view that the magazine gave Fuller her public voice, Margaret found that she did not yet have much to say:

> It is for dear New England that I wanted this review; for myself, if I had wished to write a few pages now and then, I had ways and means of disposing of them. But in truth I have not much to say, for since I have had leisure to look at myself I find that, so far from being a great original genius, I have not yet learned to think to any depth, and that the utmost I have done in life has been to form my character to a certain consistency, cultivate my tastes, and learn to tell the truth with a little better grace than I did at first.[93]

Editorship of *The Dial* was *counter*-productive in other ways, draining off time and confirming Margaret's ambivalence about her own literary powers, her grim conviction that 'I have no art'. This was not because the magazine had no female contributors; it published works by Caroline Sturgis, Emerson's first wife Ellen, Sophia Ripley, and much of Fuller's own work. But the writing of her own which Fuller thought suitable for the journal went against her native grain of analytical pungency; it was high-blown in the worst Transcendentalist style, which was characterised by 'inchoate structure, prodigal imagery, wit, paradox, symbolism . . . and a manifesto-like tone'.[94]

Part of the difficulty was that 'the Transcendentalists were exceedingly weak in the genres most in favor today (poetry, drama, prose fiction)',[95] but were attempting to revive styles little known today, and to create new genres. I shall argue in Chapter 5 that Fuller finally succeeded in creating just such a fresh form with her travel dispatches from Europe; but except for travelling a good deal in Cambridge, to paraphrase Thoreau, there was little to draw out this talent during her New England years. Although she wrote some pieces during this time which were later anthologised – such as her 'Essay on Critics' in the first issue – or which she reworked in a more powerful style – particularly 'The Great Lawsuit,' on which she based her best-selling *Woman in the Nineteenth Century* (1845), she also had to put by her own most important projects for the sake of encouraging the work of others. Her biography of Goethe, begun before she took over the editorship, was never finished. Taking on the nursing, maternal function of editor did little to advance her own craft, and much to make her doubt it.

This is particularly sad because the year 1839, when *The Dial* was first mooted, began so well for Fuller. After leaving Providence at the end of 1838, Margaret allowed herself a few months' rest, on accumulated earnings, with her mother in Groton. Most of Fuller's brothers were now established at university or in their professions, and only Ellen, Mrs Fuller and Lloyd were left at home. Although Fuller took on two boarding pupils to help pay expenses, and although Lloyd would always be a responsibility, her domestic duties were much reduced.

Released from the worst pressure of caring for and supporting the family after her father's death, Fuller's creative energy bounded into productive effort on her translations of Eckermann's conversations with Goethe. 'For seven years I have never been able to pass two months so much as I pleased and never expect it again, and I have been as industrious as any beaver.'[96] 'The hours of this summer,' Fuller wrote in 1839 to her friend Caroline Sturgis, 'the first leisure summer since I was of your age, and perhaps the last truly leisure hours of my life are to me the gold of Ophir, the spices of Ceylon.'[97] That summer she began to plan a biography of Goethe, encouraged by Harriet Martineau and Emerson: 'I know that not possibly can you write a bad book, a dull page, if you only indulge yourself and take up your work somewhat proudly.'[98] This *was* generous of Emerson. Despite his later memory of her me as mountainous, at this point – when her reputation was no threat to his, an ungenerous cynic might claim – Emerson did try to cultivate Fuller's self-confidence.

It was *The Dial* that tarnished the gold and dulled the spices of the summer of 1839 – or which at least failed to materialise into the looked-for treasure. Reviewers were often hostile: the Philadephia *Gazette* called the editors of *The Dial* 'zanies,' 'Bedlamites,' 'considerably madder than the Mormons'.[99] Meanwhile Transcendentalist stalwarts were complaining that the magazine was too conventional: Alcott insisted on introducing his contribution in the second issue with the disclaimer, 'A fit organ for such as myself, is not, but is to be.'[100] Within a year Fuller was prostrate with near-constant migraine and frustrated by her sense of still achieving nothing. In the letter of March 1840 which expresses her pessimism about *The Dial*, she told William Henry Channing:

> My dear friend, you speak of your sense of 'unemployed force.' – I feel the same. I never, never in life have had the happy feeling of really doing any thing. I can only console myself for these semblances of actions by seeing that others seem to be in some degree aided by them. But Oh! really to feel the glow of action, without its weariness, what heaven it must be! I cannot think, can you, that all men in all ages have suffered thus from an unattained Ideal. The race must have been worn out ere now by such corrosion. May you be freed from it! for me, my constant ill-health makes me daily more inadequate to my desires and my life now seems but a fragment.[101]

The conventional interpretation of this low ebb in Fuller's life is that she was distraught after rejection by both Samuel Ward and Emerson. In my previous two books I have documented the tendency to explain away women writers' professional disappointments and successes alike as conditioned by personal failures in love affairs. Both John Crowe Ransom and Ted Hughes account for Emily Dickinson's dedication to poetry as a nun-like decision to renounce the emotional world proper to women after rejection by a lover.[102] In Dickinson's case there is very little evidence of any lovers, speculations about the Philadelphia clergyman Charles Wadsworth and the Springfield editor Samuel Bowles making up in fantasy for what they lack in fact. But that is precisely what allows the myths to breed:

'Where the allurements of romance coincide with a knowledge vacuum, legends flourish.'[103]

Something very similar has gone on in many previous accounts of this period in Fuller's life. Because both Emerson and Ward were involved in preparing the *Memoirs*, with Emerson ruining many sources and Ward actively purloining them, there is a knowledge vacuum about Fuller's relationships with these men. But whether this alone indicates that the relations were amorous is dubious, I think. It is even more doubtful whether disappointment with Ward and/or Emerson accounts for Fuller's low state of mind by 1840, after the high expectations of 1839.

Fuller had known Ward – whom she called affectionately her 'Rafaello' – for many years; they had planned to travel to Europe, together with her friend Eliza Farrar, before her father's death put an end to her hopes. She was also intensely involved with Anna Barker, Ward's eventual fiancée. The announcement of Ward and Barker's engagement in 1839, and their marriage in October 1840, is usually blamed for Fuller's depression and ill-health throughout 1840 – together with Emerson's continuing inability to come down from his high horse of self-reliance and give Fuller friendship on the terms of intense sympathy she craved.

Although few of Fuller's letters to Ward from this period remain, the surviving ones (of definite attribution) are disappointed but not desperate. Their tone is rather cold but rational:

> If you love me as I deserve to be loved, you cannot dispense with seeing me . . . I will not think of you, but fix my mind on work . . . We did not begin on the footing of rational good-will and mutual esteem, but of intimacy; and I should think, if we ceased to be intimate, we must become nothing to one another. We knew long ago that age, position and pursuits being so different, nothing but love bound us together, and it must not be *my* love alone that binds us.[104]

> I never should make any claim upon the heart of any person on the score of past intercourse and those expressions of affection which were the flower and fruitage of its summer day. If autumn has come, let come also chill wind and rain like those of today. But on the *minds* of those who have known me once I have always a claim. My own entire sincerity in every passage of life gives me a right to expect that I shall never be met by unmeaning phrases or

attentions . . . I had thought too, that in ceasing to be intimates we might cease to be friends. I think so no longer.[105]

The most overblown letter of the period – beginning 'You love me no more', and signed 'Isola' – is not addressed, nor does it begin 'Dear . . .' anyone; but the convention has been to assume from the contents that Ward is the intended recipient.[106] This is arguing backwards from the desired conclusion. If Ward had the opportunity to suppress damaging letters, as he did, why would he have left this one alone? Possibly he never saw this letter, which was never sent. If he did, very likely he recognised that it was not addressed to him. It was, after all, Anna Barker, whom Fuller called 'my beloved'.[107] But presumably Ward would also have suppressed the letter if he recognised his wife as the intended recipient.

Equally well, the letter could be addressed to Caroline Sturgis: Fuller was angry with Sturgis, who had refused to confirm that she loved Fuller when pressed during their holiday at Nahant in summer 1839. Alternatively the unheaded letter could be a fantasy, perhaps a literary exercise, or an outpouring of feelings which was never meant to be sent – as is probably also true of Emily Dickinson's similarly florid 'Master' letters.[108]

I do not think that speculation about Fuller's loves can be profitable, given the sorry state of the correspondence; nor do I think that dejection about love explains Fuller's depression during the following winter, spring and summer. It was primarily professional rather than personal disappointment, I think, which extended Fuller's moratorium into the 1840s, her thirties. Rather than severing her moratorium, *The Dial* prolonged it. Rather than releasing her from her emotional languor, the *Dial* project exacerbated it.

But one reason why *The Dial* was bad for Fuller *was* personal: she had to repress her exuberance much of the time in order to work with Emerson. (Emerson had refused to take on the editorship himself because he wanted to concentrate on the first book of *Essays*, but he was nonetheless a force to be reckoned with.) Along with the maternal burdens of pacifying squabbling contributors[109] and making the journalistic household run on time, this corseting of her mind may have produced the fits of headache which afflicted her during the *Dial* years. Whatever the effect on her health – which worsened in the early 1840s, making her lose a great deal of work-time through migraine – Fuller's letters to Emerson demonstrate how she had to rein herself back to keep him sweet.

> I am on the Drachenfels [figuratively, a peak of exhilaration], and
> cannot get off; it is one of my naughtiest moods. Last Sunday, I
> wrote a long letter, describing it in prose and verse, and I had
> twenty minds to send it you as a literary curiosity; then I thought,
> this might destroy relations, and I might not be able to be calm
> and chip marble with you any more, if I talked to you in magnet-
> ism and music . . .[110]

Fuller's 'naughtiest moods' had to be tamed as much with Emerson
as if she were still a child under Timothy's tutelage. Emerson's moral
and literary principles were an extension of the Law of the Father,
and Fuller often used paternal imagery in writing to him.

> I felt that you did not for me the highest office of friendship, by
> offering me the clue to the labyrinth of my own being. Yet I
> thought you appreciated the fearlessness which shrinks from no
> truth in myself and others, and trusted me, believing that I knew
> the path for myself . . . Then indeed, when my soul, in its childish
> agony of prayer, stretched out its arms to you as a father, did you
> not see what was meant by this crying for the moon: this sullen
> rejection of playthings which had become unmeaning?[111]

> Why do I write thus to one who must ever regard the deepest
> tones of my nature as those of childish fancy or worldly
> discontent?[112]

Emerson, to his credit, sometimes recognised his own inadequacy to
meet Fuller's demands. Though he once rebuked her, 'You, instead
of wondering at my cloistered and unfriendly manners, should defend me if possible from friendship'[113] – presumably out of the
motive of friendship, which does seem rather muddled thinking on
the part of the Sage of Concord – to the letter above he appears to
have replied:

> You have a right to expect great activity great demonstration and
> large intellectual contributions from your friends, and tho' you do
> not say it you receive nothing. As well be related to mutes as to
> uncommunicating egoists.

When Fuller reproached Emerson with 'inhospitality of soul,' he
replied in still more penitent vein:

> If I count and weigh, I love also. I cannot tell you how warm and
> glad the naming of your names [Fuller's and Sturgis's] makes my
> solitude. You give me more joy than you could trust my tongue to
> tell you.

This was sincere, and as much as Fuller was going to get. So long as
she went on making demands of Emerson rather than of herself,
how could she emerge from the adolescence of her moratorium?
Like a first-year university student seeking to impress her professor
with erudite profundities, Fuller produced her most pretentious
and obscure pronouncements for Emerson:

> It has been justly remarked by Schlegel and other apprehensive
> critics, that, as all the world was in our Shakspeare [*sic*], and he
> expressed the gift of the bard or seer with the tact of the man of
> the world, so there lies beneath very slight expressions of his
> thought a double meaning like that supposed in the Swedenborgian
> construction. So that while the obvious meaning covers but a
> point, a line may be drawn from it to the limit of the Universe: As
> in this passage, so slight to a vulgar observer. "Old Signior, walk
> aside with me. I have studied eight or nine wise words to speak
> with you, which these hobby horses must not hear." Are not all
> audiences assembled in hall of state, saloon, or lecture-room de-
> scribed in this fine compound term with a picquancy [*sic*] which
> requires the illustration of no other word. Is it not this term, and
> none other, which must ever after being once acquainted with it,
> rise in the mind, on each day's intercourse with the world?
> O admirable Shakespeare, who, having not even [*sic*] for a hobby
> thyself, didst not disdain to write for hobby horses.[114]

Perhaps the root of Fuller's disenchantment with Emerson – 'Waldo
is still only a small and secluded part of Nature, secluded by a doubt,
secluded by a sneer'[115] – was that he could not give her to herself. The
imagery of her remark in this chapter's title is bridal. The enigma
was not that Emerson would not be her lover, or her intimate friend;
rather that he could not be the father who gives the daughter away.
Instead, Fuller did most of the giving: of intensity in friendship, of
labour for *The Dial*, which absorbed the time she had wanted for her
never-completed biography of Goethe.

To Frederic H. Hedge, one of the journal's recalcitrant contributors, she wrote, 'I know you are plagued and it is hard to write, just

so is it with me, for I am also a father.'[116] (With a fine display of calling the kettle black, Hedge wrote disparagingly in the *Memoirs* that 'Without external pressure, perhaps, [Fuller] would never have written at all. She was dogmatic, and not creative.'[117]) Margaret Fuller had to become her own father as well as the journal's. So long as she allowed Emerson to cast her in the roles of mother and muse to *The Dial*, daughter and handmaiden to his own thought, Fuller would never write lines she could deliver with conviction.

Only by changing the setting of the drama – making the quest literal and geographic, not abstract and ideal – could Fuller write her own life. Since 1840 she had wanted to go West and visit the Indian tribes.[118] In order to give herself to herself, she would have to make a physical break with her surroundings. Thoreau ended his own (voluntary) moratorium the year after he left Harvard but took up no profession, by just such a move – although he only 'travelled a great deal in Concord' to reach Walden Pond. So long as Fuller remained in Boston, she would never have the means to 'simplify, simplify' her life:

> This week I have not read any book, nor once walked in the woods and field. I meant to give its days to setting outward things in order, and its evenings to writing. But, I know not how it is, I can never simplify my life; always so many ties, so many claims![119]

Unlike Thoreau, Fuller did not end her moratorium by a deliberate act. Rather, the outside forces of financial, family and health worries pushed her to end her work on *The Dial*. This was not the 'event . . . to transform [her life], all unconsciously, apparently "accidentally", from a conventional to an eccentric story.'[120] What was? Was there such a decisive event in Fuller's life, or simply 'a perfectly natural progression towards more social works, in New York and Italy, consonant with teachings imbibed in early life?'[121] If the latter, was her feminism the waystation between the intense, moribund individualism of her New England period and her outwardly turned European years?[122]

4

Writing a Life For Women

There are men, women and Margaret Fuller.

Edgar Allan Poe[1]

I wish Woman to live . . . Now there is no woman, only an overgrown child.

Fuller, *Woman in the Nineteenth Century*[2]

Woman is the flower, man the bee. She sighs out melodious fragrance, and invites the winged laborer. He drains her cup, and carries off the honey. She dies on the stalk; he returns to the hive, well fed, and praised as an active member of the community.

Fuller, undated journal entry

Margaret Fuller's Cinderella years were ended by a fairy godfather. If Fuller was Miranda, as Showalter suggests, she had another Prospero who hoisted her from the desert island rather than marooning her on it. Horace Greeley's invitation to become the literary editor of his recently established *New York Daily Tribune* transplanted her from the 'wrong soil' on which she was born, the flinty chalk of New England intellectual life. It may seem ironic that it took a man's intervention to transform a woman whom I present throughout as a self-made heroine – writing a woman's life such as had not been known before in America. But Greeley offered her the post because he was impressed with her first major work on the Woman Question, 'The Great Lawsuit' (*The Dial*, July 1843) – which Greeley reprinted in his new paper – and with her treatment of the lives of white and Native American women (Indian being the term she uses) in her *Summer on the Lakes* (1844).

Writing about women's lives, and writing new lives for women, thus enabled Fuller to write a new life for herself. This became all the more true with the success of her expansion of 'The Great Lawsuit' into a bestselling book, *Woman in the Nineteenth Century* (1845), also printed with Greeley's encouragement and aid. This chapter will discuss those three works, and the gradual awakening of Fuller's abilities which they, and this period, represent.

111

But I will also suggest that Fuller was still only half-awake. The language and conclusions of 'The Great Lawsuit' – and a lesser degree of *Summer on the Lakes* and *Woman in the Nineteenth Century* – still reflect the baleful influence of the cult of True Womanhood. That this was so should not be surprising, or a cause for castigating Fuller, as some earlier feminist biographers tended to do.[3] Fuller wrote during a period of intense conservative backlash, to which we in the 1990s should be sympathetic after our own similar experience in the '80s.[4] For the most part misogyny was camouflaged by the True Woman cult's decorous language of feminine moral superiority, but occasionally the facade developed the odd chink. In *The American Lady* (1836) Charles Butler wrote that the proper woman was:

> she who stands dripping and famished before her husband, while he devours, stretched at ease, the produce of her exertions; waits his tardy permission without a word or look of impatience, and feeds, with the humblest gratitude, and the shortest intermission of labour, on the scraps and offals which he disdains; she, in a word, who is most tolerant of hardship and of unkindness.[5]

In order to reach her intended audience, Fuller had to speak their language, and that was the diction and discourse of the True Woman. The 'hegemony' of a cultural discourse, in the term used by the Italian social philosopher Antonio Gramsci, affects not only the woman writer's audience, but also her own opinions. A similar set of Gramscian ideas have been applied to the English Victorians by Deirdre David,[6] who judges that Barrett Browning, Eliot and Martineau were 'neither ideological slaves to patriarchal thought, nor distinctly separate from patriarchal culture. They were both collaborators and saboteurs in the world that enabled their very existence as women intellectuals'.[7] Is this also true of Margaret Fuller? Is it the price a woman writer must pay for being allowed to play the Dark Lady?

It would be unfair, I think, to say that Fuller was partly colluding in her own oppression, as David implies of Barrett Browning, Eliot and Martineau. Her attitudes towards women *were* considerably more radical than any of those three, though she is closest to Eliot (see Chapter 1). But it is certainly true that Fuller must be judged against the background of her time as well as that of her own personal development. This chapter begins with the personal experience, moving on to the social environment, and then considering together Fuller's three principal works on the Woman Question: 'The Great Lawsuit,' *Summer on the Lakes*, and *Woman in the Nineteenth Century*.

It is also perfectly true that Fuller's high abstraction and individualistic, self-reliant solutions to women's social disadvantage are still cast in the Emersonian mould. 'As his disciple, Fuller used all the arguments that Emerson promulgated about the individual and applied them to women.'[8] 'The Great Lawsuit' is marred by the Transcendentalist tendency to see reality through the lens of symbols.[9] (Fuller's classes for women, the Boston conversations, presented the Greek gods as stereotypical ciphers of this sort, for example, with Aphrodite standing for 'instinctive womanhood' and Zeus for 'active will'.[10]) Although 'The Great Lawsuit' contains striking and powerful statements, it also carries a heavy freight of vagueness and conceptual sloppiness.

The hegemonic discourse of the 'columnar self', as Emily Dickinson was later to phrase it,[11] still sets the tone in 'The Great Lawsuit,' and to a lesser extent in Fuller's other writings on the Woman Question. They represent a natural outgrowth of the intense liberal individualism which found vent in Emerson's essays and lectures, to be amplified later by Thoreau's 'Civil Disobedience' (1849). (This is most true of 'The Great Lawsuit', least of *Woman in the Nineteenth Century*, to which Fuller appended a gritty denunciation of the double standard after her visits in 1844 to the prostitutes in Sing Sing prison, along with shocking specific examples such as the father who had kidnapped his own children so as to bludgeon his wife into submission.) Drawing on the work of the feminist political philosopher Carole Pateman[12], this chapter will also suggest that these liberal individualistic solutions were never intended for women. Fuller eventually moved beyond them, to a more socialistic outlook which considered the need for structural change as well as individual handicaps to fulfilment. Chapter 5 will consider her mature social thought, and the flowering of both life and thought which came when she left New England.

As Bell Chevigny suggests, Fuller's feminism was a way-station, but nonetheless an important staging-point.[13] Without changing at this particular junction, she couldn't have got there – Italy, and her radical socialism – from here – Boston, and inward-turned individualism. Further, Fuller's feminism, while not programmatic, established – together with the model of her life and the drama of her death – an ideal which inspired the founding of many 'Margaret Fuller Clubs' and the Seneca Falls Convention of 1848. Even if her own writings were ambivalent on concrete political issues such as the vote, they inspired more practically minded women. Elizabeth Cady Stanton and Susan B. Anthony judged that Fuller 'possessed more influence upon the thought of American women than any woman previous to her time.'[14]

THE PERSONAL CONTEXT

Carolyn Heilbrun typifies the moratorium in gifted women's lives as 'marked by a profound sense of vocation, with no idea of what that vocation is, and by a strong sense of inadequacy and deprivation'.[15] I suggested in Chapter 3 that neither the role of friend, teacher, nor muse satisfied Fuller's sense of vocation. Crucial as her editorship of *The Dial* proved to be in forming early nineteenth-century American literature, it did not set the canon for herself. Indeed, her deeper acquaintance with Emerson, Thoreau, Alcott, the three Channings, and other members of her Boston intellectual circle only ratified her sense of 'difference':

> Have I never yet seen so much as *one* of my spiritual family? The other night they sat round me, so many who have thought they loved, or who begin to love me. I felt myself kindling the same fire in all their souls. I looked on each, and no eye repelled me. Yet there was no warmth for me on all those altars. Their natures seemed deep, yet there was not one from which I could draw the living fountain. I could only cheat the hour with them, prize, admire, and pity. It was sad; yet who would have seen sadness in me?
>
> Once I was almost all intellect; now I am almost all feeling. Nature vindicates her rights, and I feel all Italy glowing beneath the Saxon crust. This cannot last long; I shall burn to ashes if all this moulders here much longer. I must die if I do not burst forth in genius or heroism.[16]

Yet in the early 1840s Fuller's use of 'manly' as a term of praise still frequently punctuates her letters and writing,[17] as it had throughout the 1820s and 1830s. By the time she wrote *Woman*, published in 1845, she had her doubts about 'manly', *the* 'spermatic' term: 'So invariable is the use of this word where a heroic quality is to be

1. Marchese Giovanni Angelo Ossoli, husband of Margaret Fuller

2. Ralph Waldo Emerson: daguerreotype, 1848

3. Samuel G. Ward, with whom Margaret Fuller is said to have been in love in the late 1830s

4. Thomas Wentworth Higginson

5. Nathaniel Hawthorne

6.   George Sand: portrait by A. Charpentier

7.   Frédéric Chopin: portrait by Teofil Kwiatkowski

8. Giuseppe Mazzini

9. Adam Mickiewicz

10. Elizabeth Barrett Browning

described, and I feel so sure that persistence and courage are the most womanly no less than the most manly qualities . . .'.[18] But at the turn of the moratorium, her sense of difference was not coded into a feeling of *gender* difference. Nor could it be, so long as she was tolerated as Transcendentalism's Dark Lady but unable to achieve anything besides a career of 'auxiliary usefulness' as editor of *The Dial*, handmaiden to the male muses.

Part of Fuller's sense of difference and alienation was due to her circumstances. She, a woman, the supposed creature of the hearth, had no permanent home after the sale of the family's house in Groton. Throughout the late 1830s and early 1840s, she inhabited a succession of boarding houses, rented cottages, and friends' guest chambers. Emerson, Hawthorne, and Thoreau – of whom the latter in particular protested against the tyranny of bricks and mortar – are all strongly associated with places and houses in Concord; Fuller, the woman, was the unwilling nomad. There is some private place to remember the public men by.

Much of this time Margaret nevertheless had the care and lodging of her mother, her sister Ellen, Ellen's husband Ellery Channing, her mentally handicapped brother Lloyd, and an assortment of other brothers at various stages of their college and business careers. Fuller had a great many more domestic duties than the male Transcendentalists, without the stable homelife in which to perform them. 'I have not lived my own life, neither loved my own love, my strength, my sympathies have been given to others, their lives are my aims'.[19] But Transcendentalism as a philosophy was no more able to value Fuller's competence in everyday 'trivalities' than were Emerson and Thoreau[20] in their frugal capacity for sympathy. Not only did Fuller lack the space and time to concentrate: she felt Emerson would look down on her all the more for complaining about her lack of space and time.

> About our poor little Dial, as often before, it irks me to think . . .
> My article on Festus lies half-finished . . . But there is so much to
> interrupt, and (*if Serenissimo will allow the words*) to distress and
> perplex me just now, that I am not sure of being able to concentrate my thoughts upon it.[21]

Emerson's capacity for friendship – never deep enough to satisfy Fuller – was drained still drier by the death of his five-year-old son

Waldo in January 1842. His brother Charles had died in youth; his first wife Ellen Tucker had died after three years of marriage; now his first child was dead. On the day after, Emerson wrote to Fuller:

> My little boy must die also. All his wonderful beauty could not save him. He gave up his innocent breath last night and my world this morning is poor enough. He had Scarlatina on Monday night. Shall I ever dare to love any thing again.[22]

This death affected Fuller deeply, too. As a frequent visitor to the Emerson household, and one with an early-instilled talent for looking after small children, she had spent much time with the little boy. His death redoubled her hopelessness in this final period of her moratorium:

> His father will meet him again, but to me he seems lost, and yet that is weakness. I *must* meet that which he represented, since I so truly loved it. He was the only child I ever saw, that I sometimes wished I could have called mine . . . But it is all gone, and is another of the lessons brought by each year, that we are to expect suggestions only, and not fulfilments . . .[23]

But these final few years of her waiting were also marked by a sense of new serenity, produced in part by another religious experience in 1840, after the one of 1831. In March 1842 she wrote:

> My inward life has been rich and deep, and of more calm and musical flow than ever before. It seems to me that Heaven, whose course has ever been to 'cross-bias' me as Herbert hath it, is no niggard in its compensations.[24]

In this peace of mind, however, there was a terrible exhaustion, a quiet desperation:

> I do not suffer keen pains and spasms as I used to do, but on the other hand have not half the energy in the intervals . . . Now that my mind is so calm and sweet there seems to be no fire in me to resist or to consume . . .[25]

Although Fuller had handed over the editorship of *The Dial* to Emerson in order to make time at last for her writing, her creative tides were at low ebb in the years 1842–3. But the letters of this period convey the sense of a mind cocooned. Like a caterpillar's body, her energies had dissolved, but something was working within the shell.

It was this intense inner striving, in the best Puritan tradition, which made possible her emergence in 1844 as literary editor and social critic for the most influential journal in the country, the *New York Daily Tribune*, and as a successful author. What ended Fuller's moratorium was not a *deus ex machina* – even though Greeley appears at first to have played that part – nor an unconscious accident of the sort Heilbrun identifies in other women writers' lives. It was the power of concentration and bleak inner fortitude which she had first acquired in her hated Groton. So it should comes as no surprise that the work with which Fuller marked the end of her waiting life and the beginning of her best writing life, 'The Great Lawsuit,' is a hymn to women's equal powers of self-reliance with men.

THE DOMINANT DISCOURSE

'The Great Lawsuit' was not, of course, the first attempt to write a new kind of life for women. Writing women's lives – the biographies of women of achievement – went back at least to the Irish-born essayist Anna Jameson's *Memoirs of the Loves of the Poets: Biographical Sketches of Women Celebrated in Ancient and Modern Poetry* (1829) and *Memoirs of Celebrated Female Sovereigns* (1831). By living the example of a woman who earned her own *living* by the pen, and later by writing more extensively about prostitution and female labour questions, Jameson was a positive influence. But like Martineau, though perhaps less consciously, she was also something of an 'appeaser'.[26] Even on behalf of queens, Jameson had been self-effacing: 'On the whole it seems indisputable that the experiments hitherto made in the way of female government have been signally unfortunate; and that women called to empire have been, in most cases, conspicuously unhappy or criminal . . .'[27] And Jameson's style was acceptably True Womanish:

> These little sketches (they can pretend to no higher title) are submitted to the public with a feeling of timidity almost painful . . . to illustrate a subject . . . the influence which the beauty and virtue of women have exercised over the characters and writings

of men of genius. Will it be thought unfeminine or obtrusive, if I add yet a few words?[28]

In their content and manner, Jameson's lives of women reinforced rather than challenged the accepted restrictions on women's lives. Without Jameson's fluttering, though occasionally with a surfeit of pedantry, Fuller evoked heroic women, living and dead, real and mythical: Joan of Arc, Queen Elizabeth, George Sand, Mme de Roland, Mme de Staël, Jameson herself, and most unexpectedly, the Virgin Mary. 'I have aimed to show that no age was left entirely without a witness of the equality of the sexes in function, duty and hope.'[29] Fuller prefigured the biographical strand in modern feminism which has aimed to restore to present-day women the previous female lives which had been written off by men – as would be done with her own life.

> She finds real or fictive heroines everywhere. Her heroines are all in some respect flawed or stunted. But that such women, however, inadequate, have existed or been imagined indicates, for Fuller, the heroic or mythic human possibilities yet to be realized.[30]

The example of the lives which women could live, and had lived, demonstrated the gap between the possible and the actual True Woman. Higginson thinks Fuller appended the subtitle of 'The Great Lawsuit' ('Man vs. Men, Woman vs. Women') in order to deflect charges that the title was confrontational, implying battle between the sexes. The real clash, to Fuller, is between the true nature of woman and the shabby imitation thereof in individual women's lives, lived in society as we know it.[31] To a modern mind, this is puzzling. We might expect the subtitle to mean something like 'the stereotype of woman versus the actual lives of real women;' and we may find Fuller's apparent conservatism problematic.

But this is to ignore the context in which Fuller wrote, the reaction against the ideal of Republican Motherhood and the dominance of the True Woman paradigm (see Chapter 2). Although this was the ideology of the backlash, women of Fuller's time were also told that their position was one of privilege such as had never been known before. Vestiges of the eighteenth-century faith in progress away from the barbarous conditions which women were thought to have suffered in earlier times; the American sense of divine mission and exceptionalism; the promotion of a gentle 'feminine' evangelicalism rather than the hellfire Christianity of the eighteenth century[32] – all these factors combined to assure early nineteenth-century American women that they were the happiest of mortals.

The example of evangelicalism illustrates how two-edged a sword was women's supposed moral superiority. Ordained devotees of the cult of the True Woman, both male and female – and roughly one-third of its published authors *were* women – preached that moral regeneration was in female power to convey:

We look to you, ladies, to raise the standard of character in our own sex; we look to you to guard and fortify those barriers, which still exist in society, against the encroachments of impudence and licentiousness. We look to you for the continuance of domestic purity, for the revival of domestic religion, for the increase of our charities and the support of what remains of religion in our private habits and publick [*sic*] institutions.[33]

'Domestic' was the clueword. Prayer groups, women's sewing circles, mission societies, Sunday schools, maternal associations such as that founded in Dorchester (Massachusetts) in 1816: these extensions of the home role were initially thought to be gainful occupations outside the home for women. But any female interloper on the public, male domain was soon to be prosecuted, and these 'concessions' withdrawn.

In the early years of the nineteenth century, women had preached, especially among the Baptists and Methodists. American female itinerant preachers, such as Martha Howell and Clarissa Danforth, were successful – paralleling the Methodist experience in England, fictionalised by George Eliot in *Adam Bede*. But Eliot's Dinah is eventually forbidden to preach by the Methodist hierarchy, and so it was in actual fact, too, in both England and America. As new sects became more structured, and as those structures became bastions of male authority, the ministry of women was increasingly threatening and threatened. Even some Quakers, whose church government is minimal and whose women had been allowed an equal voice since the seventeenth century, came to reject the ministry of women in the early nineteenth century.

Early revivalists of the Great Awakenings had allowed women to take a key part in meetings and to lead prayers; but by 1823 they were forbidden to do either in a pamphlet on 'Female Influence', published by the Presbyterian Utica Tract Society and typical of the changes in the hotbed of evangelicalism, the Burnt-Over District of Western New York state. In the repressive 1820s and 1830s even maternal and moral reform societies were beginning to be thought suspect.[34] To step outside the domestic sphere, hardliners argued, would sully the purity which alone gave women the right to call themselves morally superior to men, and capable of the other sex's moral reform.

The last of the partial exemptions which remained intact in the early 1840s – and indeed flourishing – was education. Improvement of the female intellect was acceptable as a means to an imperative end. As Fuller herself confirmed the dominant view, American daughters were exhorted to strive constantly for spiritual and intellectual perfection, not only for the sake of their own salvation, but for the good of their fathers, brothers, and beaux – whose contact with the sharp world of business excused them from any such strictness with themselves. 'Improvement in the daughters will best aid the reformation of the sons of this age.'[35] (This jars oddly with Fuller's assertion that 'not one man in the million, shall I say? no, not in the hundred million, can rise above the belief that Woman was made *for* Man . . .'[36] and her complaint that 'Too much is said of women being better educated, that they may become better companions and mothers *for men*'.[37])

Catharine Beecher, founder of the Hartford Female Seminary and later of the Western Female Institute in Cincinnati, justified female education by women's aptitude as natural missionaries, spreading a civilising influence from the holy hearth. This imperial role for women was given a patriotic force by Philo Stewart, co-founder of Oberlin, the first college to educate men and women together. 'The work of female education,' wrote Stewart, 'must be carried on in some form, and in a much more efficient manner than it has been hitherto, or our country will go to destruction.'[38]

In the cult of True Womanhood a strong religious component co-existed more or less peacefully with what might appear the ideological opposite, Locke's doctrine of the mind as a *tabula rasa* or blank slate. Since the child's personality was entirely a reflection of what the educator put into it, mothers as principal childrearers bore a ponderous responsibility. Both the true man and the true woman were formed by their mothers. This perilous power in women's hands had to be tamed, by educating them to be reliable propagandisers of the cult. The 'concession' made in favour of education was not so much a privilege afforded to women as a further mechanism of control. Education was certainly not intended to prepare women for the professions and public life; it was meant to make them more reliable stewards of the master's most important resources, his children.

But by operating within the constraints of the cult of the True Woman, early nineteenth-century reformers had secured some educational advancement for women. Colluding with the doctrine of separate spheres, 'domestic feminists' such as Catharine Beecher helped to breed up a class of educated heretics within the cult, women who would *not* accept separate spheres. Further, the legitimacy of evangelical fervour, and the partial exceptions made in favour of philanthropic causes and education, had allowed some women a taste of life outside the home. Ladies' societies gave women experience in drawing up regulations, electing officers, corresponding with other charitable organisations, and overseeing accounts.[39]

The rise of 'Moral Reform' (see Chapter 5) and of the abolitionist movement – in some cases, such as that of the Grimké sisters, as an outgrowth of religious convictions and concern at the spread of venereal disease through sexual exploitation of slave women by white men – gave further opportunities for public participation. Women formed auxiliary societies, collected signatures, organised bazaars, and began boycotts of slave-grown products. But at the same time abolitionist women who overstepped their bounds were severely chastised. The Grimké sisters – among whose vociferous opponents was Catharine Beecher – were threatened and harassed during their ground-breaking lectures to mixed audiences, and the abolitionist Abby Kelley's violation of proper womanly silence at the 1840 meeting of the Connecticut Anti-Slavery Society provoked the male chairman to rage:

> I will not sit in a chair where women bear rule. I vacate this chair. No woman shall speak or vote where I am moderator. I will not countenance such an outrage on decency . . . It is woman's business to take care of children in the nursery. She has no business to come into this meeting, and by speaking and voting lord it over men. Where woman's enticing eloquence is heard men are incapable of right and efficient action. She beguiles and blinds man by her smiles and her bland and winning voice.[40]

In the same year the World Antislavery Convention in London voted to bar women. There Lucretia Mott, Lydia Francis Child, and other women in the American abolitionist delegation were denounced by the British clergyman George Harvey in phrases still to be heard almost word-for-word in England today about women's ordination:

> It is a matter of conscience with me . . . I have certain views in relation to the teaching of the Word of God, and of the particular sphere in which woman is to act . . . If I were to give a vote in favour of females, sitting and deliberating in such an assembly as this, I should be acting in opposition to the plain teaching of the Word of God.[41]

Abolitionism in Britain had confined women to a function of purely 'auxiliary usefulness', but British delegates were joined in their opposition to female representation by the 'moderate' wing of the American abolitionist movement. Against William Lloyd Garrison's insistence that abolitionism was a moral crusade which would be tainted by the hypocrisy of assigning women to an inferior sphere, more politically minded American abolitionists thought that any hint of feminism would alienate powerful groups whose support the anti-slavery movement needed. Exclusion from the Convention was a humiliation which prodded Mott, Susan B. Anthony and others into a more entrenched concern for women's rights; but its immediate effect was retrenchment.

In the political sphere, too, the early nineteenth century was a period of retreat for women. During the American Revolution enthusiasm for the logical consequences of the idea that all *men* are created equal had undermined the common-law position inherited from England, that married women had no legal, economic or political existence. Women married to Tories who had been exiled, and their property confiscated, were sometimes able to regain their own share if they swore loyalty to the new republic. This implied that married women's property rights were not entirely subsumed in their husbands' and that women's political commitment could have some meaning, even if they were not full citizens. In 1790 the state of New Jersey even went so far as to adopt a franchise statute referring to voters as 'he or she'.[42] In the aftermath of the Revolution divorce, overruled by the Privy Council in 1773 as contrary to the law of England, also became a right for those women in the New England and mid-Atlantic seaboard states whose legislatures had legalised it.

With the end to the Revolution and no further need for female support in the war effort; the rise of an entrepreneurial capitalism which confined women's economic activity more closely to the home; and the development of the True Woman ideology, these political and economic gains were generally shortlived. By the 1830s and 1840s, ironically the high tide of liberal individualism, the political and economic rights of American women had never been fewer. At the same time when white American men had gained near-total control over their wives' property, they were benefiting from the abolition in almost all states of property requirements for the franchise. Rhode Island, for example, one of the few states which still limited white male suffrage to freeholders, extended the vote to all nativeborn men after the Dorr rebellion of 1842. The contrast between the sexes was sharper in America than in England, where the 1832 Reform Act still left lower middle-class and working-class men disenfranchised. (There, too, however, the forces of misogyny were in the ascendant: the 1832 Act specified for the first time in statute form that the voter must be male.)

The feminist historians Bonnie S. Anderson and Judith P. Zinsser have written a summary of this high period of European liberalism which rings even truer for America in the same period:

Women were meant for the home; men for public life. Supported by the economic changes of the period, these ancient ideas held firm in an era in which much else was swept away. Slavery, the divine right of monarchs, distinctions between aristocratic and bourgeois men, and literal views of religion all came under powerful and sustained attack during this period. But traditional ideas of women endured, and even were strengthened in the new developments of the age: in law codes and republican governments, in medical and scientific thought, in images of women, even in the clothing of the period. Men's lives changed radically as new kinds of work expanded in business, the professions, government bureaucracies and industry. For men, these changes were often liberating, and many benefited from the democratic gains the laws gave them. Women lost power, both relatively and absolutely . . . Created in the spirit of reform, the new codes often discarded traditional inequalities among men. Aristocratic privileges were limited or abolished, religious qualifications and tests were often removed, distinctions were based on money rather

than birth, and the principle of equality before the law was established. But these gains were for men only.[43]

In both Britain and America existing practices and old common-law
rights affording some degree of safety to women were eroded.
Equity trusts, which had protected American married women's
property from predatory husbands, were ended, and the English
common-law right of dower, by which a widow automatically received one-third of her husband's estate, was replaced in 1833 by
a provision stipulating that the husband could bar this right of
inheritance during his lifetime. Elizabeth Cady Stanton's autobiography records her dismay when she discovered how few legal
rights American women retained in the 1830s.

> As my father's office joined the house, I spent there much of my
> time when out of school, listening to the clients stating their cases,
> talking with the students, and reading the laws in regard to woman
> . . . Fathers, at their death, would will the bulk of their property to
> the eldest son, with the proviso that the mother was to have a
> home with him. Hence it was not unusual for the mother, who
> had brought all the property into the family, to be made an
> unhappy dependent [sic] on the bounty of an uncongenial daugh-
> ter-in-law and a dissipated son. The tears and complaints of the
> women who came to my father for legal advice touched my heart
> and early drew my attention to the injustice and cruelty of the
> laws. As the practice of the law was my father's business, I could
> not exactly understand why he could not alleviate the sufferings
> of these women. So, in order to enlighten me, he would take down
> his books and show me the inexorable statutes. The students,
> observing my interest, would amuse themselves by reading to me
> all the worst laws they could find, over which I would laugh and
> cry by turns. One Christmas morning I went into the office to
> show them, among other of my presents, a new coral necklace
> and bracelets. They all admired the jewelry and then began to
> tease me with hypothetical cases of future ownership. 'Now,' said
> Henry Bayard, 'if in due time you should be my wife, those
> ornaments would be mine; I could take them and lock them up,
> and you could never wear them except with my permission. I
> could even exchange them for a box of cigars, and you could
> watch them evaporate in smoke.'[44]

Property in jewellery was the least of married women's problems; they also had little property in the fruits of their own body. The disjuncture between the child's need for a mother and the mother's minimal rights to custody of the child on divorce troubled many reformers. In this way the ideology of domesticity and the True Woman might have provoked legal change, as occurred in England with the Infants' Custody Act of 1837. But in America there was no such *cause célèbre* as that of the Act's instigator Caroline Norton, denied not only legal custody of her three children on her separation from her violent husband but also all access to them. Between 1836 and 1850 many states began to permit married women to hold inherited property, but not their own earnings or the custody of their children. And in many cases these statutes were not feminist-inspired; rather, they were promulgated by anxious fathers with rapacious sons-in-law.

FULLER'S WRITINGS ON THE WOMAN QUESTION

Slave women, too, had no right to their own children, and Fuller did not jib at the comparison.' . . . [T]here exists in the minds of men a tone of feeling toward women as toward slaves,' she wrote in *Woman in the Nineteenth Century*.[45]

> As the friend of the negro assumes that one man cannot by right hold another in bondage, so should the friend of Woman assume that Man cannot by right lay even well-meaning restrictions on Woman. If the negro be a soul, if the woman be a soul, apparelled in flesh, to one Master only are they accountable.[46]

Indeed, slavery is more honest: 'In slavery, *acknowledged* slavery, women are on a par with men.'[47] Fuller was not the first to make this uncomfortable comparison. Drawing on ideas first advanced by the Irish feminist Anna Wheeler (b. 1785), William Thompson's *Appeal of One-Half the Human Race, Women, against the Pretensions of the Other Half, Men, to Retain Them in Political, and Thence in Civil and Domestic Slavery* (1825) likewise remarks:

> As little as slaves have had to do in any part of the world in the enacting of slave-codes, have women in any part of the world had

to do with the partial codes of selfishness and ignorance, which everywhere dispose of their right over their own actions and all their other enjoyments, in favour of those who made the regulations; particularly that most unequal and debasing code, absurdly called the contract of marriage . . . From regulating the terms of this pretended contract, women have been as completely excluded as bullocks, or sheep, or any other animals subjugated to man, have been from determining the regulations of commons or slaughter-houses.[48]

Earlier still, Charles Brockden Brown, writing in the 1790's, had identified marriage as a 'compact of slavery'.[49] But there is no firm indication that Fuller had read Thompson or Brown by the time she wrote her texts on women's position;[50] and in the True-Womanised climate of the 1840's, such sentiments were much more shocking – particularly when they came from a woman. Even more controversial was Fuller's scepticism about the justifications put forward by men to legitimate their political and economic dominance: that women are incapable of fiscal wisdom or political nous. These, she judged, are only psychological mechanisms which the dominant sex, or race, must use in order to excuse its own arbitrary power to itself. 'The aversion of the injurer for him he has degraded',[51] originally used by Fuller to explain the white man's denigration of the Indian, implicitly extended to race and gender.

Fuller was not an abolitionist at this time, but the examples of slaves and Indians had galvanised her thought on women. In 1843 she made a journey to Niagara Falls and the Great Lakes with her friends Caroline Sturgis, Sarah Ann Clarke, and Clarke's brother William. The book which resulted, *Summer on the Lakes* (1844), represents a forward hop, if not a leap, in both style and thought. Although the book lacks what Fuller admired – 'the Spartan brevity and sinewy grasp of Indian speech'[52] – it is liberally sprinkled with Thoreauvian salt:

[At Niagara] what I liked best was to sit on Table Rock, close to the great fall. There all power of observing details, all separate consciousness, was quite lost. Once, just as I had seated myself there, a man came up to take his first look. He walked close up to the fall, and, after looking at it for a moment, with an air of thinking how he could best appropriate it to his own use – he spat into it.[53]

The people on the boat were almost all New Englanders, seeking their fortunes. They had brought with them their habits of calculation, their cautious manners, their love of polemics. It grieved me to hear these immigrants who were to be the fathers of a new race, all, from the old man down to the little girl, talking not of what they should do, but of what they should get . . .[54]

The range of Fuller's thought on women was stretched by the example of the squaws of Mackinac Island, among whom she was able to wander freely. Unlike the Enlightenment, which explored various constellations of domestic power relations – matrilineal Iroquois society, polyandry among the Nairs of Malabar, collective marriage in eastern Iran[55] – the early nineteenth-century cult of True Womanhood lumped together all 'uncivilised' women's positions as barbarous. Fuller agreed that Indian women were lumbered with drudgery: their 'peculiarly awkward gait, and forms bent by burthens . . . so different from the steady and noble step of the men, [mark] the inferior position they occupy'.[56] But she also observed more tenderness towards children among Indian braves than in white men, and considerable respect for matrons who were mothers of warriors. Indian children were called by the mother's name, and divorce was easy, more advantageous to women than men. On the boat for Sault Ste. Marie Fuller met an Indian woman (with whom she quite markedly did *not* identify, since she says that she was the only lady on board the ship). The woman had left her husband because he drank and wasted their earnings; she earned a living for herself and her child as a chambermaid. 'Now and again, she said, her husband called on her, and asked if he might live with her again, but she always answered, no. Here she was far freer than she would have been in civilized life.'[57] In *Woman in the Nineteenth Century* Fuller worked her observations of such autonomous Indian women into the following interpretation of a story first reported by Anna Jameson:

A woman dreamt in her youth that she was betrothed to the Sun. She built her a wigwam apart, filled it with emblems of her alliance, and means of an independent life. There she passed her days, sustained by her own exertions, and true to her supposed engagement. In any tribe, we believe, a woman, who lived as if she was betrothed to the Sun, would be tolerated, and the rays which made her youth blossom sweetly, would crown her with a halo in age . . .[58]

But if *white* Western women were not freer than Eastern, Fuller thought it was probably their own fault – or that of their mothers.

> [T]hey have not learnt to ride, to drive, to row, alone. Their culture has too generally been that given to women to make them 'the ornaments of society . . .' We could not but look with deep interest on the little girls, and hope they would grow up with the strength of body, dexterity, simple tastes and resources that would fit them to enjoy and refine the western farmer's life. But they have a great deal to war with in the habits of thought acquired from their mothers from their own early life. Everywhere the fatal spirit of imitation, of reference to European standards, penetrates, and threatens to blight whatever of original growth might adorn the soil.
>
> If the little girls grow up strong, resolute, able to exert their faculties, their mothers mourn over their want of fashionable delicacy. Are they gay, enterprising, ready to fly about in the various ways that teach them so much, these ladies lament that 'they cannot go to school, where they might learn to be quiet.' They lament the want of 'education' for their daughters, as if the thousand needs which call out their young energies, and the language of Nature around, yielded no education.[59]

Fuller herself is not entirely free from such prejudices: she remarks that the female ferry-person across the Kishwaukie River was 'unfortunately not of the most picturesque appearance'.[60] At the same time that she attacks Western women's concern for frills and furbelows, she castigates poor pioneer women for letting themselves go, becoming 'slatterns' through overwork.[61] Still unable to see women's position as socially conditioned, Fuller remains within the True Woman tradition by looking to Western women for their own salvation.

> It is . . . evident that . . . the women have great power at home. It can never be otherwise, men being dependent upon them for the comfort of their lives. Just so among ourselves, wives who are neither esteemed nor loved by their husbands, have great power over their conduct by the friction of every day, and over the formation of their opinions . . . This power is good for nothing, unless the woman be wise to use it aright. Has the Indian, has the white woman, as noble a feeling of life and its uses, as religious a

self-respect, as worthy a field of thought and action as man? If not, the white woman, the Indian woman, occupies an inferior position to that of man. It is not so much a question of power, as of privilege.[62]

That Fuller judged 'it is not so much a question of power' in the case of Indian women may be understandable. Indian men also lacked political power: they were denied the vote in Fuller's time, although the Chippewas had petitioned the Michigan government for citizenship. But even here Fuller was resolutely apolitical: 'This would be in vain, unless they could be admitted, as brothers, to the heart of the white man'.[63] Individual before social reform remains her creed in *Woman*, despite that essay's greater awareness of social ills.

[T]he only efficient remedy must come from individual character. These bad institutions, indeed, it may always be replied, prevent individuals from forming good character, therefore we must remove them. Agreed; yet keep steadily the higher aim in view. Could you clear away all the bad forms of society, it is vain, unless the individual begin to be ready for better.[64]

Like 'The Great Lawsuit' and *Summer on the Lakes, Woman in the Nineteenth Century* is more concerned with individual regeneration than practical achievements, although the new sections written especially for the book-length version of *Woman* – roughly one-third of the total of this expanded version of 'Lawsuit' – are again more down-to-earth than the earlier work. Barbara Welter has surmised that *Woman* is a how-to manual in the best American self-improvement style.[65] But Fuller's book did differ drastically from the mainstream mentor literature of the day – such as Margaret Coxe's *The Young Lady's Companion* or Dr Alexander Walker's *Beauty* (which subdivided female perfection into pulchritude of 'the locomotive system', 'the nutritive system', and 'the thinking system'.[66]) Fuller preached activism rather than submission, self-cultivation rather than self-abnegation. The cult of True Womanhood was the dominant discourse whose influence Fuller could not escape; but her version of what constituted genuine femininity was as different from the standard milk-and-water version as her earnest self-discipline was from the conscious dilettantism of the popular novelist Caroline Lee Hentz, who fluttered in her novel *Ernest Linwood*: 'Book? Am I writing a book? No indeed! This is only a record of my heart's life, written at random and carelessly thrown aside, sheet after sheet, sibylline leaves from the great book of Fate.'[67] Nevertheless, despite her own intense intellectualism and concentration, Fuller wrote:

> The especial genius of Woman I believe to be electrical in movement, intuitive in function, spiritual in tendency. She excels not so easily in classification, or recreation, as in an instinctive seizure of causes, and a simple breathing out of what she receives that has the singleness of life, rather than the selecting and energizing of art.[68]

This is a crucial passage. Is it mere wishful thinking from Fuller, known to all and sundry as an oversized cerebrum? Or did Fuller – whose genius was anything but intuitive, and whose life was never a simple breathing out of what she had received – believe this to be true of woman in general but not of her exceptional self? This is a common enough strategy for Dark Ladies: George Sand's public pronouncements – though not her novels – distanced her from other women. In reply to the female socialists who had demanded the vote and requested that she stand as a candidate for the National Assembly after the 1848 revolution, she wrote:

> As for you women who pretend to begin by the exercise of your rights, permit me to tell you again that you are amusing yourselves with childishness. Your house is on fire, your home is in peril, and you want to go expose yourself to railleries and public affronts when you should be defending your home and setting up again your outraged household gods . . . To what ridiculous attacks, to what possible vile scandals, would such an innovation [votes for women] give rise? Good sense thrusts it aside, and the pride that your sex ought to have makes it nearly a crime for you to think of braving such outrages.[69]

In the last sentence Sand writes '*your* sex', not 'our sex.' Perhaps a similar estrangement from her own femaleness underlies Fuller's reply in *Woman* to the question of what occupations women should pursue – 'Let *them* be sea-captains,' that chillingly prescient choice of image.

Or did Fuller mean to include herself, and all exceptional women, under the rubric of 'electrical', 'intuitive', 'spiritual' female nature? If so, how does her view differ from the dominant discourse, the cult of True Womanhood? Can a conception which accepts that male and female natures are separate by nature be said to be anything other than part of the regressive ideology which confined women to their own 'rightful' sphere in the home?

Although Fuller's intellectual colleagues may have viewed her as an exceptional woman, a Dark Lady, she wrote that 'I love best to be a woman; but womanhood is at present too straitly-bounded to give me scope.' Elizabeth Cady Stanton and Susan B. Anthony described her as 'the largest woman, and not a woman who wanted to be a man'.[70] Her authorial persona in *Woman*, Miranda – whose name, Elaine Showalter thinks, means not the passive 'one to be wondered at', as in Latin, but the active 'seeing one', as in Spanish – dismisses a man's compliment to her as 'above her sex'.

> When they [men] admired any woman, they were inclined to speak of her as 'above her sex' . . . I look upon it as a signal instance of this, that an intimate friend of the other sex said, in a fervent moment, that I 'deserved in some star to be a man'. He was much surprised when I disclosed my view of my position and hopes, when I declared my faith that the feminine side, the side of love, of beauty, of holiness, was now to have its full chance, and that, if either were better, it was better now to be a woman . . . Let it not be said, wherever there is energy or creative genius, 'She has a masculine mind.'[71]

When Fuller did express androgynous doubts about her identity, it was to claim a superior 'manliness' for women over men:

> I wish I were a man, and then there would be *one*. I weary in this play-ground of boys, proud and happy in their balls and marbles. Give me heroes, poets, lawgivers, Men.
>
> There are women much less unworthy to live than you, Men; the best are so unripe, the wisest so ignoble, the truest so cold![72]

Unlike Sand, Fuller did usually identify with other women: why not, when they were the superior sex? She wanted to recognise her own nature in the 'electrical' female: *both* wishful thinking and a sincere pronouncement.

Although some twentieth-century feminists have taken Fuller to task for dominating the Boston Conversations in an unsisterly manner, she was after all being paid to teach. Ednah Dow Cheney, a student at the Boston Conversations, left behind a testimonial to Fuller's sympathy and identification with other women:

> One day when she was alone with me, and I feel as if I could now feel her touch and hear her voice, she said, 'Is life rich to you?' and I replied, 'It is since I have known you.' Such was the response of many a youthful heart to her, and herein was her wonderful influence. She did not make us her disciples, her blind followers. She opened the book of life to us and helped us to read it for ourselves . . .
>
> The first mistake that the world has made in its effort to comprehend this large nature is in considering her, not as a typical woman, but as an exceptional one, whose powers were masculine, and who wielded some magic sword which she alone had strength to grasp . . . With all the force of her intellect, all the strength of her will, all her self-denial and power of thought, she was essentially and thoroughly a woman, and she won her victories not by borrowing the peculiar weapons of man, but by using her own with courage and skill.[73]

In a letter of July 1844 to Emerson, commenting on his second volume of essays, Fuller likewise identified with the female force:

> You have been showing me your great results, sculptured out into such clear beauty. But your excellence never shames me, nor chills my next effort, because it is of a kind wholly unattainable to me, in a walk where I shall never take a step. You are intellect, I am life . . . I shall be content whenever I am in a state of unimpeded energy and can sing at the top of my voice, I dont [sic] care what.[74]

But can this be a strategy for liberation? Reductionism of this sort, particularly if it reserves 'the rational' for men, is more often a policy for confining women to the hearth or the pedestal. But Fuller's relational feminism, her belief in separate male and female natures, was at one with what has been called the Romantic strategy for women's liberation, the call for gentler men and more self-reliant women.[75] The cult of True Womanhood celebrated virtues antithetical to critical thought, and Jacksonian society valued the practical person above the intellectual. But a Romantic feminism could allow Fuller to be both intellectual and female: knowledge was to be attained through intuition and sensibility, not the cold steel of reason. Further, Romanticism prescribed for men the sensibility of the best women, the virtues of the sensitive mind rather than the strong arm.[76]

A 'rationalist' feminism tries to end women's subordination primarily through political change – transforming education, instituting equal political standing – and bases this programme on a rights argument. Mary Wollstonecraft is this sort of feminist, and indeed Wollstonecraft's call for female suffrage is far clearer than Fuller's, though issued fifty years earlier. (Although Timothy Fuller had read Wollstonecraft, he prevented Margaret from doing so on grounds of decorum, and it is unclear how much or little Fuller knew of the earlier woman's work. But similar rights-orientated arguments were made by other writers in Fuller's own time, such as Marion Reid in *A Plea for Woman* [1843].[77])

A 'romantic' feminism, by contrast, retreats from politics and seeks liberation through psychological means: consciousness-raising and personal experience. It views political change as hollow without inner transformation, particularly where men are concerned This is Fuller's primary set of concerns, and it is in its psychological and sexual insights that *Woman* best stands the test of time. (Fuller's views on sexuality will be discussed at greater length in Chapter 5, where her writings on prostitution are considered, along with her other essays on social reform.)

In fact Wollstonecraft's project includes 'a revolution in female manners', 'the radical transformation of womanhood itself';[78] and Fuller does sometimes take a more rationalist line, particularly about education. In demanding equal university-level facilities for both sexes, her programme is superficially similar to Wollstonecraft's. But Wollstonecraft had something to prove which Fuller didn't. In Wollstonecraft the demand for equal education stems from the assertion that full humanity is demonstrated by rationality. Women appear frivolous, shallow and irrational, Wollstonecraft concedes, but she is then open to the charge that they really *are* inferior – unless she replies that it is only because their minds have been neglected.

Fuller, of all people, can least claim that women's minds have been neglected. But she is also unable to rely on the putative transformative powers of equal education: in the early nineteenth century the *increase* in girls' academies co-existed with *decreased* opportunities after school. The cult of True Womanhood could afford to grant educational opportunities; as I argued earlier, they were actually a means of controlling rather than freeing women. By the early to mid-nineteenth century intellectual equality could be conceded, but in the economic and political sphere there was no place for the True Woman:

> Hers be the domain of the moral affections, the empire of the heart, the co-equal sovereignty of intellect . . . Leave the rude commerce of camps and the soul-hardening struggles of political power to the harsher spirit of man, that he may still look up to her as a purer and brighter being.[79]

Fuller is a Romantic feminist in contending that the content of girls' education should be *affirmatively* different, not merely a watered-down version of the classic texts fed to boys. Having been privileged to learn the father speech, Latin, she need not worship the priestly tongue mindlessly. (See Chapter 2.) Romanticism values diversity and assigns positive value to gender differences. It does not define female nature solely in contrast to male. This is the impetus behind Fuller's description of female nature as electrical, vital, magnetic, full of life. It is intended as the most affirmative of descriptions, not the mere negative of masculine identity. *Life* is what Fuller writes into her definition of woman.

This still has resonance for modern feminism. Carol Gilligan pursues a similar strategy, for example, in refusing to equate boys' development with that of all children, and in depicting a separate but equal female ethic of connection and relatedness (see Chapter 2). Simone de Beauvoir held that female identity is constructed in linguistic and social codes as the negative end of a pole where 'masculine' occupies both the positive and the neutral positions. If, in addition, evil is defined as the mere absence of good – Emerson's formulation – then women, also defined purely in negative terms, will very likely be identified with evil. Modern feminists such as Nel Noddings still struggle with this pernicious legacy: 'Surely creatures who have themselves been branded as evil or peculiarly susceptible to evil must develop a special perspective on evil, especially when they are also, and paradoxically, exalted as possessing a special and natural form of goodness.'[80]

Fuller's attempt to state a vibrant and positive ideal of femaleness borrows from the dominant discourse, the cult of True Womanhood, but ultimately transcends it. The qualities which Fuller claims for women by nature and right are too dynamic to sit comfortably in the hands-in-lap posture of the True Woman.

Fuller's feminism is Romantic in another sense: it emphasises independence and self-assertion, almost to the point of proto-existentialist alienation. *Woman* is ambivalent as to whether women will achieve freedom through each other's support or their own individual striving, but it is clear that they will not achieve it in league with men. 'Men do *not* look at both sides, and women must leave off asking them.'[81] (This is another reason why political lobbying – of an all-male legislature – will be of little effect, to Fuller's way of thinking.)

The liberal individualism of this view extends to Fuller's feelings about marriage. If there is no society – and Fuller accepts this view in a letter written in the early 1840s – and if there are only individuals, all social institutions are problematic. What holds them together? In the case of marriage, Fuller argues, the glue is greed. She is sceptical of both men's and women's motives for marriage, which is treated by society as a good for sale, she argues. As proof she cites the phrase '*get* married' – implying that marriage is an object to be had, not a relation to be lived. The now-familiar argument that marriage is legalised prostitution largely originates with Fuller, although it was given more 'scandalous' prominence by Victoria Woodhull, the first woman to run for President.[82]

As well as in 'The Great Lawsuit' and *Woman in the Nineteenth Century*, this bald view of marriage as it is, though not as it might be, appears in Fuller's story 'Aglauron and Laurie'. The heroine of the story, Emily, is a Lydia Bennet figure: the spoilt youngest child of a self-centred father and a weak mother. Both parents are delighted with the status conferred on the family by Emily's engagement at fifteen to Leven, a much older man. But the marriage, entered into for the crassest motives by all parties, soon palls. Although uneducated and superficial, Emily still embodies the female 'electrical' striving for some impossible alternative only vaguely sensed but violently desired:

> . . . I was scarcely in his power when I awoke, I perceived the unfitness of the tie, its closeness revolted me . . . I had never known what it was to be resisted, and the thought never came to me that I could now, and for all my life, be bound by so early a mistake. I thought only of expressing my resolve to be free . . . For

all but me have been trained to bear the burden from their youth up, and accustomed to have the individual will fettered, for the advantage of society. For the same reason you cannot guess the silent fury that filled my mind when I at last found that I struggled in vain, that I must remain in the bondage I had ignorantly put on . . . I felt alone, bitterly, contemptuously alone. I hated men, who had made the laws that bound me. I did not believe in God, for why had he permitted the dart to enter so unprepared a breast? I determined never to submit, though I disdained to struggle, since struggle was in vain.[83]

The distance Fuller has travelled from the cult of True Womanhood is obvious in this forlorn portrayal of a conventional marriage. Unlike poor Emily, Miranda, the authorial persona of *Woman*, was taught by a wise father that 'I must depend on myself as the only consistent friend'.

This self-dependence, which was honored in me, is deprecated as a fault in most women. They are taught to learn their rule from without, not to unfold it from within . . . [T]he position I early on was enabled to take was one of self-reliance.[84]

Everything most and least attractive in Fuller's thought on the Woman Question is contained in Miranda's remarks. Insistent callers from the True Woman Mission Society are politely told that no one is at home to them; but is it enough for women to be left alone?

Fuller's feminism is imbued with the extreme liberal individualism of her time and place. I have already shown that the rights gained by early nineteenth-century liberal individualism benefited men only. My argument was historical, confined to the contrast between the economic and political rights which contractarian liberalism had secured for men and the actual decline in women's rights under the aegis of liberalism. Was this merely coincidental, a historical oddity? The feminist political philosopher Carole Pateman thinks not.

The liberal Lockean ideas of the social contract, individual rights, and separation of public and private realms underpinned Anglo-American political discourse in Fuller's time, as they do now. Rare foreign plants such as Fourierite socialism occasionally sprang up from windblown seeds in New England soil, resulting in such odd growths as the utopian community at Brook Farm. But the underly-

ing ideas of Transcendentalism are individualist, expressed most
classically in Thoreau's 'Civil Disobedience': 'For government is an
expedient by which men would fain succeed in letting one another
alone; and . . . when it is most expedient, the governed are most let
alone by it.'[85]

'Men' means just what it says. The idea of a social contract, by
which the only legitimate functions of government are those delegated to it by the governed, is a story of freedom for men but
subordination for women, Pateman argues. 'Men alone have the
attributes of free and equal individuals.'[86] Liberal theory views the
government as formed freely by consenting individuals, but stipu-
lates that those individuals are heads of households.[87] As early as
1700, following John Locke's *Two Treatises on Government* (1689) to
their logical conclusion, Mary Astell demanded, 'If Absolute Sovereignty be not necessary in a State, how comes it to be so in a Family?'[88] But the structure of the household – the Law of the Father – is
not created by consent and is not open to question in Lockean liberal
theory. Women are excluded from the public realm, the political,
and confined to the household, the personal. But in liberal individualism the personal is not political.

Contractarian rhetoric about free individuals masks the social
reality of women's servitude, Pateman argues. This is clearest in the
example of the marriage contract. Women cannot choose not to
marry when no other professions but the oldest one are open to
them. But the contract of marriage is then used in liberal thought
to assert that the wife freely chose her position. In Fuller's time (and
indeed until 1991 in England) this justified marital rape, in law. By
accepting the marriage contract, the wife 'hath given up her body to
her husband . . . which she cannot retract', Chief Justice Matthew
Hale held in the seventeenth century. By pronouncing the words 'I
do', a woman was held to have ceded permanent property rights
over her own body. So long as the marriage contract remained valid
– and as I discussed earlier, the early nineteenth century closed off
possibilities of divorce opened in the late eighteenth century – the
wife's permanent consent to sexual relations did as well: all in the
name of her original 'choice' and 'freedom.'

Choice, freedom, self-reliance: these are men's terms, not women's language, Pateman claims. In more practical ways, too, the
ideal of self-reliance was not for women in Fuller's time: they couldn't
afford it. There was no reliable economic means to independence.
Emily Dickinson eulogised 'a columnar self' but relied most 'amply'

on her father's and brother's provision, as she had to. For Emerson self-reliance was all very well: he had wealth inherited from his first wife, sufficient means to buy and maintain a spacious house in Concord, and possibilities of income from lecturing and preaching, fields barred to women in Fuller's time.

Fuller had to be economically self-reliant – and to provide for her father's children from the limited means available from a woman's profession, teaching. It did her health no good, and probably caused her death. The boat on which she went down, the *Elizabeth*, was an old-fashioned wooden-bottomed merchantman; Fuller could not afford a modern steamer or packet ship. When the *Elizabeth* foundered on a sandbar off Fire Island, the bottom ruptured under the cargo of Italian marble and a statue of John Calhoun – that advocate of nullification, states' rights to self-reliance.

If we are all free and independent, as liberal individualism asserts, then whatever we do or do not achieve is a result of our own efforts: there are no other barriers. If there are few successful women writers, artists, politicians, heroes – then the reason must be that they choose freely to stay out of the public eye, to do all by inspiring man to do all, in Emerson's terms. Thus Fuller's liberal individualism undermines her search for inspiration in other gifted women's lives. Although a few quirky women may achieve greatness, most do not want greatness thrust upon them – and this is evident from the fact that so few have achieved greatness, her opponents in the True Woman cult would argue.

There is no rejoinder to this within liberal individualism. As another feminist philosopher, Joan Cocks, has written, the explanation of women's disadvantage 'require[s] a move liberal theory had not the competence to make, one which its entire methodological apparatus was designed to forbid: a reference to relations between social collectivities irreducible to relations between individuals as the sole authors of their own thought and action'.[89]

The individual is a male concept, and it relies on women *not* being individuals, Pateman asserts. This is a similar argument to that put forward by Carol Gilligan (see Chapter 2). The key concepts for women are different, Gilligan says:

> The moral imperative . . . [for] women is an injunction to care, a responsibility to discern and alleviate the 'real and recognizable trouble' of this world. For men, the moral imperative appears

rather as an injunction to respect the rights of others and thus to protect from interference the rights to life and self-fulfilment.[90]

Many of women's caring responsibilities, such as blood relationships, are not voluntary and consensual. They cannot be renounced, at least not without guilt. This was certainly true of Fuller's own life. She spent most of her adult years caring for her father's family, only the last two years of her life in looking after her own. An individualistic rhetoric of self-reliance, of cutting off, of denying the claims of others, doesn't allow Fuller to do justice to her own life, or permit those who follow her – including Emerson and the other editors of the *Memoirs* – to see her achievement. It is not the ethic she lived by, to her entire credit.

Of course it is important that Fuller should have registered a protest against the compulsory selflessless expected of one sex only. As Higginson said, 'Feminine self-sacrifice is a very common fruit on every soil, and certainly on that of New England.' But by espousing the morality of self-development so fervently, she allows her own altruism to be undervalued, as it was by every early biographer but Higginson. There is little room for altruism in liberal individualism, founded as it is on Hobbes's metaphor of men (and women) as mushrooms, only shallowly grounded in their soil, with no interconnecting roots.

Clearly Fuller should not be blamed for failing to foresee a twentieth-century analysis of the actual harm that individualism does to women: that would be hopelessly anachronistic. Rather I think she should be praised for eventually beginning to sense the inadequacy of Transcendentalist self-reliance in her own way, in her own time. The next chapter will examine that transformation in her thought at greater length; this chapter concludes with her own time's reaction to *Woman in the Nineteenth Century*.

REACTIONS TO *WOMAN IN THE NINETEENTH CENTURY*

Fuller's expectations for *Woman* were modest: no more than 'a sincere and patient attention from those who open the following pages at all',[91] and the hope that the first edition would clear in two or three years. Within a week the entire stock vanished from the bookshops, placarded with advertisements extolling Fuller's book as the *magnum opus* of the age. Sales were done no harm by noisily scandal-ised reviewers such as Charles F. Briggs:

> No unmarried woman has the right to say any thing on the subject. Let any wife, if one can be found to say it, declare that she would not have it so. But Miss Fuller is not a competent oracle.[92]

Fuller had argued the reverse: 'A profound thinker has said, that no married woman can represent the female world, for she belongs to her husband. The idea of Woman must be represented by a virgin.'[93] However, she had qualified this piece of apparent braggadocio:

> But that is the very fault of marriage, and of the present relation between the sexes, that the woman *does* belong to the man, instead of forming a whole with him. Were it otherwise, there would be no such limitation to the thought . . . Would she [woman] but assume her inheritance, Mary would not be the only virgin mother.[94]

Briggs was unimpressed: 'It would be as reasonable to say that none but a deaf man could give a true idea of music. Woman is nothing but as a wife.'

In *Woman* Fuller had called marriage a stick with which to beat free-living women such as Wollstonecraft and Sand. Now it was used to bludgeon her, too. Sophia Peabody Hawthorne, once so great an admirer that she had made Fuller the first confidante of her engagement (see Chapter 1), speculated that poor Margaret had been driven to hysteria by spinsterdom, as soon as 'The Great Law-suit' appeared in print.

> What do you think of the speech which Queen Margaret Fuller has made from the throne? It seems to me that if she were married truly, she would no longer be puzzled about the rights of woman. This is the revelation of woman's true destiny and place, which can never be *imagined* by those who do not experience the relation.[95]

Likewise, when 'Lawsuit's' successor *Woman* appeared the British intelligentsia either condemned Fuller – Dickens called the book 'rank with unwomanly sentiments' – or yawned visibly. Elizabeth Barrett wrote to Robert Browning, 'How I hate those 'Women of England,' 'Women and their Mission' and the rest. As if any possible good were to be done by such expositions of rights and wrongs.'[96] But many American reviewers thought Fuller had broached marriage and prostitution with great chastity. Although she judged conventional marriage harshly, she did posit great hopes for a higher, more durable spiritual form of companionship. (Wollstonecraft, by contrast, had 'sullied' her reputation not only with the birth before her marriage to Godwin of her illegitimate daughter by Gilbert Imlay, but also with her pronouncement that no marriage can last.[97]) A writer for *The Christian Examiner* pronounced of Fuller: 'She has discussed a delicate topic delicately and fearlessly; without prudish folly, without timidity, as a true woman should. No tongue will dare to cavil at her'.[98]

'As a true woman should': Fuller was judged,for good or ill, by the standards of the established church, the cult of True Womanhood. (Other members of that cabal did judge Fuller for ill: 'Her most direct writing is on a subject no virtuous woman can treat justly. No woman is a true woman who is not wife and mother.'[99]) Fuller was not so much a collaborator with patriarchal culture, as David implies of English women writers, but rather a Salman Rushdie: one born into a religion who is not allowed to opt out of it, not permitted to be judged by any other standards – even if he rejects it.

Some reviewers were willing to excuse Fuller on the grounds that she was too odd a bird to have any harmful effect on more ordinary women. This was the tone of Poe's patronising comments:

Woman in the Nineteenth Century is a book which few women in the country could have written, and no woman in the country would have published, with the exception of Miss Fuller. In the way of independence, of unmitigated radicalism, it is one of the 'Curiosities of American Literature' . . . Miss Fuller has erred, too, through her own excessive subjectiveness. She judges woman by the heart and intellect of Miss Fuller, but there are not more than one or two dozen Miss Fullers on the whole face of the earth.[100]

Poe thought Fuller's manner 'nervous, forcible, thoughtful, suggestive, brilliant', but the visionary style of *Woman* offended not a few readers. Fuller had written to Emerson that she realised she could never achieve his 'sculptured' excellence: 'I shall be content whenever I am in a state of unimpeded energy and can sing at the top of my voice, I dont care what.' This is perfectly consistent with the fact that although Fuller's work habits were disciplined, *Woman* seemed to lack structure. In fact Fuller's style comes perilously close to

Caroline Lee Hentz's 'record of my heart's life, written at random and carelessly thrown aside, sheet after sheet, sibylline leaves from the great book of Fate'.

The *Christian Examiner* reviewer complained that *Woman* 'is rather a collection of clever sayings and bright intimations, than a logical treatise'. Sneering with impunity in the journal which he himself edited, Orestes Brownson was considerably more poisonous.

> As talk, it [*Woman in the Nineteenth Century*] is very well, and proves that the lady has great talkative powers, and that, in this respect at least, she is a genuine woman . . . Miss Fuller does not know what she wants, any more than does many a fine lady, whom silks, laces, shawls, dogs, parrots, balls, routs, jams, water-places, and despair of lover or husband or friends have ceased to satisfy.[101]

At Groton, when Fuller had nursed one brother through threatened loss of sight in one eye, sewn clothes for six siblings, and made the family's soap from lye and fat, she had not been exactly surfeited with pug-dogs, Nottingham lace, or spa cures. But that Fuller was merely a victim of the vapours was clear to Brownson from her 'interminable prattle', her inability to diagnose her own ailment, and the amorphous formlessness of her argument. Even Fuller's defenders conceded that the book was too loosely written.

This has been the prevailing modern opinion until recent feminist work. Perry Miller shrugged that 'her style [was] as verbose as her emotions were chaotic'.[102] Marie Urbanski, in contrast, thinks that *Woman* has a very definite form: that of the sermon. The boundary between sermon, essay, and lecture was fluid for the male Transcendentalists: Emerson recycled one into another. Fuller had heard many of the great Unitarian preachers – William Ellery Channing, Frederic Henry Hedge, the abolitionists, Emerson himself – and might well have chosen this exalted but familiar form to fit her highly spiritual content. There is evidence in a previously unpublished letter that she had tried writing sermons herself.[103]

As Urbanski argues,

> What makes *Woman* a unique feminist work is its revolutionary spiritualism . . . the transcendental view of the immanence of God within men and women . . . It is only by viewing *Woman* as a

transcendentalist work that it can be understood. This accounts for what some readers consider its flaws, and what others consider its merits.[104]

This judgement seems to work: it would have been seconded by Fuller's enemies as much as her friends. What Brownson detested most in *Woman* – even more than its supposed *ennui* with parrots, dogs and watering-places – was its Transcendentalist attitudes towards nature. Fuller's argument foreshadows Thoreau's: 'If a plant cannot live according to its nature, it dies; and so a man',[105] but with the substitution of 'woman.' As Fuller writes at the end of *Woman,*

> Let us be wide, and not impede the soul. Let her work as she will. Let us have one creative energy, one incessant revelation. Let it take what form it will, and let us not bind it by the past to man or woman, black or white . . .
>
> If any individual live too much in relations, so that he becomes a stranger to the resources of his own nature, he falls after a while into a distraction, or imbecility . . . With a society it is the same . . .
>
> It is therefore that I would have Woman lay aside all thought, such as she habitually cherishes, of being taught and led by men. I would have her, like the Indian girl, dedicate herself to the Sun, the Sun of Truth . . .[106]

Brownson denounced the glorification of nature as a lamentable illusion.

> Nothing can be falser or more dangerous than this delusion. Nature does not suffice. Nature cannot be trusted. Away with your wretched cant about 'faith in man, in man's nature,' 'his lofty capacities,' 'glorious affinities,' and 'Godlike tendencies'. Nature, we repeat, is rotten, trust it not.[107]

Ironically, in view of the Burkean conservative tone of this polemic, Brownson had been a Saint-Simonian socialist, a former admirer of Fanny Wright and Robert Owen. The Saint-Simonians denounced existing family life and attempted to found communities embodying collectivist principles, such as Wright's Tennessee colony. Having recanted and become a Catholic convert, Brownson was perhaps all the more virulent towards proponents of radical change.

But more practically minded reformers than Fuller thought she had wasted her efforts in *Woman*. Other writers of the day, such as Marion Reid, had already demanded the vote. By ignoring the franchise issue – or only tackling it negatively, urging that 'all arbitrary barriers be thrown down' – Fuller had actually done women a disservice, argued her erstwhile acquaintance at the Greene Street school in Providence, the novelist John Neal.

> I tell you that there is no hope for woman, till she has a hand in making the law – no chance for her till her *vote* is worth as much as a mans [*sic*] vote. When it is – woman will not be fobbed off with sixpence a day for the very work a man would get a dollar for . . . All you and others are doing to elevate woman, is only fitted to make her feel more sensibly the long abuse of her understanding, when she comes to her senses. You might as well educate slaves – and still keep them in bondage.[108]

Fuller was less hurt by Neal's vigorous criticisms than by Caroline Sturgis's complaint that her style was lifeless:

> I have read it [*Woman in the Nineteenth Century*] through but the style troubles me very much . . . There is a recurrence of comparisons, illustrations, and words, which is not pleasing. There seems to be a want of vital powers as if you had gathered flowers and planted them in a garden but had left the roots in their own soil.[109]

Little wonder that Fuller was wounded by this admonition: heightened vitality was, after all, her great aim in personal and professional life. The demands of daily journalism were to transform Fuller's style into 'directness, terseness and practicality,'[110] as Horace Greeley judged it. Visiting Sing Sing prison and the New York asylums for the insane was to flesh out her skeletal and over-abstract thought on social issues. And the life, too, would at last be sweet.

5

'To Drink the Air and Light'

We are made to keep in motion, to drink the air and light.

Margaret Fuller[1]

The last chapter of Fuller's life was as rich as the posthumous accounts by Emerson, Hawthorne and James were impoverished, as
profound as they were shallow. Before being wrecked on other
shallows – the sandbars off Fire Island which caught and held her
ship, the *Elizabeth* – Fuller achieved a tragic synthesis following the
long years of her moratorium. From an unexpected affinity with
'fallen women' she moved to concern for a fallen foreign nation,
Italy. On her eighteenth birthday, she held in her arms a shortlived baby, her youngest brother Edward, born that day; on her
fortieth and last birthday she was tending a man dying of smallpox
– Captain Seth Hasty of the *Elizabeth*. Her final letter was about
female heroism, that of Mrs Hasty – matching her own attempt to
write a heroic life for herself and other women.

It is always tempting to see order after the event, but that would
be especially inappropriate when Fuller despaired of finding any life
for herself, her husband Giovanni Ossoli and their son after the fall
of the Roman republic. In the end there was none: 'I see nothing but
death before me,' the last survivor to leave the wreck heard her say.
The life of action failed her in her death, against which she could
take no action. But there is a tragic unity to these final five years – the
subject of Chapter 5 – and to the death itself – in Chapter 6. The line
between thought and action, person and persona, becomes ever
more blurred, the longer she stays away from New England. This
creates a new coherence in Fuller's thought, and a dramatic unity in
her life.

THE POLITICS OF SEXUALITY

The transformation of Fuller's social views – indeed, the emergence of anything which can be called *social* views rather than an intensely individualistic philosophy – began with her observations of other women. Being the Dark Lady among so many prominent men had threatened to separate Fuller from the quotidian reality of women's actual lives, despite her intense female friendships. The rarefied exchanges of the Boston Conversations – whose topics included 'Constancy', 'Faith', 'Education', 'Health', 'Mistakes', 'Woman' and 'Daemonology' – likewise left Fuller stranded like Socrates in his airborne basket in Aristophanes's *The Clouds*.

It was observation of pioneer and Indian women's concrete daily existence which tugged Fuller down to earth. There may be a further link between Fuller's Western experiences and her thought on sexual politics[2]: on Mackinac Island she was freer than in Boston to wander without fear of sexual harassment or molestation. New England women captured by Indians, such as Mary Rowlandson, wrote that 'not one of them ever offered the least abuse of unchastity to me in word or action'.[3] Prostitution did not exist before the settlers arrived; rape was rare among native Americans, and punished draconianly. Sexual politics might well have been another arena which made Fuller wonder about much-vaunted 'progress', particularly where women were concerned.

But the ultimate ballast was her visits to the prostitutes in Sing Sing prison, beginning in the autumn of 1844, during the final revisions of *Woman in the Nineteenth Century*, just before Fuller took up her position on the *New York Daily Tribune*. At this time Fuller was spending seven weeks at Fishkill Landing on the Hudson, not far from the prison in Ossining. Living with her close friend Caroline Sturgis and finishing her book, she lived what she described as 'this pleasant life of the free nun'. At the suggestion of her old Brook Farm acquaintance Georgiana Bruce, who was then working as a matron at Sing Sing, Fuller, Sturgis and William Channing paid a social call to women who were neither nuns nor free.

Sing Sing was the first of many 'benevolent institutions' which Fuller was to report on in her career at the *Tribune*: insane asylums, prisons, almshouses. Although most of her social columns were Greeley's suggestion, Greeley was only the catalyst in Fuller's development. Her thought was generally abstract in the Boston years and more concrete in the New York period – when she wrote on prejudice against the Irish, capital punishment, hygiene and other very specific issues. But Blanchard quite rightly points out that Fuller's social consciousness was rooted in her sympathy for Goethean political radicalism, her exposure to practical Unitarianism, and her readings in Jefferson, at her father's behest.

> Some biographers have tended to attribute Margaret's apparently new interest in social reform to a sudden enlightenment brought about by Horace Greeley and the squalid realities of the New York streets. What a mercy it was (they imply) that Margaret Fuller escaped from the Never-Never-Land of Boston Transcendentalism into the real world. This is true only to the extent that the massive social problems of the larger city provided a focus for an already developing social consciousness.[4]

As always with the moratorium years, roots were growing in the dark; without them the flower would have remained stuck in the bud when exposed to light.

Fuller was particularly 'ready' to meet the prostitutes of Sing Sing, and it was the politics of sexuality which roused Fuller's interest in the politics of politics. In 'The Great Lawsuit' Fuller had preached the Emersonian creed of self-reliance. But when 'we women have no profession except marriage, mantua-making and schoolkeeping',[5] to be *economically* self-reliant without following one of these three 'trades' could only mean one possibility: the enterprise which the women of Sing Sing pursued. Realisation of this anomaly in her own thought combined with Fuller's detestation of hypocrisy – 'Give me truth, cheat me by no illusion' – to ignite her fiery denunciation of the double standard.

It was prostitution which emblematised all other social ills, and which propelled Fuller into her increasing public concern and sympathy for socialism. Evangelical writers conflated prostitution with other forms of social chaos, including socialist radicalism; conversely Owenite socialists saw prostitution as the paradigm of exploitation in industrial capitalism.[6] The symbolic importance of prostitution holds true not only chronologically, in relation to Fuller's own development, but also in terms of the economic and demographic background to mid-nineteenth-century prostitution, which reflected deeper tends in American political and social life. Before discussing Fuller's thought on prostitution, we need to look at this backdrop.

Fuller was by no means the first to attack the system of commercialised prostitution, and in the passages on prostitution which she appended to *Woman in the Nineteenth Century* she acknowledged her admiration for a predecessor. Anna Jameson, whom I presented in Chapter 4 as a frequent collaborator with the cult of the True Woman, was atypically outspoken in her condemnation of male hypocrisy about prostitution. It was this sort of assault which Fuller most respected in Jameson's work – 'the decision with which she speaks on a subject which refined women are usually afraid to approach, for fear of the insult and scurrile jest they may encounter'.[7] As Jameson put it:

> We are told openly by moralists and politicians, that it is for the general good of society, nay, an absolute necessity, that one-fifth part of our sex should be condemned as the legitimate prey of the other, predoomed to die in reprobation, in the streets, in hospitals, that the virtue of the rest may be preserved, and the pride and the passions of men both gratified.[8]

Fuller's concern about prostitution was by no means unique, nor was her analysis as systematic or programmatic as that of existing activists. The New York Female Moral Reform Society, founded in 1834 to convert prostitutes to evangelical Protestantism, proposed to keep vigil at brothels and to publish a list of clients in the society's journal, the *Advocate of Moral Reform*. The journal was staffed and edited almost entirely by women, a deliberate policy: even the typesetter and the book-keeper were female. The Society attacked the double standard vigorously and denied allegations that nice women should remain nicely ignorant of the mere existence of prostitution. By the 1840s the American Female Moral Reform Society, as it became, had over 500 branches, providing cannon fodder for intensive political lobbying of the New York state legislature to make seduction imprisonable – and succeeding in their demands by 1848.

'Moral reform' became an acceptable outlet for challenging other forms of patriarchy. The Society also pilloried the male monopoly of the professions and claimed that low wages for women caused prostitution.[9] Displaced from cottage industries such as spinning and weaving by industrialisation, or recently arrived as impoverished immigrants, working-class women faced a choice between domestic service, millwork, and prostitution: their equivalent of the middle-class woman's dilemma – marriage, mantua-making or schoolkeeping. Many working-class girls used casual prostitution to eke out low earnings or get through periods of unemployment.

Compared to the New York Female Moral Reform Society, Fuller's attitudes were mainstream. But unlike many American crusaders against prostitution in her period, she did not play on nativist fears of immigration by claiming that it was foreign women who were corrupting American manhood.[10] Nor did she denounce prostitution out of what moderns might wrongly regard as the repressive attitudes of a daughter of the Puritans. The New England colonists encouraged sexual activity as joyful and fruitful, if channeled within marriage; indeed, abstaining from marital sex was an offence, as much for a husband as for a wife. One New England church excommunicated a man who denied conjugal relations to his wife for two years.[11]

Nonetheless, the double standard was well rooted in New England soil. Women were more likely than men to be prosecuted for adultery (sex between a man and a married woman) and fornication (between a married man and a single woman, or two single people). Women were more likely to be whipped or imprisoned if found guilty – partly because men, who had more property, could pay a fine instead. Rape was only punished by the death penalty if the woman was married or engaged – another man's property.

But what made the double standard particularly pernicious in the nineteenth century was the decline of the New England communitarian ideal in favour of the deracinated, deregulated marketplace. Among the Puritans each member of the community, man or women, was responsible for the moral health of the group as a whole. This legitimised prying into what the more private-minded nineteenth century would regard as nobody else's business. 'Acting on these precepts, Clement Coldom of Gloucester, Massachusetts, "heaved the door off the hinges" to see what his neighbor John Pearce was doing with "the widow Stannard" at night.'[12]

This institutionalised nosiness meant that Puritan men's misdeeds were as likely to be uncovered as women's, even if they might be less strictly punished. But disestablishment of the Protestant churches after the American Revolution lessened the religious imperative to uncover a neighbor's nakedness. Ironically, the nineteenth-century ideology of domesticity, retreating into the sanctity of the private home, also covered up male mis-steps *outside* the home. The wife's blissful domestic ignorance would be threatened if a husband's wrongdoing were revealed, it could be argued.

At the same time the expanding anonymous cities provided the ideal camouflage, and a market for prostitution. Buyers couldn't always find sellers in the early colonies: in 1720 William Byrd was unable to locate a prostitute in Williamsburg.[13] In Philadelphia, prostitution was not even a crime in the early nineteenth century: it was simply not a sufficiently widespread problem. Seventeenth- and eighteenth-century New England statutes recognised and punished the existence of prostitution, but it remained small-scale before the stimulus of three wars – the French and Indian War, the American Revolution and the War of 1812 – and of increasing maritime trade and urbanisation. By the mid-nineteenth century Dr William Sanger estimated that there were 6000 prostitutes in New York City, one for every sixty-four men.[14] Slightly earlier, in 1883, the Protestant reformer John McDowall had warned in *McDowall's Journal* and the *Magdalen Report* of ten thousand depraved harlots in the city.

Broadly, men benefited from more permissive attitudes towards their behaviour, together with a change in the ratio between the sexes towards a surplus of females except on the frontier. By the mid-nineteenth century, New York men could buy a published guide to the best brothels, couched in the politest terms:

> Mrs. Everett, No. 158 Laurens St.: This is a quiet, safe and respectable house, and altogether on the assignation order, and conducted on true Southern principles. She accommodates a few charming and beautiful lady boarders, who are from the sunny South, and equal to any of its class in the city. The proprietress strictly superintends the operations of the household, which is always in perfect order. The beautiful senoritas are quite accomplished, sociable and agreeable, and pattern after the much admired landlady. Gentlemen visitors from the South and West, are confidently recommended to this pleasant, quiet and safe abode. The landlady possesses all the charming mannerisms which so highly characterize that soothing clime. The very best wines constantly kept on hand, and selected from the best brands the market affords.[15]

But these changes were not always welcomed by men themselves. In 1793 several hundred working men in New York vandalised brothels and gentlemen's residences in a protest against the acquittal of a *soi-disant* gentleman who had taken a seventeen-year-old seamstress to a brothel and raped her. Another riot was directed at a bawdy house which catered for both whites and blacks.

These attacks on brothels reveal the symbolic power that prostitution had begun to acquire in the late eighteenth century. Prostitutes provided a reminder of the increasing class stratification that occurred in late-eighteenth-century cities, for they came from the newly formed ranks of urban poor. In addition, the appearance of prostitutes symbolized larger changes in the meaning of sexuality as it began to move outside of the private sphere of the family and away from its reproductive moorings. Prostitution did not go unnoticed as a threat to social order at a time when, on the one hand, family and community controls over morality weakened and, on the other hand, republicanism proclaimed that individual virtue was an essential condition for political well-being.[16]

This emblematic significance of prostitution was reinforced by the rapidity of social change. In the midst of westward settlement, industrialisation, urbanisation, and disestablishment of religion, the family alone seemed to stand firm. Yet even here there was worrisome change: the marital fertility rate fell by one child in each generation between 1800 (when an average couple had seven children) and 1880 (just over four).[17] At the same time abortion rates increased from one per 25–30 live births in the early nineteenth century to one in every five or six live births by the 1850s.[18] The decline in fertility was steepest in white middle-class Protestant families, whose numbers were most under threat – particularly frightening as Irish Catholic immigrants' birthrates boomed.

These shifts help to explain the backlash cult of the True Woman, and the cult in turn laid down new laws about female sexuality. In addition to demographic and political changes, and in part because of them, 'a new ideal of female "passionlessness" emerged in Anglo-American culture in the late eighteenth century, and biological arguments supported its contention that women had desires that were more maternal than sexual'.[19] The *natural* woman was sexless; prostitutes were unnatural. The popular physician William Acton wrote that 'the majority of women (happily for society) are not very much troubled with sexual feelings of any kind . . . Love of home, of children, and of domestic duties are the only passions they feel'.[20] Both male and female writers began to stress female chastity as protection for both the individual woman and society as a whole, and evangelical fervour heightened the imperative. As a female reformer wrote, 'The purity of women is the everlasting barrier against which the tides of man's sensual nature surge'.[21]

Slightly after Fuller's time, British doctors would contest the biological 'fact' of women's milder sexuality. R.J. Culverwell, author of *On Single and Married Life*, thought women's desire was functional: 'The best test of their [the female organs'] healthy condition will be the presence of desire, and the enjoyment of the orgasm simultaneously with the husband'.[22] George Drysdale wrote in his anonymously published *Physical, Sexual and Natural Religion* (1855):

> There is a great deal of erroneous feeling attached to the subject of sexual desires in woman. To have strong sexual passions is held to be rather a disgrace for a woman, and they are looked down upon as animal, sensual, coarse, and deserving reprobation. The moral emotions of love are indeed thought beautiful in her; but the physical ones are rather held unwomanly and debasing, this is a great error. In woman, exactly as in man, strong sexual appetites are a very great virtue, as they are signs of a vigorous frame, healthy sexual organs, and a naturally-developed sexual disposition . . . If chastity must continue to be regarded as the highest female virtue, it is impossible to give any woman real liberty.[23]

But this was by no means the dominant American discourse of Fuller's True-Womanised time. Early nineteenth-century America rejected the Enlightenment view that sexuality, like everything else natural, was good – and intercourse 'a virtuous Action', according to Benjamin Franklin. Vestiges of the older joy in sexuality remained: Peter Gay has documented, at least in private sources such as diaries, that the legitimacy of eroticism between loving partners was as great in the nineteenth century as ever or as now.[24] But at least formally the ideology *did* change. As the early nineteenth century came to reject the ideal of Republican Motherhood in favour of the cult of True Womanhood, it also replaced more egalitarian notions about male and female sexuality with what Bram Dijkstra calls 'the cult of the Household Nun'.[25] The purity of the Angel in the House required a demon outside to service male sexuality. This accentuated the divide between good and 'fallen' women, but also legitimised male libido. Prostitution was a boon to society, and the whore the upholder of the wife's chastity.

Herself the supreme type of vice, she is ultimately the most efficient guardian of virtue. But for her, the unchallenged purity of
countless happy homes would be polluted.[26]

Further, the dominant discourse only applied to nativeborn white
middle-class women; women of colour, immigrants and working-
class women were not regarded as passionless, but as fair sexual
game. Native American women were also thought debased: the
heroic figures of Pocahontas and Sacajawea, both of whom saved
men, were replaced by accounts in mid-nineteenth-century travel
journals of 'dirty little squaws' leading male adventurers astray.

Fuller's view travels far onward from this dominant discourse,
yet also begins from a starting point in the cult of the True Woman
– as I argued was true of her feminism, in Chapter 4. Prostitution
posed a particular problem for anyone who accepted, as Fuller did,
that women were different from men in their moral nature: a basic
premise of the cult. Men's nature apparently included being more
immoral. 'Passionlessness was on the other side of the coin which
paid, so to speak, for women's admission to moral equality.'[27] But
prostitutes were sexual women. Either Fuller could accept that prostitutes were passionless victims of male predatory sexuality – or she
could prove the rule by the exceptions, denigrating prostitutes as
false to all that True Womanhood stood for. Both strategies would
have confirmed the cult by ratifying asexuality in the 'normal'
female.

Instead Fuller asks, 'Why can't a man be more like a woman?' She
extends the True Womanly ideal of chastity to men: 'We shall not
decline celibacy as the great fact of our age.'[28] Fuller stands the cult
of the True Woman on its head: female moral nature, rightly re-
constituted in the case of aberrant specimens such as prostitutes,
can and should instruct male. It follows the cult to its own logical
conclusions, uncomfortable for men though they may actually turn
out to be.

This aspect of Fuller's thought can be seen in other contempora-
neous nineteenth-century movements against prostitution, which
mobilised middle-class women in an attempt to control men's sexuality. 'Social purity', a single sexual standard, should prevail for both
sexes – Fuller's message, and one which more closely resembled the
lost Puritan heritage than the double standard of the day. As temper-
ance would become, sexual continence was a revivalism-fuelled,
female-dominated movement to control the excesses of male behav-

iour which threatened women in their domestic sanctum, consciously drawing on the cult of the True Woman to 'feminise' politics.

Fuller implicitly accepts the ideal of the True Woman as the redemptive goal for passion-filled women – prostitutes – and men alike. However, she does not regard 'fallen' women as past all hope because they have fallen from so high a plane – as many devotees of the cult argued, and as medical opinion of the time confirmed.[29] Reviewing the report of the Matron of the Female Department of Sing-Sing, Eliza Farnham, in an 1845 essay for the *New York Tribune*, she approves of punishment designed to break the masculine braggadocio to which unnatural 'scenes of violence and depravity' had habituated the prostitutes in their early years, diverting them from the channel in which a True Woman's life should flow. Although Farnham was committed to rehabilitation, and although she instituted gentle reforms such as starting a library and suspending the rule of silence, the 'cure' she proposed may remind a modern reader uncomfortably of the 'calming' treatment imposed on the heroine in Charlotte Perkins Gilman's story 'The Yellow Wallpaper.' It is worth reproducing at some length, to demonstrate some limitations of Fuller's thought: her inability to understand that many working-class women used prostitution as a casual stopgap, her acceptance of the notions that these women *are* in some sense fallen and that punishment and redemption are in order. Fuller approved of what Farnham had written:

Of the females especially, a large majority have been reared and habituated to scenes of violence and depravity, that would themselves be the greatest terror to better constituted minds. Years of such excitement have prepared them to enjoy only scenes like those in which they have previously participated. Thus trained, aggression and resistance are the spontaneous and continued fruits of their minds. They come to the prison, therefore, prepared to war against physical measures, and the supremacy of animal courage, and to derive the highest enjoyment from such contest.

While in this condition, no punishment could be more severe than the unseen, quiet restraints of a moral system, which furnish no excitement to their resisting faculties, offer no provocation to endurance, no account of injuries to be revenged on some future occasion . . . An occasional burst of passion and resort to coercion; an occasional scene in which depravity makes itself in foul language or deeds of violence are holidays to them. Something of the old life is again felt in their veins; something of the old spirit is kindled . . .

But one primary object of our system is to cause this state to be superseded by one of greater activity in the moral and intellectual powers; to kindle purer and more elevated desires in the mind . . . Indeed the keenest suffering which the incarcerated ever experienced is that which flows from these sensibilities when the horrors of former years pass in review before the mind, and the future threatens equal terrors when they shall find themselves without protection, without sympathy, overwhelmed with disgrace and the consciousness of guilt. But painful though it be, it is the first indication of promise, the first step in the path of reform. It is the price which all who are susceptible of improvement must pay for the comparative tranquillity and sense of comfort which our system furnishes to those who are capable of enjoying them. Thus the gentler features of the system do not become sources of comfort until there is an adaptation to receive them as incentives also, and aids to reformation . . .

Many of the offenders were admonished and warned of the consequences that would follow a repetition of their offences. This treatment often secured all that was desired, and where it failed, the second act was promptly followed by the penalty which had been previously promised. Some of the punishments have been very slight, such as the deprivation of a meal; of books; the prohibition of exercise, etc. In a very few cases they have been severe. Such are the long terms of solitary confinement and the cropping of the hair. This last has been resorted to in but one instance, but with excellent effort . . .[30]

The aim of the punishment was to turn the Magdalen into a household nun. Unlike the New York Female Reform Society, but like the more punitive prostitutes' reform groups in England, Fuller appears to accept that the 'corrupt' women were morally blameworthy. Indeed, she rises to new heights of woman-blaming in a letter written before meeting the prostitutes to Georgiana Bruce: 'For these women in their degradation express most powerfully the present wants of the sex at large. What blasphemes in them must fret and murmur in the perfumed boudoir, for a society beats with one great heart'.[31] The same sentiment appears in her comment on other women's penal institutions in a *Tribune* article on 'Our City Charities': 'Here are the twelve hundred, who receive the punishment due to the vices of so large a portion of the rest.'[32]

When Fuller actually met these women, she liked them: 'I like them better than most women I meet, because, if any good is left it is so genuine, and they make no false pretensions, nor cling to shadows.'[33] But with her Transcendentalist tendency to see individuals as symbols of something greater, Fuller had as yet little concrete sense of the women's 'degradation'. There is no mention of venereal disease in her article on 'Prison Reform', for example – although it was the epidemic of venereal disease, largely undetectable in women but 'caused' by prostitutes, which so terrified men. Nor did she demonstrate any great interest in experiments with other forms of sexuality and family organisation, such as the Oneida community's principle of group marriage – backed by a splinter group of the New York Female Moral Reform Society. Had she been in favour of radical reforms to marriage, including divorce, Greeley would probably have refused to publish them: his opposition to divorce cost Elizabeth Cady Stanton the support of his editorials, when she backed an unsuccessful divorce bill in 1860. (Greeley also opposed female suffrage, which may explain Fuller's tactful omission of the topic from *Woman*, whose publication he sponsored.)

But where Fuller's thought *is* new, and at its most challenging, is where it is most at odds with the cult of the True Woman while apparently accepting the cult's credo. The respectable wife is not far off the prostitute, Fuller suggests in the letter above and the quotation below from *Woman in the Nineteenth Century*; the respectable husband benefits from the labour of both.

A little while since I was at one of the most fashionable places of public resort. I saw there many women dressed without regard to the season or the demands of the place, in apery, or, as it looked, in mockery of European fashions. I saw their eyes restlessly courting attention. I saw the way in which it was paid; the style of devotion, almost an open sneer, which it pleased those ladies to receive from men whose expression marked their own low position in the moral and intellectual world. Those women went to their pillows with their heads full of folly, their hearts of jealousy, or gratified vanity; those men, with the low opinion they already entertained of Woman confirmed. They were American *ladies*; that is, they were of that class who have wealth and leisure to make full use of the day, and confer benefits on others. They were of that class whom the possession of external advantages makes of pernicious example to many if these advantages be misused.

Soon after, I met a circle of women, stamped by society as among the most degraded of their sex. 'How.' it was asked of them, 'did you come here?' for by the society that I saw in the former place they were shut up in a prison. The causes were not difficult to trace: love of dress, love of flattery, love of excitement. They had not dresses like the other ladies, so they stole them; they could not pay for flattery by distinctions, and the dower of a worldly marriage, so they paid by the profanation of their persons. In excitement, more and more madly sought from day to day, they drowned the voice of conscience.

Now I ask you, my sisters, if the women at the fashionable house be not answerable for those women being in prison?[34]

This analysis does demonstrate awareness of class issues; yet after blaming 'virtuous women' for the existence of 'fallen women', Fuller goes on to state what appears to be a contradiction:

Women are accustomed to be told by men that the reform is to come *from them*. 'You,' say the man, 'must frown upon vice; you must decline the attentions of the corrupt; you must not submit to the will of your husband when it seems to you unworthy, but give the laws in marriage and redeem it from its present sensual and mental pollutions.'

This seems to us hard. Men have, indeed, been, for more than a hundred years, rating women for countenancing vice. But, at the same time, they have carefully hid from them its nature . . . As to marriage, it has been inculcated on [*sic*] women for centuries, that men have not only stronger passions than they, but of a sort that it would be shameful for them to share or even understand; that, therefore, they must 'confide in their husbands,' that is, submit implicitly to their will; that the least appearance of coldness or withdrawal, from whatever cause, in the wife is wicked, because liable to turn her husband's thoughts to illicit indulgence; for a man is so constituted that he must indulge his passions or die! . . .

On this subject, let every woman, who has once begun to think, examine herself; see whether she does not suppose virtue possible and necessary to Man, and whether she would not desire for her son a virtue which aimed at a fitness for a divine life, and involved, if not asceticism, that degree of power over the lower self, which shall 'not exterminate the passions, but keep them chained at the feet of reason.'[35]

What women are really to blame for is not seeing through male hypocrisy. And the reply to the evil must be total abolition of prostitution – rather than its regulation, institutionalisation, and legitimisation by women. So long as women are held responsible for mitigating the worst evils of prostitution, and for satisfying men sexually so that their recourse to prostitutes is minimal, there will be no advance.

In immediate practical terms, showing beneficence towards prostitutes, Fuller falls in behind the Sing Sing style of reform. She is, after all, always concerned with immediate, practical *action*. As Greeley said,

> I have known few women, and scarcely another maiden, who had the heart and the courage to speak with such frank compassion, in mixed circles, of the most degraded and outcast portion of the sex. The contemplation of their treatment, especially by the guilty authors of their ruin, moved her to a calm and mournful indignation, which she did not attempt to suppress nor control. Others were willing to pity and deplore; Margaret was more inclined to vindicate and to redeem.[36]

But ultimately her demands are much more radical: 'I will not decline celibacy as the great fact of our time,' for *both* sexes.

This aspect of Fuller's thought was *not* typical of her time, but it can be seen in later feminists. English campaigners against the Contagious Diseases Acts of 1864, 1866 and 1869 likewise rejected the mere regulation of prostitution, as benefiting men only. They, too, called for an abolition of the sexual double standard and the establishment of a single joint code of sexual behaviour. If the prostitute was the unwitting guardian of the domestic hearth, this root-and-branch stance – which Fuller shares – means a radical willingness to see conventional marriage die the death. In contrast, Emerson wrote, 'We cannot rectify marriage because it would introduce such carnage in our social relations.'[37]

In her 1875 lecture 'Social Purity', Susan B. Anthony argued, 'There is no escape from the conclusion that, while woman's want of bread induces her to pursue this vice [prostitution], man's love of the vice leads him there. For every abandoned woman, there is always *one* abandoned man and oftener many more.'[38] This is pure Fuller and, before her, Jameson:

> Man, born of Woman, the father of daughters, declares that he will and must buy the comforts and commercial advantages of his London, Vienna, Vienna, Paris, New York, by conniving at the moral death, the damnation, so far as the action of society can insecure it, of thousands of women for each splendid metropolis.[39]
>
> The rhetorical gentleman and silken dames . . . quite forgetting their washerwomen, their seamstresses, and the poor hirelings for the sensual pleasures of man that jostle them daily in the streets, talk as if Woman need to be fitted for no other chance than that of growing like a cherished flower in the garden of domestic love . . . I would point out as a primary source of incalculable mischief, the contradiction between her assumed and her real position . . . In the strong language of Carlyle, I would say that 'Here is a LIE, standing up in the midst of society.'[40]

With Jameson, the New York Moral Reform Society, Anthony, and others, Fuller helped to construct sexuality as gender- and class-specific. She contributed to the proliferation of nineteenth-century discourses on sexuality which Michel Foucault has identified as typical of the age which we usually think of as having put piano legs into skirts.[41] In her own sexual life, too, the New York years show her as something other than the angular spinster of *Memoirs* myth and memory. In this case, it appears to have been her exposure to the issue of sexuality which prepared her to change her life – whereas in Chapter 4 I suggested that forces of change in her own life prepared her to tackle the abstract issues around the Woman Question.

In February 1845, shortly after moving to New York, Fuller met and apparently fell in love with James Nathan, a German commercial traveller of doubtful honesty. (Even his nationality seems dubious: in one letter Fuller says that Germany was his 'adopted' country.[42]) Nathan professed concern for the reform of prostitutes, so that the link between Fuller's abstract concern for the politics of sexuality and the awakening of her own are directly linked: this was the ground on which they met.

Fuller wrote to or saw Nathan almost every day between February and June, when he sailed for Europe with an 'English maiden' supposedly under his protection (actually his mistress). He left as the *Tribune's* foreign correspondent, a position which Fuller used her influence to obtain for him; but his reports were bland and unprofessional. Nevertheless, she continued to hope for the best from him personally and professionally, until late 1846, when she discovered that he was engaged to a woman in Hamburg. By then she was herself in Europe on her final quest, which included an element of handsome-prince-seeking: hoping to meet Nathan again, on the right soil.

Nathan turned out to be a frog instead. Biographers have been almost as embarrassed by the Nathan correspondence as were Fuller's family, who suppressed it: it did not appear until 1903. Bell Gale Chevigny writes, 'It would be difficult to say which of the effects Nathan had on Fuller was stronger: the awakening of her sensuality or the putting to sleep of her mind.'[43] Certainly the letters which she wrote to him make uncomfortable reading. Nathan manipulated Fuller by playing on her True Womanly sympathy, a certain sentimentality, and her Romantic admiration for noble aspirations, judging from such evidence as this:

> Yesterday was, perhaps, a sadder day than I have had in all my life . . . Neither could I reconcile myself to your having such thoughts, and just when you had induced me to trust you so absolutely. I know you could not help it . . .
>
> Since then I have your note. Not one moment have I sinned against you; to 'disdain' you would be to disdain myself. Can I be deceived, then am I impure! . . .
>
> The child, even when its nurse has herself given it a blow, comes to throw itself into her arms for consolation, for it only feels the nearness of the relation. And so I come to thee . . . Yet the time is past when I could protect myself by reserve. I must now seem just as I feel, and *you* must protect me.[44]

Despite her protestations in *Woman* that men are not helpless in the face of their own sexuality, Fuller acknowledges to Nathan, 'I know you could not help it.' He succeeded in making *her* feel at abject fault for resisting his proposition, although she had denounced the common view that women who fail to satisfy men in their sexual demands are to blame:

> Your hand removes at last the veil from my eyes. It is then, indeed, myself who have caused all the ill. It is I who by flattering

myself and letting others flatter me that I must ever act nobly and nobler than others, have forgot that pure humility which is our only safeguard. I have let self-love, pride and distrust creep upon me and mingle with my life blood . . . I came from the battle field fancying myself a victor . . . I will now kneel . . . in this same moment I submit . . . I have not been good and pure and sweet enough.[45]

The battle-field from which Fuller had just returned was the critical reaction to publication of *Woman in the Nineteenth Century*. Whose Waterloo that turned out to be is open to doubt. With the ambivalence which Gilbert and Gubar identify as typical of even successful women – and remember that the entire first edition of *Woman* sold out in a week – Fuller may well have internalised reviewers' criticisms that she was not humble enough for a True Woman. Still smarting from unexpected hostility towards the book from her closest female friend, Caroline Sturgis, Fuller, though now the most widely read critic of her time, admitted to her favourite brother Richard, 'Sometimes I get very tired of my lonely and comfortless life . . .'[46] Nathan knew how to take advantage of that guilt and loneliness.

Fuller's letters to Nathan demonstrate the same distressing pattern of subservience found in other gifted women's correspondence with real or imagined lovers.

I dont [*sic*] know that any words from your mouth gave me more pleasure, a strange kind of pleasure, than these, 'You must be a fool, little girl.' It seemed so whimsical that they should be addressed to me who was called on for wisdom and dignity long before my leading strings were off and so pleasant too. Indeed thou art my dear brother and must ever be good and loving as to a little sister.[47]

With their implorings, their use of a sentimental pet name (Daisy), their metaphors of volcanoes, and their atypical humility, Emily Dickinson's 'Master' letters share the same frenetically abject tone. (Fuller is also supposed to have written a letter addressed to her 'Master', Beethoven – in which the famous deprecatory phrase 'I have no art' occurs.[48]) After George Sand's lover Alfred de Musset had spent *her* advance visiting whorehouses in Venice, diverting himself further by chasing her round their hotel room with a knife, she wrote in similar grovelling vein of his noble character in *Lettres d'un voyageur* (1837): 'You were bound to be a poet, you have been one in spite of yourself. In vain did you abjure the cult of virtue; you will be known as the most handsome of its young Levites. . . . [in] the white garment of your purity.'[49]

But Fuller had always maintained that 'Thought will never make us be born again'. Even if she made a fool of herself over Nathan – whose attentions were explicitly sexual but whose high-mindedness she vociferously protested, even against his own word – I think there is something strong and healthy in her newfound willingness to let herself go. Nor did her infatuation for Nathan scar the burgeoning pleasure she felt in her newly independent life. Letter after letter from New York is joy-ridden, even after Nathan had left her:

> [To James Nathan] Sept. 29th [1845]: These are the loveliest days of the American year, the breezes are melody and balm, the sunlight pours in floods through foliage itself transparent gold. The water is so very blue and animated; the sail-boats bound along, as if they felt like me. I have been inexpressibly happy these last few days. The weather within has been just the same as without. I am generally serene and rather bright, but *these* feelings are joy. Even for thee, I seldom feel regret . . .[50]

In the final five years of her life, Fuller followed the advice which Emerson prescribed to others in his 1841 essay on 'Heroism' but ignored for himself:

> Life is a festival only to the wise. Seen from the nook and chimney-side of prudence, it wears a ragged and dangerous front . . . Heroism . . . is a self-trust which slights the restraints of prudence in the plenitude of its energy and power to repair the harms it may suffer.[51]

> There is no weakness or exposure for which we cannot find consolation in the thought, – this is a part of my constitution, part of my relation and office to my fellow creature. Has nature covenanted with me that I should never appear to disadvantage, never make a ridiculous figure? Let us be generous of our dignity, as well as of our money.[52]

It was Nathan's vitality which appealed to Fuller, as superabundant life always did.

> I am with you as never with any other one. I like to be quite still and have you the actor and the voice. You have life enough for both; you will indulge me in this dear repose.[53]

> But let me sometimes hold you by the hand to linger with me here, and listen while the grass grows; it does me so much good, this soft warm life close to the earth. Perhaps it is that I was not enough a child at the right time, and now am too childish, but will you not have patience with that? The tulips are out now, and the crimson ones seem to me like you. They fill gloriously with the sunlight, and the petals glow like gems, while the black stamens in the cup of the flower look so rich and mystical. I have gathered two and put them in my vase, but the perfume is almost overpowering.[54]

This sensual image – carried forward in a later letter's reference to 'the fruit . . . on my tree, to which you so sweetly likened yourself, glanc[ing] like cornelians and corals among the leaves'[55] – prefigures more concrete power in Fuller's prose. In her thought and life, too, she sought greater vitality, and hoped that Nathan would confer it on her – that he would give her to herself. Fuller wrote to Nathan that she had been told, presumably by reviewers, that she was 'unnatural': that 'if I had the experience of passionate life, it would alter my view'.[56] Although her behaviour with Nathan was abject, her decision to take a risk on 'passionate life' was bravely consistent with both her previous development and her earlier deprivation – odd though it is to find her exchanging self-reliance for Svengali:

> I hear you with awe assert the power over me and feel it to be true. It causes awe, but not dread, such as I felt sometime since at the approach of this mysterious power, for I feel deep confidence in my friend and know that he will lead me on in a spirit of holy love, and that all I may learn of nature and the soul will be legitimate . . . I feel *chosen among women* . . . Are you my guardian to domesticate me in the body, and attach it more firmly to the earth . . . I hang lightly as an air plant. Am I to be rooted on earth, oh choose for me a good soil and a sunny place, that I may be a green shelter to the weary and bear fruit enough to pay for staying.[57]

SOCIAL AND LITERARY CRITICISM

Prostitution was the social concern which symbolised all others to many Americans, including Fuller, and sexuality was a key issue in many alternative analyses of society. The old Enlightenment interest in the position of women as indicative of a society's progress also found expression in the early nineteenth-century proto-socialist theories of Charles Fourier and Robert Owen. As Fourier wrote, 'The degree of emancipation of women is the natural measure of general emancipation.' Fourier advanced a progressive theory of social evolution through stages, each characterised by a particular form of conjugal relations. Healthy sexual passion was the mainspring of history to Fourier. Marriage or sexual partnership was more than a mirror of social progress, as the Enlightenment had held: it was actually the cause of social evolution. 'Social progress and changes of period are brought about by virtue of the progress of women towards liberty, and social retrogression occurs as a result of a diminution in the liberty of women.'[58]

I do not for a moment intend to argue that there is an inalienable link between feminism and socialism: only that logically and chronologically, Fuller's form of feminism led her into social concern. Many English Fourierites rejected any campaign for women's political rights: 'It is as vain for women to expect freedom in the present state of social organisation . . . as it is for the labouring multitude to expect ease and plenty from universal suffrage and annual parliaments.'[59] The French revolution of 1848 has been judged a substantial defeat for feminists, with male socialists providing most of the heavy artillery against women's suffrage.[60] We have already seen that George Sand, a committed sponsor of Fourierite socialism, abused women who demanded political participation. But the large American following which Fourier attracted was more often feminist than in Europe – though with Fourier's more shocking thoughts on sexuality edited out by his chief American disciple, Albert Brisbane – and in Fuller's case the link between feminism and socialism holds good.

Further, the Romantic feminism which Fuller espoused (see Chapter 4) set up quintessentially 'female' qualities – sympathy, compassion, charity – as a model for all humanity. The reverse of that proposition was that women should support the socialist ventures which embodied those values. As Barbara Taylor puts it in *Eve and the New Jerusalem*, 'A good woman, it was implied, was a born communist.'[61] The cult of True Womanhood supposedly venerated those values, but only as balm to the weary brow of the husband, wounded in the skirmishes of entrepreneurial capitalism. Beginning in the cult but transcending it, Fuller became more and more radically convinced of the cult's hypocrisy. Wanting all along to be a good woman, she became a made communist if not a born one.

Fuller had read Fourier while writing *Woman in the Nineteenth Century*, and had been a regular visitor at the Fourierite community of Brook Farm in the early 1840s. (Beginning as a vaguer sort of Utopia, during the period described by Hawthorne in *The Blithedale Romance*, Brook Farm was remodelled along the lines of Fourier's 'phalansteries' in 1844.) But she rejected invitations to become a permanent resident at Brook Farm and showed little interest in class or political issues until her New York period. Of a poor widow and her daughter whom Fuller visited on a True-Womanly mission of mercy during her New England years, she wrote, 'These grub-like lives, undignified even by passion, – these life-long quenchings of the spark divine, – why dost Thou suffer them?'[62] As a visitor to Rhode Island witnessing the Dorr rebellion for 'universal' male suffrage in 1842, she felt nothing but disdain:

I came into the very midst of the fuss . . . I shall in future be able to believe real, what I have read with a dim disbelief of such times and tendencies. There is, indeed, little good, little cheer, in what I have seen: a city full of grown-up people as wild, as mischief-seeking, as full of prejudice, careless slander and exaggeration, as a herd of boys in the play-ground of the worst boarding-school. Women whom I have seen, as the domestic cat, gentle, graceful, cajoling, suddenly showing the disposition, if not the force, of the tigress . . . I don't know when I have felt such an aversion to my environment, and prayed so earnestly day by day, – 'O, Eternal, purge from my inmost heart this hot haste about ephemeral trifles . . .'[63]

Seven years later, Fuller would be in the crowds demanding manhood suffrage in Rome; after the fall of the Roman Republic, she would write with equally withering scorn of Americans who had lost the popular touch:

[This is] a meanness and weakness too common to Americans abroad. Too often I have had occasion to blush at their apostasy, their ingratitude to the principles, the institutions which have made them all of good they are. They disdain the 'people', forgetting that if they have risen to peculiar privileges it was owing to freedom which kept the career open to talent . . .[64]

What accounts for this sea-change? Fuller's blasé attitude towards the Dorr rebellion does not stem from any feminist scepticism about how 'universal' manhood suffrage really was: that would be a modern reading-in. Manhood suffrage was all that the Roman Republic enacted, but Fuller mentions scarcely a qualm about the unrepresented position of Italian women. As in the above passage, 'freedom' is the key, I think. Before Fuller attained any liberty of her own, she had no emotional room to spare for empathy. In New York, to a degree, and even more fully in Europe, she finally got enough independence to share around.

Throughout her moratorium Fuller had suffered from the isolation imposed by restrictions on women's activity, her father's preference for the rural life, and domestic burdens. Conversation, she felt, was her element, and she needed the stimulus of other minds to draw forth her most systematic thought. After all, that impetus, available in universities and professions, was taken for granted by Emerson, Channing and Clarke – quick to criticise Fuller's need for conversation though they were in the *Memoirs*, as evidence of a flimsy feminine mind. The Five Points slums, the Hopper Home for released female convicts, the Bloomingdale Asylum for the Insane, Mount Pleasant State Prison, Sing Sing; evenings with Isaac Hopper, a Quaker who helped to run the Underground Railroad for freeing slaves; lectures by Cassius Clay, the antislavery publisher; galleries, studios, soirées – New York became Fuller's Free University, 'this great field which opens before me'.[65]

Poverty and crime had been available for Fuller's inspection in Boston, the crucible of many reform movements between 1835 and 1848, with abolitionism only the most prominent. Massachusetts had a long history of millenarian movements, dating back to the '82 pestilent heresies' numbered by Puritan divines in 1638. The Second Advent Movement, mesmerism, phrenology, the Graham health food movement, 'Dunkers, Muggletonians, Come-outers, Groaners . . .'[66] – all flourished in early nineteenth-century Boston. To some extent Fuller found this stimulating; the maleficent effect of New England on her should not be overstated.

Surely there never was a place where there was less of an approx-
imation to a harmony in views and tastes than here in Boston. It
is a time of dissonance, of transition, of aspiration. No three
persons think alike. The preference, to be given to this over another place I should think would be that there is here a restless
almost earnest spirit of enquiry as to: What shall a man [do] to
worthily fill the place assigned him in the universe?[67]

But in New England Fuller's circumstances and mental state were
more constricted: in New York she experienced a new Whitmanesque
vigour, a sense of being large, embracing multitudes – 'the life blood
rushing from an entire continent to swell my heart'.[68] Nor, even (or
especially not) through *The Dial*, did Boston offer the wide national
readership that the *Tribune* afforded her. Journalism forced her out
of herself and into the world which she had been too timidly True
Womanish to approach during her New England years, when she
had written to Clarke: 'But with all my aspirations after independence I do not possess sufficient at present to walk into the Boston
establishments and ask them to buy my work.'[69] Her career as a
reporter made her the self-reliant woman she had worshipped from
afar in 'The Great Lawsuit' and *Woman in the Nineteenth Century*. By
the end of her New York period, she had written over 250 articles,
some of which she hastily collected into her two-volume *Papers on
Literature and Art* (1846) before leaving for Europe, along with a few
essays previously published elsewhere. The tone of her introduction
to this work shows a playful pride in her own professionalism,
compared to her diffident twitterings about *The Dial*.

To those of my friends, who have often expressed a wish that I
'could find time to write,' it will be a satisfaction to know that,
though the last twenty months is the first period in my life when
it has been permitted me to make my pen my chief means of
expressing my thoughts, yet I have written enough, if what is
afloat, and what lies hid in manuscript, were put together, to
make a little library, quite large enough to exhaust the patience of
the collector, if not of the reader. Should I do no more, I have at
least sent my share of paper missives through the world.[70]

This was the best received of her books, and the most favourably
reviewed by the English press. The *Spectator*, generally known for its

'magisterial seriousness', and inclined to dismiss Dickens and Tennyson as lightweights, wrote:

> We have seen enough to assure us that Margaret Fuller is worthy to hold her place among the highest order of female writers of our day . . . The present volumes present to us the thoughts of a full and discerning mind, delicately susceptible of all impressions of beauty; earnest, generous, and serene; expressing itself in language of varies compass, for the most part singularly graceful and appropriate.[71]

But some reviewers – James Russell Lowell included - thought the introduction to the book immodest: un-True Womanly, in fact. Journalism had actually inculcated professionalism in Fuller, a simultaneous modesty about what she had achieved and a newly confident conviction that she could do better:

> I have not put dates to any of the pieces, though, in the earlier, I see much crudity, which I seem to have outgrown now, just as I hope I shall think ten years hence of what I write to day. But I find an identity in the main views and ideas, a substantial harmony among these pieces, and I think those who have been interested in my mind at all, will take some pleasure in reading the youngest and crudest of these pieces, and will readily disown for me what I would myself disown.
>
> Should these volumes meet with a kind reception, a more complete selection from my miscellanies will be offered to the public in due time. Should these not seem to be objects of interest I shall take the hint, and consign the rest to the peaceful seclusion of the garret.[72]

At the same time, journalism widened the angle of her vision beyond the narrow liberal individualism of 'The Great Lawsuit', *Summer on the Lakes*, and *Woman in the Nineteenth Century*. From her concern for prostitutes, Fuller went on to report on other oppressed groups: immigrants, slaves, servants, the unemployed. Greeley was much taken with her empathy: 'As the elephant's trunk serves either to rend a limb from the oak or pick up a pin, so her wonderful range of capacities, of experiences, of sympathies, seemed adapted to every condition and phase of humanity.'[73] Despite a certain genteel condescension, her pieces on the character of the Irish, the autobiography of Frederick Douglas, and United States cultural imperialism share a common radical theme with *Woman:* the right to self-development. Fuller denounces the supposed 'laziness' of the Irish, 'contentment' of the slave, and 'superiority' of the white race as lies – and she never has much patience with lies. Her defence of the Irish – 'fundamentally one of the best nations of the world – drew angry correspondence, but Fuller remained convinced of the need for an independent Irish republic. Her opposition to capital punishment provoked a shotgun-pellet barrage from one 'T.L.', complaining that *she* was 'personal and abusive' while lampooning her 'vanity', 'ignorance,' 'cant', 'drivel', 'slop', 'unmeaning rhapsodies' and praise for 'the chaste "creations" of that most chaste and "spiritual" creature, George Sand.'[74]

From disdain for the violent invective of all abolitionists, Fuller moved partway towards acceptance of their arguments by 1845, when she published seven pieces against slavery. Her chafing against hypocrisy and platitude, first obvious in *Summer on the Lakes*, is evident in these selections from an article on the United States exploring expedition to the South Seas. Beginning with delicate irony, Fuller cannot long prevent herself from launching into more direct attack:

> It is deeply interesting to us to know how much and how little God has accomplished for the various nations of the larger portion of the earth, before they are brought into contact with the civilization of Europe and the Christian religion. To suppose it so little as most people do, is to impugn the justice of Providence . . . [C]ontact with Europe has proved so generally more of a curse than a blessing [for] . . . our red man, to whom the white extends the Bible or crucifix with one hand, and the rum-bottle with the other . . . [and] [t]he Hindoo, the South American Indian, who knew their teachers first as powerful robbers . . . 'Believe or die" 'Understand or we will scourge you;' 'Understand and we will only plunder and tyrannize over you . . .' Would you speak to a man? first learn his language.[75]

This denunciation of cultural imperialism occurs in a book review – that of *The Narrative of the United States Exploring Expedition*. Societal affairs and literary questions were often intermingled in Fuller's thought and writing. Fuller's *Tribune* pieces are difficult to categorise as either about arts or about politics. Nominally she was under contract to produce one political and two literary lead articles every week for Greeley; but she moves from one to another in the course of a single piece. The theme of freedom connects the two particularly clearly in Fuller's article on Byron, whose own free living and heroic dying united life and art, she felt: 'Men do not now look in poetry for a serene world . . . No! dissatisfied and repressed, they want to be made to weep, because in so doing they feel themselves in some sense free.'[76]

In all spheres, Fuller wanted to see people live out their natures – the theme of *Woman*. She rejected false constraints on women, debasing poverty, stereotypes about the Irish or the slaves, and what she regarded as hackneyed writing. When she denounced an author, it was for facile platitude: the criticism which angered James Russell Lowell was her complaint that 'his verse is stereotyped.' With journalistic practice, her earnestness diminished and her old childish habit of teasing returned. In this case Longfellow was its butt:

> Mr. Longfellow has been accused of plagiarism. We have been surprised that anyone should have been anxious to fasten special charges of this kind upon him, when we had supposed it so obvious that the greater part of his mental stores were derived from the works of others.[77]

The verses which occasioned Fuller's giggles were these, from Longfellow's 'Prelude to the Voices of the Night':

> *Beneath some patriarchal tree*
> *I lay upon the ground;*
> *His hoary arms uplifted be,*
> *And all the broad leaves over me*
> *Clapped their little hands in glee*
> *With one continuous sound.*

In mocking the popular Longfellow Fuller braved the opinion of her time, for which Julia Ward Howe was still apologising forty years later: 'Our friend's appreciation of her contemporaries was influenced . . . by idiosyncrasies of her own which could not give the law to the general public.'[78] 'But this idea of leaves clapping their little hands with glee is taken out of some book; or at any rate it is a book thought . . .' Fuller complained. 'Thought will never make us be born again,' she had written elsewhere: book thought least of all.

In what has been called the 'tomahawk' age of criticism, when the American literary world was still small enough for all its members to hate each other personally, Fuller, the pre-eminent literary critic of her time, was generally impartial and fair-minded, Higginson thinks. She abhorred reviewers' and writers' cliques, 'that system of mutual adulation and organized puff'.[79] Her criteria were consistently Romantic: originality, heroism, openness, frankness, sincerity, uniqueness, democratic American fellow-feeling. She admired strength of style and emotion, commenting favourably of Poe: 'His narrative proceeds with vigor . . . Even the failures are those of an intellect of strong fiber and well-chosen aim.'[80] But she feared that the native American hue of resolution was soon to be sicklied over with the pale cast of commercial thought:

> Gentleness is dignified, but caution is debasing . . . Publishers are afraid; authors are afraid; and if a worthy resistance is not made by religious souls, there is danger that all the light will soon be put under bushels, lest some wind should waft from it a spark that may kindle dangerous fire.[81]

Unlike other Bostonians, Hawthorne in *Our Old Home* and James in particular, Fuller had no visceral reverence for the Mother Country: '[T]ake it as a whole, there is in English literature, as in English character, a reminiscence of walls and ceilings . . .' (The rest of this quotation demonstrates that Fuller was still true to her Roman roots: '[T]hat repels a mind trained in admiration of the antique spirit.') On the other hand, she thought American readers too fond of simplistic homilies, and American writers too ready to pander to popular taste, for profit. This explained Emerson's comparative dishonour in his native land, she generously judged. (Her own popularity, compared to his lack of sales, was a subject she tactfully avoided.)

What Fuller liked most in Emerson the writer – not always present in Emerson the man – was his openness. But as with Longfellow, she complained of a certain inertia.

> Here is undoubtedly the man of ideas, but we want the ideal man also; want the heart and genius of human life to interpret it, and here our satisfaction is not so perfect. We doubt this friend raised himself too early to the perpendicular and did not lie along the ground long enough to hear the secret whispers of our parent life.

We could wish he might be thrown by conflicts on the lap of
mother earth, to see if he would not rise again with added
powers . . . The mind is kept open to truth, and life only valued as
a tendency toward it.[82]

Nonetheless, Fuller pronounced Emerson the most melodic and sub-
tle poet of the day, and the greatest writer of fiction, Hawthorne –
who would do more to destroy her own good standing than any
other contemporary writer. But like the literary men who would
outlive her and kill her reputation, she set little store by the popular
female poets. The great irony of Fuller's denigration by the writers
who were to be canonical – and whom she helped to make canonical
– was that she shared their critical values – though not their consternation at the supposed feminisation of American literature.

But like George Sand, whose novels abound in lively female characters even if her public pronouncements scorned women's rights,
Fuller wanted to see women live in literature – not necessarily as
authors, but as something other than legless angels. Of Shakespeare,
for example – beginning to be idolised after eighteenth-century neglect – Fuller complained that he presented no heroic women. Even
Portia was insufficient, she said, though Cordelia came nearest to
tragic stature.

The literature of the day, too, written by both men and women,
English and American, was still influenced by the True-Womanly
gospel. In her widely read *The Women of England: Their Social Duties
and Domestic Habits* (1839) Sarah Stickney Ellis opined: 'Never yet,
however, was woman great, because she had great requirements;
nor can she ever be great in herself – personally, and without instru-
mentality – as an object, not an agent.'[83] Beginning in Transcendentalism, with its Kantian-inspired distrust of the idea that any human
being is merely a means and not an end, Fuller had great requirements all along. In New York she began to fulfil them, and to create
new ones for herself. But it was in Europe that Fuller would do her
damnedest to prove the Ellis view wrong. Living the events up to
and after the 1848 revolutionary period as well as reporting them in
her dispatches for the *Tribune*, she would achieve in her writing and
in her life an intensity and immediateness which had eluded her.
With her sense of life as art and life as art,[84] the 'romantic persona'[85]
of the dispatches, as it has been called, was no conscious masquer-
ade: it became Fuller herself.

THE HEART OF BRIGHTNESS

In the spring of 1846 Fuller left New York for Europe, as the *Tribune*'s new foreign correspondent, and tutor to the son of the reforming Quaker friends whom she accompanied, Marcus and Rebecca Spring. This was the reprise of the dream of freedom which she had abandoned ten years earlier (see the second quotation at the head of Chapter 3). But the lineaments of the dream were now sketched with greater realism:

> I do not look forward to seeing Europe now as so very important to me. My mind and character are too much formed. I shall not modify them but only add to my stores of knowledge. Still, even in this sense, I wish much to go. It is important to me, almost needful in the career I am now engaged in. I feel that, if I persevere, there is nothing to hinder my having an important career even now. But it must be in the capacity of a journalist, and for that I need this new field of observation.[86]

The script which Fuller first wrote for herself began as a travelogue, not an epic: a recital of the usual Grand Tour sights and sounds, augmented with objects of social concern. However, in order to vivify the hackneyed genre of travelogue, Fuller injected the qualities she always valued in writing: originality, frankness, the personal voice. As Fuller the woman came to have more of a life in Europe, her dispatches of her life in Europe came to be better written. At the same time her 'Things and Thoughts in Europe' became the most personal and revealing of any of the columns appearing in the *Tribune*. 'Months of living abroad, with little news from home, eventually caused her to lose touch with the American public and to imagine and address them as she did intimate friends with whom she maintained a regular correspondence.'[87] Letters, journals, diaries: these were the female-dominated literary forms from which the novel developed. By Fuller's time the 'respectable' novel was coming to be claimed by men. Fuller rejuvenated its sources and recast them into another form, one which no man of her time could rival.

> Fuller eventually revealed her joys, fears, anger, sorrow, and despair in ways no other journalist of the day was willing to. This became one of the features of the new eclectic genre represented

by the dispatches, a genre overfull, excessive, extravagant in the original sense of the term. That is, the dispatches wander far outside the boundaries of conventional travel writing and take on the qualities of the history, the sermon, the political manifesto, the historical romance, and especially the diary.[88]

This personal, philosophical journey becomes a kind of picaresque novel in Fuller's hands. Other travel writers of the day, such as Mrs Trollope – whom Fuller disliked – commented freely on the oddities of the natives, but Fuller was willing to bare her own quirks and puzzlements. Her writing in these last years is more twentieth-century than nineteenth: more akin to Paul Theroux, Bruce Chatwin, or Peter Matthiessen than it is like Mrs Trollope or Dickens in America.

Fuller's first dispatches from Scotland and England continued her *Tribune* observations on cultural and educational concerns, but actually in a less hard-hitting style than she had adopted in New York. Her first visits were to the Mechanics' Institutes in Liverpool and Manchester, following on in her American pattern of describing and assessing benevolent institutions for the poor. There is everything of the reformer, not the radical, in these early dispatches, and still considerable of the True Woman:

> For a very small fee the mechanic, clerk, or apprentice, and the women of their families can receive good and well-arranged instruction, not only in common branches of an English Education, but in mathematics, composition, the French and German languages, the practice and theory of the Fine Arts, and they are ardent of availing themselves of instruction in the higher branches . . . Only for the last year in Manchester and for two in Liverpool, have these advantages been extended to girls; but now that part of the subject is looked upon as it ought to be, and begins to be treated more and more as it must and will be wherever true civilization is making its way . . . Among other things they are taught, as they ought to be in all American schools, to cut out and make dresses.[89]

[T]alking by night in the streets of Manchester to the girls from the Mills, who were strolling bare-headed, with coarse, rude and reckless air through the streets, seeing through the windows of its gin-palaces the women seated drinking, too dull to carouse. The homes of England! their sweetness is melting into fable; only the new Spirit in its holiest power can restore to those homes their boasted security of 'each man's castle,' for Woman, the warder, is driven into the street, and has let fall the keys in her sad plight.[90]

Fuller's social observations were complemented by discussions with anyone who was anyone in British political and literary society: Martineau, Wordsworth, De Quincey, Joanna Baillie, Carlyle, the exiled Mazzini (whom she pronounced 'by far the most beauteous person I have seen'[91]) – all received her. Fuller – once too shy to approach Boston publishers with her work – enjoyed this enormously:

> I find myself much in my element in European Society. It does not indeed come up to my ideal: but so many of the encumbrances are cleared away that used to weary me in America, that I can enjoy a freer play of faculty, and feel, if not like a bird in the air, at least as easy as a fish in water.[92]

But again, any sort of radical consciousness is largely absent during her stay in England and Scotland, and there is little political energy in her reports of these conversations. It is as if the spirit of the place – what she had called English literature's 'reminiscence of walls and ceilings' – had imbued her with a foreign caution.

The only heroic bent evident in these early dispatches is in Fuller's description of her brush with death on Ben Lomond, when she became separated from Marcus Spring and was lost overnight in the peat bogs. This adventure is a good example of her creation of a self-reliant and romantic *literary* persona, exemplified by bravery in *life*:

> I thought I should not live through the night, or if I did, live always a miserable invalid. I had no chance to keep myself warm by walking, for, now it was dark, it would be too dangerous to stir. My only chance, however, lay in motion, and my only help in myself . . . [T]he mist fell and I saw nothing more, except such apparitions as visited Ossian on the hill-side when he went out by night and struck the bosky shield and called to him the spirits of the heroes and white-armed maids with their blue eyes of grief. – To me, too, came those visionary shapes: floating slowly and gracefully, their white robes would unfurl from the great body of

mist in which they had been engaged, and come upon me with a
kiss pervasively cold as that of Death. What they might have told
me, who knows, if I had but resigned myself more passively to
that cold, spirit-like breathing![93]

'We are made to keep in motion,' and without motion Fuller would
have been unmade.

But elsewhere in her dispatches from England and Scotland Fuller
is very down-to-earth. Of the elderly Wordsworth, once a supporter
of the French Revolution, Fuller remarks with approbation that he
'spoke with more liberality than we expected of the recent measures
about the Corn Laws . . . His neighbors were pleased to hear of his
speaking thus mildly'.[94] When Fuller visited Carlyle in company
with the abolitionist Springs, she left it to Rebecca to correct Carlyle's
complacent remark, 'If people consent to be slaves, they deserve to
be slaves.' In an 1845 article reviewing Carlyle's life of Cromwell
for the *Tribune*, she had criticised Carlyle for excusing Cromwell's
massacre at Drogheda and for worshipping naked unprincipled
power. Her own hero-worship was of a different stripe then:

> We know you do with all your soul love kings and heroes, Mr
> Carlyle, but we are not sure you always know the Sauls from the
> Davids. We fear if you had the disposal of the holy oil, you would
> be tempted to pour it on the head of him who is taller by the head
> than all his brethren.[95]

Oddly, exposure to poverty in Glasgow and London initially mel-
lowed Fuller rather than radicalised her. Fuller arrived in England
ready to view Carlyle as a reactionary. Even his friend Emerson,
who provided her letter of acquaintance to Carlyle, held this opinion
of him: 'Carlyle is no idealist in opinions, but a protectionist in
political economy, aristocrat in politics, epicure in diet, goes for
murder, money, punishment by death, and all the pretty slavery,
and all the pretty abominations, tempering them with epigrams.'[96]
But Fuller became more receptive towards Carlyle: 'I approached
him with more reverence after a little experience of England and
Scotland had taught me to appreciate the strength and high [sic] of
that wall of shams and conventions which he, more than any man, or
thousand men, – indeed, he almost alone – has begun to throw
down.'[97] She was more willing to accept his own heroic stature in
person than in print:

[T]he work of construction is left to those that come after him: nay, all attempts of the kind he is the readiest to deride, fearing new shams worse than the old, unable to trust the general action of a thought, and finding no heroic man, no natural king to represent it and challenge his confidence . . . Carlyle, indeed, is arrogant and overbearing, but in his arrogance there is no little- ness, no self-love: it is the heroic arrogance of some old Scandinavian conqueror – it is his nature and the untamable impulse that has given him power to crush the dragons.[98]

What is most sympathetic in these English and Scottish dispatches is Fuller's continued interest in and concern for women. The Northern English custom of female pallbearers for dead women and children – documented as late as the mid-twentieth century in the Yorkshire fishing village of Staithes[99] – impressed her with its appropriateness, in the burial of a dead child.

[I]n Liverpool . . . I saw . . . the body of an infant borne to the grave by women; for it is a beautiful custom here that those who have fulfilled all other tender offices to the little being, should hold to it the same relation to the very last.[100]

Her own chore-filled days at Groton, when she was unable to enjoy the summer days because she had to remain indoors sewing for her brothers and sister, gave her a quick sympathy for poor women's labours in washing clothes. With incisive tenderness she details the choice open to the mother in the damp English climate; leave the children in dirty clothes, or expose them to continual dampness indoors from washed garments which might take days to dry in the single room that housed the entire family. There is an immediate practical understanding and fellow-feeling in Fuller's account, the first quotation below, which contrasts with the more detached tone of a later male observer of London poverty, Charles Booth, in the second quotation:

I went to see . . . an establishment for washing clothes, where the poor can go and hire, for almost nothing, good tubs, water ready heated, the use of an apparatus for rinsing, drying and ironing, all so admirably arranged that a poor woman can in three hours get through an amount of washing and ironing that would, under ordinary circumstances, occupy three or four days. Especially the drying closets I contemplated with great satisfaction, and hope to see in our own country the same arrangements throughout the cities and even in the towns and villages. – Hanging out the clothes is a great exposure for women, even when they have a good place for it, but when, as is so common in cities, they must dry them in the house, how much they suffer! . . . An eminent physician told me he knew of two children whom he considered to have died because their mother, having but one room to live in, was obliged to wash and dry clothes close to their bed when they were ill. The poor people in London naturally do without washing all they can, and beneath that perpetual fall of soot the result may be guessed. All but the very poor in England put out their washing . . .*they* cannot put out their washing, because they cannot earn enough money to pay for it, and, preliminary to something better, washing establishments like this of London are desirable.[101]

. . . [S]o long as the low class exists at all, it must evidently lodge somewhere. This class tends (very naturally) to herd together; it is this tendency which must be combated, for by herding together, they – both the quarters they occupy, and their denizens – tend to get worse. When this comes about destruction is the only cure, and in this neighbourhood there has been of late years a great change brought about by the demolition of bad property. If much remains to do, still much has been done in the clearing away of vile spots, which contained dwellings unfit for human use and matched only by the people who inhabited them.[102]

Booth favours the grand social remedy – in this case, though certainly not always, with little inkling of the human cost; Fuller, the small-scale woman-centred reform.

This focus on practical action is again apparent in her dispatches from France, where she visited and approved of the day nurseries (crèches) and evening schools. By 1848 the male literacy rate in France was 87 per cent, the female 79 – comparing very favourably with American figures and far outstripping English rates.[103] Between 1821 and 1850 the population of the Department of Seine rose by half, but the number of primary schools tripled, and the percentage of children attending for free quintupled. During the 1830s a system of primary schools for adults and apprentices was set up: by 1850 there were 66 of them, enrolling 4500 pupils. In the seven years between 1827 and 1834 government spending on education performed an exponential leap from 50 000 francs to over 1.5 million.

Many visitors concurred with French middle-class opinion about improper working-class fascination with the printed word, as expressed by a writer for the *Universel* in 1829:

> The rage to read has invaded everywhere. I learned this fact recently before the door to my kitchen and the lodgings of my doorman, where I threatened twenty times, without issue, to hang the culprits if they did not bring my dinner. Reading has now reached the blacksmith's shop, the quarries, the sheds of wood-joiners' apprentices, and the stoneman's closet under the stairs.[104]

But Fuller could be expected to be delighted by it, and was. She was particularly moved by a visit to a 'School for Idiots,' though she disapproved of that title:

> Idiots, so called long time by the impatience of the crowd – for there are really none such, but only beings so below the average standard, so partially organized that it is difficult for them to learn or to sustain themselves. I wept the whole time I was in this place . . . I thought sorrowfully of the persons of this class whom I have known in our country, who might have been so raised and solaced by similar care.[105]

Fuller was probably crying for her youngest, mentally handicapped brother Lloyd, whom she had tried to establish in a series of positions – at Brook Farm, as a printer's apprentice, and elsewhere. Again, she is at her most touching, and most moved, when most private in her public correspondence. But this element of intense personal sympathy is not confined to the living, or those of her own flesh and blood.

While in Paris Fuller was granted a special request to see and handle the manuscripts of Jean-Jacques Rousseau in the Library of the Chamber of Deputies. This impressed her deeply:

> I saw them and touched them – those manuscripts just as he has celebrated them, written on the fine white paper, tied with ribbon – yellow and faded age has made them, yet at their touch I seemed to feel the fire of youth, immortally glowing, more and

more expansive, with which his soul has pervaded this century. He was the precursor of all we most prize; true, his blood was mixed with madness, and the course of his actual life made some detours through villanous [sic] places, but his spirit was intimate with the fundamental truths of human nature, and fraught with prophecy; there is none who has given birth to more life for this age; his gifts are yet untold; they are too present with us; but he who thinks really must often think with Rousseau, and learn him even more and more . . .[106]

This is typical of the new subjective style which Fuller's dispatches infuse into the standard genres of travel writing and cultural reporting. Yet with her fine eye for hypocrisy, one might expect Fuller to be a shade less obsequious before the author of the educational tract *Émile*, the man who sent his own five children to the foundling hospital. Nor would this necessarily be a modern reading-in – although Rousseau's two-facedness has made him an easy target for modern feminists such as Carole Pateman.[107] Wollstonecraft had pilloried Rousseau's libertinism towards Sophie, the girl who is to be educated only as a sexual plaything for Émile. In France itself feminist ideas were discussed energetically before, during and after the Revolution of 1789, and in the prologue to the 1848 revolution.

But surprisingly, Rousseau's female contemporaries and their successors were often more inspired than repelled by his theories of education. They took as their text not *Émile*, but *La Nouvelle Héloïse*, whose heroine, Julie, transcends her feeling for her lover and devotes herself to the sentimental education of the husband chosen by her parents, and of the children she bears him. 'The theme of the moral regeneration of the citizen through the influence of the family became an extremely powerful one; and it was this theme, rather than the artificiality and weakness of Sophie, which constituted Rousseau's appeal to these [women] writers.'[108] Julie was, in fact, a True Woman; and in both France and America, the moral regeneration of the nation was to be accomplished from the home. Fuller still accepted this hegemonic discourse to a great extent, as I argued in Chapter 4, although she subverted it from within.

Fuller also found Rousseau appealing because he conceived of democracy as a mechanism for individual self-development, her abiding ideal. Further, he wore the *toga virilis:* he admired the legacy of republican Rome. His limited economic egalitarianism – from which he excluded women and servants; his emphasis on each individual being master over himself and no others – from which he exempted wives; his assertion that all men love liberty – though women require protection and guidance: these are mixed blessings to a female admirer, but Fuller felt them to be benisons, as did Sand and many other gifted women of the time. If Sand and Fuller wrote quest plots for themselves, it was partly because Rousseau inspired them with the conviction that all could be made new.

Sand herself was another member of Fuller's far-flung spiritual kindred. While still in America, Fuller – at cost to herself of sarcastic remarks such as those of 'T.L.' about 'that most chaste and 'spiritual' creature, George Sand' – had praised the purity of Sand's idealism and social concern, contrasting her constructive genius with Balzac's dissecting pettiness:

> He [Balzac] delights to analyze, to classify . . . To him there is no virtue and no vice; men and women are more or less finely organized; noble and tender conduct is more agreeable than the reverse because it argues better health, that is all . . . Thus Balzac with all his force and fullness of talent never rises one moment into the region of genius. For genius is in nature positive and creative, and cannot exist where there is no heart to believe in realities . . . No more of him! – We leave him to his suicidal work . . .
>
> To the weak or unthinking the reading of such books [as Sand's novels] may not be desirable, for only those who take exercise as men can digest strong meat. But to anyone able to understand the position and circumstances, we believe that this reading cannot fail of bringing good impulses, valuable suggestions, and it is quite free from that subtle miasma which taints so large a portion of French literature, not less since the Revolution than before. This we say to the foreign reader. To her own country Sand is a boon, precious and prized both as a warning and a leader, for which none there can be ungrateful. She has dared to probe its festering wounds, and if they be not past all surgery, she is one who, most of any, helps toward a cure.[109]

The family reunion with her French spiritual *cousine* left Fuller with strongly favourable impressions:

> She was dressed in a robe of dark violet silk, with a black mantle on her shoulders, her beautiful hair dressed with the greatest taste, her whole appearance and attitude, in its simple and lady-

like dignity, presenting an almost ludicrous contrast to the vulgar caricature idea of George Sand . . . All these details I saw at a glance; but what fixed my attention was the expression of *goodness*, nobleness, and power, that pervaded the whole, – the truly human heart and nature that shone in the eyes. As our eyes met, she said, '*C'est vous,*' and held out her hand. I took it, and went into her little study; we sat down a moment, then I said, '*Il me fait de [sic] bien de vous voir,*' and I am sure I said it with my whole heart, for it made me very happy to see such a woman, so large and so developed a character, and everything that *is* in it so *really* good. I loved, shall always love her. She looked away, and said, '*Ah, vous m'avez écrit une lettre charmante.*' This was all the preliminary of our talk, which then went on as if we had always known one another . . . We did not talk at all of personal or private matters. I saw, as one sees in her writings, the want of an independent, interior life, but I did not feel it as a fault, there is so much in her of her kind. I heartily enjoyed the sense of so rich, so prolific, so ardent a genius. I liked the women in her, too, very much; I never liked a woman better.[110]

In addition to her veneration of Sand for having 'bravely acted out her nature', Fuller also admired Sand's concern for social reform: during her life the novelist donated over a million pounds in charity to persecuted republicans, Parisian artisans, needy peasants on her small estate, Nohant, and exiled nationalist leaders such as Mazzini and Chopin's countryman, the poet Adam Mickiewicz. Mickiewicz was closer to Sand, in fact, than to his bristly compatriot Chopin. He wrote of the relationship, 'Chopin is her evil genius, her moral vampire, her cross.'[111]

Fuller's own acquaintance with Mickiewicz was the most satisfying connection she made in Paris – just as that with Mazzini was the deepest she carried away from London. His brilliant eloquence and ability to extemporise for hours on romantic, nationalist themes combined with a mystical, authoritarian Catholicism but a simultaneously greater concern for women's rights than more left-wing reformers possessed. Like Fuller herself, Mickiewicz subscribed to an apocalyptic feminism. Both he and Fuller were disillusioned with Emersonian self-reliance: Mickiewicz wrote that Emerson 'isolates us too much, not taking into account epoch, nation or earth. Emerson's man dangles one knows not where.'[112]

Mickiewicz pronounced Fuller a 'true person' – a pleasant change from the usual diagnosis of 'true', or false, *woman*. Excelling even Sand, she was the only 'woman to whom it has been given to touch what is decisive in the present world and to have a presentiment of the world of the future'. In a character analysis which he sent her after their meeting, Mickiewicz declared,

> Her resting point is in the old world; her sphere of action is in the new world; her peace is in the world to come. She is called on to feel, think, act in these three worlds. The only woman truly initiated into the antique world . . .[113]

There was something of Mariolatry in this: Mickiewicz also mused on her virginity, wondering whether she would be 'permitted to remain chaste'. But Fuller, with an increasingly un-Bostonian outlook on sexuality, found this no bar to her admiration for the Pole.To Emerson, whose poems she had to Mickiewicz, she wrote, 'I found in him the man I had long wished to see, with the intellects and passions in due proportion for a full and healthy human being, with a soul constantly inspiring . . . [I]t was only with Mickiewicz that I felt any deep-founded mental connection.'[114]

Both Mazzini and Mickiewicz, with their satisfyingly heroic characters and causes, would reappear in Fuller's life as even more brilliant supernovae, during her stay in Italy. Mazzini would return as one of the three triumvirs of the Roman republic, Mickiewicz to raise a regiment of Polish exiles who would fight with the Romans. Ironically, however, when Fuller left Paris, she wrote: 'When I was with him [Mickiewicz] I was happy; and thus far the attraction is so strong that all the way from Paris I felt as if I had left my life behind, and if I followed my inclination I should return at this moment and leave Italy unseen.'[115]

As in England, Fuller showed herself most sympathetic to women's situation in France when she was confronted by it directly. French feminists had founded newspapers such as the *Voix des femmes* and *Opinion des femmes*, a congress of women's trades unions, and co-operative workshops, laundries, restaurants and social rooms,[116] but Fuller did not report on these exciting transformations. It is surprising that apart from one briefly described meeting with the socialist feminist Pauline Roland (1805–52), Fuller showed herself largely uninterested in the tremendous amount of women's political activity in the run-up to the 1848 revolution.

Nor did she show any curiosity about unionisation, again given a feminist slant by the organising work of Flora Tristan (1803–44). Fuller knew about the skilled craftsmen's union movement in Paris: she had published in an 1845 article in the *Tribune* her translation of a letter signed 'journeymen carpenters of Paris'. (Originally this article appeared in the German immigrants' newsletter *Deutsche Schnellpost:* it was also Fuller's first sight of the names of Marx and Engels.) This movement, like many others, was supported by women – in this case, the carpenters' 'mothers', who provided food and shelter for striking carpenters and controlled the union dues. The immediate occasion of Fuller's article was the furore over the arrest of one such 'mother', and the later jubilation over her release. Clearly Fuller knew that women were intensely involved in French labour movements, but there is little trace of feminist socialism in her dispatches from Paris.

But Fuller does report what she did see directly – the famine suffered by the lower classes during the difficult winter of 1847–8; the abysmal condition of French prostitutes; and the sufferings of the cottage weavers of Lyons. There she visited lodgings inhabited by a weaving family – working together all day in the same room, cooking in a corner, and sleeping on shelves under the ceiling – and exclaimed in her dispatch:

> The more I see of the terrible ills which infests [*sic*] the body politic of Europe, the more indignation I feel at the selfishness or stupidity of those in my own country who oppose an examination of these subjects – such as is animated by the hope of prevention ... And there are those who dare to say that such a state of things is *well enough*, and what Providence intended for man – who call those have hearts to suffer at the sight, energy and zeal to seek its remedy, visionaries and fanatics![117]

In this thirteenth dispatch – beginning with a private recital by Chopin in Paris, passing through the weavers' room in Lyons, and travelling on through a shipwreck (this time outlived) to Naples – Fuller locates her voice and home.'[H]ere at Naples I *have* at last found *my* Italy – . . . this priest-ridden, misgoverned, full of dirty, degraded men and women, yet still most lovely Naples . . .'[118] Initially, in discovering her home, Fuller very nearly *loses* her authorial voice. Dispatch 14 begins, 'There is very little that I can like to write about Italy. Italy is beautiful, worthy to be loved and embraced, not talked about.'[119] Italy was the land of action; Boston was the city of thought and endless talk. As Higginson correctly surmised, Fuller always valued *action* most; as she wrote from Rome, 'We are made to keep in motion, to drink the air and light'. When she first arrived in her ancestral home, as she felt it to be, the last thing she wanted to do was to *talk* in print. 'It is difficult to speak with any truth of Italy: it requires *genius, talent*, which is made to serve most purposes now, entirely fails here.'[120]

But although describing indissolubly romantic events, Fuller soon finds a much less florid style in Italy than in her own bleak home. It is almost as if she is speaking her own language for the first time. During her *Dial* years and before, in her correspondence with James Freeman Clarke over pieces which she submitted for his *Western Messenger*, she wondered if too much early exposure to European literature had hampered her native speech in print. Now that she is speaking little but Italian, her English suddenly flares into light:

At night the Corso, in which we live, was illuminated, and many thousands passed through it in a torch-bearing procession. I saw them first assembled in the Piazza del Populo, forming around its fountain a great circle of fire. – Then, as a river of fire, they streamed slowly through the Corso, on their way to the Quirinal to thank the Pope [for limited representative measures], upbearing a banner on which the edict was printed. The stream of fire advanced slowly with a perpetual surge-like sound of voices; the torches flashed on the animated Italian faces. I have never seen anything finer. Ascending the Quirinal they made it a mount of light. Bengal fires were thrown up, which cast their red and white light on the noble Greek figures of men and horses that reign over it. The Pope appeared on his balcony; the crowd shouted three vivas; he extended his arms; the crowd fell on their knees and received his benediction; he retired, and the torches were extinguished, and the multitude dispersed in an instant.[121]

The scene in which Fuller was caught up was an opening act of the 1848–9 revolutions played out in Italy and all over Europe. With the replacement in 1846 of a previous conservative pontiff by the initially progressive Pius IX (Pio Nono), Romans' hopes were raised for a more representative government. But the Good Father turned out to disappoint. It was the initial victory of reform through the flight of the discredited Pope in November 1848 and the establishment of a Roman republic with manhood suffrage in February 1849, the republic's subsequent destruction after invasion by the French, and the re-establishment of a conservative papal regime in July 1849, which Fuller chronicled for an attentive American audience. Although the high tide of Italian immigration to America did not occur until later in the nineteenth century, Americans were receptive to another budding republic's struggles. Greeley chaired a committee to prepare a letter to the Pope, 'as Republicans and lovers of Constitutional Freedom'.[122] Like her countrymen, Fuller viewed Italy as an appropriate object of benevolent distant concern, though during her time in Italy she increasingly came to see despotism in Rome as a direct warning to the young American republic itself:

> I take pride here that I may really say the Liberty of the Press works well, and that checks and balances naturally evolve from it which suffice to its government. I may say the minds of our people are alert, and that Talent has a free chance to rise. It is much. But dare I say that political ambition is not as darkly sullied as in other countries? Dare I say that men of most influence in political life are those who represent most virtue or even intellectual power? . . . Must I not confess in my country to a boundless lust of gain? . . . Then there is this horrible cancer of Slavery, and this wicked War [the Mexican War of 1846–48], that has grown out of it [as an extension of slaveholding territory]. How dare I speak of these things here? I listen to the same arguments against the emancipation of Italy, that are used against the emancipation of our blacks; the same arguments in favour of the spoliation of Poland as for the conquest of Mexico. I find the cause of tyranny and wrong everywhere the same – and lo! my Country the darkest offender, because with the least excuse, forsworn to the high calling with which she was called, – no champion of the rights of men, but a robber and a jailer; the scourge hid behind her banner; her eyes fixed, not on the stars, but on the possessions of other men.[123]

Although here she rejected the imperialist Mexican War,[124] Fuller, like most of her intellectual circle, was responsive to *progressive* nationalism even before meeting Mazzini and Mickiewicz. The aspect of *Woman in the Nineteenth Century* which had provoked more censure from newspaper editors than any – including her espousal of prostitutes' concerns – was her identification with the romantic figure of the Lithuanian nationalist Emilija Plater (1806–31), who raised a regiment against the Russians in 1831.[125] National self-identity was, to Fuller, a God-given right; for Rome, the centre of the Church, to be ruled by any other than the Roman people was an affront to the deity. The doctrine of popular sovereignty, the links between romanticism and nationalism, and the dictates of progressive religion coalesced in Fuller's thought to make her an ardent sympathiser with the nationalist cause long before she reached Italy: witness her espousal of Irish independence in the *Tribune* essays she wrote in New York.

To a modern mind, nationalism seems a strange doctrine for a feminist, and Fuller's willingness to accept Italian *men* as 'the people' difficult to understand. Feminist writers such as Carol Gilligan and Nel Noddings would claim that women's moral allegiance is to specific people in particular relationships, not to abstractions such as king and country. This is the view not only of feminists, but of E.M. Forster in his assertion that if he had to choose between betraying his friends and betraying his country, he hoped for sufficient bravery to be a traitor to his country. The moral primacy of personal relations, 'personalism,' is opposed to both nationalism and cosmopolitan ideologies such as Marxism, which dictates loyalty to an internationally common class rather than a nation.[126]

Having seen nationalism in its various debased forms of imperialism and inter-ethnic violence, we may well find it hard to accept as a progressive force. Yet it remains broadly true that nationalism was associated with revolution before 1850, with reaction only after. The nationalists whom Fuller knew were the revolutionaries, like Mazzini (1805–72), imprisoned in 1830 and afterwards exiled first in France and then in England. The founder of the 'Young Italy' movement, which numbered 60 000 supporters by 1833, Mazzini embodied the ideals of the Italian *Risorgimento*, or movement for national rebirth, as expressed in this letter which he wrote to Pio Nono in September 1847.

> I am not a subverter, nor a communist, nor a man of blood, nor a hater, nor intolerant, nor exclusive adorer of a system, or of a form imagined by my mind. I adore God, and an idea which seems to me of God, Italy an angel of moral unity and of progressive civilization for the nations of Europe . . . I have studied the

Tradition of Italy, and have found there Rome twice directress of the world – first through the Emperors, later through the Popes . . . I believe in yet another manifestation of the Italian Idea; and I believe that another European world ought to be revealed from the Eternal City . . . Look around you; you will find superstitions and hypocrites, but not believers. The intellect travels in a void. The bad adore calculation, physical good; the good pray and hope; nobody *believes*.[127]

Belief is an act, in these words of Mazzini's, and the Roman tradition demands heroic acts of its believers. Little wonder that Fuller found this deeply stirring.

Mazzini's followers were drawn from all social strata: this was both evidence of and a component in his appeal. In April 1847 – appropriately enough, in St Peter's, the heart of the papal domain – Fuller had made the acquaintance of one of the aristocratic recruits: Marchese Giovanni Angelo Ossoli. In the summer of 1847 Fuller separated in northern Italy from her travelling companions, the Springs, and returned to Rome to be with Ossoli and the incipient revolution.

This was in itself a 'manly' action: after abandoning her tutor post with the Springs, Fuller had no income beyond the ten dollars which she earned for each *Tribune* column. Subsidising the publication of the Danish writer Harro Harring's work had been one of her last actions in New York, but Harring's publisher Stallknecht cheated her. She was too generous to demand compensation from Harring: 'I would rather lose the money entirely than that anything should be added to the pressure on Harro.'[128] The profits from her *Papers on Literature and Art* were less than she had hoped: she had been rushed into preparing too slim an edition, at too low a price. She thought of writing a biography of George Sand, but was loath to return to Paris while events in Rome held her attention.

Ossoli himself, still only 26, was dependent on the good will of a despotic father and two elder brothers in the papal service, and that good will was in short supply, with his sympathies for Mazzini. When Ossoli's father died in February 1848, administration of the family estate passed over to the eldest and least sympathetic Ossoli brother, Giuseppe; there was all the more reason for Margaret and Giovanni to keep their relationship hidden. Fuller still hoped for some small sum from the final distribution of her own father's estate after the death of her uncle, the estate's executor; but this turned out to be tiny, the estate being divided among a total of 63 heirs after the specific legacies were paid – none to Margaret. Greeley advanced her six hundred dollars by selling part of his interest in the *Tribune*. But Fuller's bankers in Paris did not notify her that the funds had been received, and she thought Greeley had ignored her request.

Further, Fuller was ill with cholera in the summer and autumn of 1847, and with nausea in the early winter of 1848. Her health, never robust, benefited from the warmth of an Italian autumn but suffered during the rains of January and February. The dispatches continue to resound with the clarion calls of romantic nationalism; the private letters are increasingly anxious. Even within the letters, there are two voices:

> I find myself so happy here alone and free.[129]

> Altho' I have been much alone in our country, yet it was never as it is here where there is no one whom I can call for aid in any case.[130]

The narrative Fuller wrote for herself was split when she was, as it were, writing for two. She was now pregnant by Ossoli.

Much has been written about Fuller's hypocrisy in keeping her relationship with Ossoli secret, as she did in both the above letters. It hardly seems to be acting out her nature, or to be consistent with the store she set on frankness, which she viewed as excusing much in the case of Sand's relationships. In the past she had taxed Caroline Sturgis with lack of openness and commitment, yet now she wrote with mawkish self-pity to the newly married Caroline Sturgis Tappan:

> At present you have really cast your lot with another person, live in a house, I suppose; sleep and wake in unison with humanity; an island flowers in the river of your life. I cannot say anything about it from my present self . . . I am all alone . . .[131]

Not until March 1849 is there evidence that Fuller had told Tappan of her child's birth, though the baby was born in September 1848 – and Tappan was the first she told.[132] Before then, Fuller dwelt in double-entendres. To a former pupil, Jane Tuckerman King, she wrote:

> I am very happy here; tranquil, and alone in Rome. I love Rome more every hour; but I do not like to write details, or really to let any one know any thing about it. I pretend to, perhaps, but in reality, I do not betray the secrets of my love . . . Much has changed since we met; my character is not in what may be called the heroic phase, now. I have done, and may still do, things that may invoke censure; but in the foundation of character, in my aims, I am always the same . . .[133]

Even more ink, and corrective fluid, have been spilled in speculations about the date of Fuller's marriage – if any. During the siege of Rome by the French, in spring 1849, Fuller showed to her close friend Emelyn Story the documents of the marriage, but these have never surfaced – if that metaphor is not too uncomfortable. In the absence of sure knowledge, romantic speculation flourishes, as has been said of Emily Dickinson. Several theses have been advanced: that Fuller never married – the 'politically correct' position, perhaps; that Fuller wed Ossoli in April 1848, as some evidence in their letters seems to indicate;[134] or that she married him after the birth of their son on 5 September 1848. This last position is corroborated by her references to Ossoli as her husband in letters after that date, as in the letter below to Arthur Hugh Clough, dating from 1850. Fuller explained her secrecy to her sister Ellen in terms of Ossoli's adherence to Roman Catholicism; that also might indicate marriage after the child's birth, as could the paper Ossoli took out affirming that Nino was indeed his son.

The question is why Fuller and Ossoli kept their marriage and their son's birth secret, if indeed they were married. Emelyn Story, to whom Fuller confided the tale in hopes that she would protect the baby if Margaret and Ossoli were killed in the siege, accepted Fuller's own account of her unwonted failure to tell the whole truth. Ossoli's family, Story related, would have opposed his marriage to Margaret: a non-Catholic, a foreigner, a radical, and an older woman. At the time of their marriage, when his father had just died, the Ossolis needed his share of the forthcoming legacy: Ossoli had no profession other than his captaincy in the Roman Republic's Civil Guard. After the fall of Rome, Ossoli lost that legacy in any case, as a political exile. This, with the disbanding of the Civic Guard, explains their continued poverty during their exile in Florence.

Whatever the truth about Fuller's marriage, I think her behaviour *is* consistent with her character – despite her usual insistence on the full truth from herself and others. Her secrecy was motivated by Ossoli's needs rather than her own reputation; and she was primarily other-directed, despite the so-called mountainous me. It jeopardised her hard-won career: the dispatches ceased for seven months in May 1848, when Fuller's advancing pregnancy forced her to leave Roman society, and she was unable to come up with any convincing excuse to the irate Greeley, deprived of European copy at the apex of the revolutionary period. It was a heroic gesture involving much sacrifice: Fuller gave birth in circumstances of great isolation, in the mountains at Rieti, with Ossoli able to be with her for only a few days. The baby Angelino had to be left in Rieti when he was three months old, so that Margaret could resume her work and avoid scandal; the risks involved in bringing him to Rome were too great. This caused her great pain:

> It is *now* I want to be with him . . . If I had a little money I should go with him into strict retirement for a year or two and live for him alone. This I cannot do; all life that has been or could be natural to me is invariably denied. God knows why, I suppose.[135]

When she was able to return to him after the fall of Rome, he was near death from malnutrition. All in all, I think we should sympathise with Fuller, rather than endlessly dissect her motives: 'I acted upon a strong impulse. I could not analyze at all what passed in my mind. I neither rejoice nor grieve, for bad or for good I acted out my character'.[136]

But neither should we lose sight of the excitement which disguise afforded. With her scepticism about conventional marriage, Fuller was perhaps even more wary of matrimony than Ossoli, as she admitted to Arthur Hugh Clough in this letter written in 1850:

> I like also much [sic] living with my husband. You said in your letter you thought I should at any rate be happier now because the position of an unmarried woman in our time is not desirable; to me on the contrary it had seemed that in a state of society where marriage brings so much of trifling business arrangements and various soporifics that the liberty of single life was most precious . . . With Ossoli I liked when no one knew of our relation, and we passed our days together in the mountains, or walked beautiful nights amid the ruins of Rome. But for the child I should have wished to remain as we were, and feared we should lose much by

entering on the jog-trot of domestic life. However, I do not find it
so; we are of mutual solace and aid about the dish and spoon part,
yet enjoy our free rambles as much as ever.[137]

This letter reverses the usual roles: it is the woman who rejects 'the
jog-trot of domestic life'. And what Fuller did gain from marriage
was the 'wife' she had long needed. In a letter of January 1850 to her
recently married brother Richard, Fuller made that comparison
explicit:

> I may say of him [Ossoli], as you say of your wife, it would be
> difficult to other than like him, so sweet is his disposition, so
> without an effort disinterested, so simply wise his daily conduct,
> so harmonious his whole nature. Add that he is a perfectly uncon-
> scious character, and never dreams that he does well.[138]

Ossoli embodied the natural goodness to which Fuller had long
aspired herself, and his influence changed her for the better, she
thought. The edginess which the *Memoirs* editors associated with her
largely disappeared, despite the very real cares of her last years.
'Thought will never make us be born again', and Ossoli's beneficent
good nature revealed itself 'by acts, not words':

> . . . I have written as little as possible about Ossoli and our
> relation, wishing my old friends to form their own impressions
> naturally when they saw us together. I have all who ever really
> knew me [sic] would feel that I am become somewhat milder,
> kinder and more worthy to all who need for my new relations
> . . . But that would be only gradually, for it is by acts, not words,
> that one so simple, true, delicate and retiring can be known . . .
> His mind has little habitual action except in a simple natural
> poetry that one not very intimate with him would never know
> any thing about. But once opened to a great impulse as it was to
> the hope of freeing his country it rose to the height of the occasion
> and staid [sic] there. His enthusiasm was quiet but unsleeping. He
> is very unlike most Italians, but very unlike most Americans too.
> I do not expect all who cared for me to care for him, nor is it of
> importance to him; he is wholly without vanity. He is too truly
> the gentleman not to be respected by all persons of refinement;
> for the rest if my life is free and not too much troubled, if he can

enjoy his domestic affections and fulfil his duties in his own way he will [be] content. Can we find this much for ourselves in bustling America for the next three or four years?[139]

Fuller feared that her family and acquaintances would think Ossoli 'beneath' her: perhaps she suspected that they would see in him only another foreign adventurer, like James Nathan. But more deeply, gifted women who choose 'wives' rather than dominant husbands are always cause for mockery. George Sand lived for thirteen years with the engraver Alexandre Manceau, also younger than herself – longer than with Chopin or Musset. Most biographers, however, have ignored Manceau as being not quite up to snuff in the glory and renown stakes. Yet Sand praised Manceau much as Fuller valued Ossoli: he was like

. . . a woman who is skilled, active and ingenious. When I am ill, I am cured by the mere sight of him preparing my pillow and bringing me my slippers. I, who have never asked to be cared for, or accepted it, need his care, as though it were in my nature to be pampered.[140]

But this solid domestic support was not available to Fuller when she most needed it, in the last months of her pregnancy. At thirty-eight, with a history of ill health, and the best local remedy bloodletting, Fuller had much to fear. The murky letters of this period, deliberately ambiguous and secretive, are clear on only one point: she did not expect to see her friends and family again. Fuller, who gave her best childbearing years to the care of her father's children, could not even bring herself to tell her mother about the pregnancy and birth. Two weeks before Nino was born, she was still unsure whether Ossoli would be with her: 'If I were sure to do well, I would rather pass this ordeal before your coming, but when I think that it is possible for me to die alone without touching a dear hand . . .'[141]

Still, her first mountain retreat at Aquila in the Abruzzi, largely isolated from the civil unrest, inspired some of Fuller's most evocative private writing. At last she had time, unwelcome though it was, to observe in silence and inaction:

I am in the midst of a theatre of mountains, some of them crowned with snow, all of very noble shapes. Along three sides run bridle paths, fringed with olive and almond groves and vineyards; here and there gleams a church or shrine. Through the valley glides a little stream, along its banks here and there little farm houses; vegetation is most luxuriant in this valley. This town is on a slope of one of the hills, it is a little place, much ruined, having been once a baronial residence, the houses of these barons are gone to decay; there are churches now unused, with faded frescoes over the arched portals . . . [I]t looks very peaceful to see [monks'] draped forms pacing up the hills, and they have a healthy red in the cheek, unlike the vicious sallowness of monks of Rome . . . There is often sweet music in these churches, they are dresst with fresh flowers, and the mountain breeze sweeps through them so freely, they do not smell too strong of incense.

Here I live with a lively Italian woman who makes me broth of turnips and gets my clothes washed in the stream. I shall stay here sometime, if the beautiful solitude continues to please. The country people say '"Povera, sola, soletta," poor one, alone, all alone! the saints keep her,' as I pass. They think me some stricken deer to stay so apart from the herd.[142]

Fuller also began working intensively on her projected history of the Roman Revolution. Whatever the outcome – still undecided – she saw this as the heroic work of her life, a subject fitting for her rhetoric.   To her brother Richard she wrote later, in March 1849:

I trust I shall not find it impossible to accomplish at least one of my desires. This is to see the end of the political struggle in Italy and write its history. I think it will come to its crisis within this year. But to complete my work as I have begun I must watch it to the end . . . I shall have done something good which may survive my troubled existence. Still it would be like the rest if by ill health, want of means or being driven prematurely from the field of observation this hope also should be blighted. I am prepared to have it so. Only my efforts tend to the accomplishment of my object and should they not be baffled, you will not see me before the summer of 1850.[143]

Nor after the summer of 1850, either. Her work was lost, of course, as was the revolution.

Nevertheless, the contrast between the timelessness of Italy and the transience of the Roman Republic makes for tragic stature and pathos in Fuller's last works, even in what she would have seen as a lesser medium, her *Tribune* dispatches after the fall of Rome:

Rome will never recover the cruel ravages of these days, perhaps only just begun. I had often thought of living a few months near St Peter's . . . walking about to see what pleasant places there were, I had fixed my eye on a clean simple house near Ponte St. Angelo. It bore on a tablet that it was the property of Angela – *libera*, its little balconies with their old wooden rails, full of flowers in humble earthen vases, the many bird cages, the air of domestic quiet, and comfort marked it as the home of some vestal or widow, some lone woman, whose heart was centered in the ordinary and simplest pleasures of a home. I saw also she was one of the most limited income . . . Now . . . the cannonade reverberates all day under the dome of St Peter's, and the house of poor Angela is leveled with the ground.[144]

A contadini [*sic*] showed me where thirty-seven braves are buried beneath a heap of wall that fell upon them in the shock of one canonade. A marble nymph, with broken arm, looked sadly that way from her sun-dried fountain, some roses were blooming still, some red oleanders among the ruin . . . I then entered the French ground, all mapped and hollowed like a honey-comb. A pair of skeleton legs protruded from a bank of one barricade; lower a dog had scratched away its light covering of earth from the body of a man, and discovered it lying face upward all dressed; the dog stood gazing on it with an air of stupid amazement.[145]

Meanwhile the Italian sun shines gloriously, and the earth teems plenteous more than ever to feed the crowd of invaders that wound her bosom, and prevent her own children from perishing the while. For me as I heard the tramp of a great force come to keep down every throb of generous, spontaneous life, I shuddered at the sense of what existence is under such conditions, and felt for the first time joy over the noble men that have perished.[146]

Walking among corpses, tending the barely living in the hospital Bene Fratelli, separated from her child, whose own life was threatened: what are Fuller's last days in Rome if not heroic?

There are no heroines in myth, one modern male psychoanalyst has argued,[147] because the heroic quest is towards the place where woman is all along. She only needs to be 'to inspire man to do all', as Emerson put it; she has no quest of her own. She is Sleeping Beauty, not the prince. The emblematic woman is one who has no life to write, in this view. But this is not far off the True Woman creed. The final years of Fuller's life are emblematic, a life a woman wrote for herself. As Higginson said,

> At the very moment when Lowell was satirizing her in his 'Fable for Critics,' she was leading such a life as no American woman had led in this century before. During our own civil war, many women afterwards led it, and found out for themselves what it was; but by that time Margaret Fuller Ossoli had passed away.[148]

The narrative Fuller constructed of her life in Europe – Italy in particular – prefigures in some ways the male quest romance of the 1880s: the penetration into an exotic ancient centre of civilisation, the adventure, the loss. But whereas the male quest narrative is into a womb-like darkness, Fuller's language is evangelistic, messianic, revivalist: a turning toward light, the Heart of Brightness, not Darkness. The Roman Revolution she saw as evidence of that movement towards light, away from the Roman catacombs of Italy's political dismemberment and appropriation by a moribund religion. 'Born of the sun, they travelled a short while towards the sun', in Stephen Spender's phrase. In her own life, at its most wintry, Italy had always been the beneficent sun. Fuller's metaphors about Italy are about taking delayed root:

> Italy has been glorious to me, and there have been hours in which I received the full benefit of the vision. In Rome, I have known some blessed, quiet days, when I could yield myself to be soothed and instructed by the great thoughts and memories of the place . . . Had I only come ten years earlier. Now my life must be a failure, so much strength has been wasted on abstractions, which only came because I grew not in the right soil.[149]

Everything flowered in her final spring:

> Florence, 5 March 1850: This has been a divine day – The most glorious sunshine, and gently flowing airs, crows cawing and searching in gay bands; the birds twittering their first notes of love; the fields enameled with anemones, cowslips and crocuses – the Italian spring is as good as Paradise. How dreadful it will be hereafter to shiver and pine up to the middle of May; yet I *must* go and brave that and many an ugly thing beside.[150]

6

Dreaming a Woman's Death

Fuller wrote in her autobiographical romance that 'Every Roman was an emperor.' When she and Ossoli left Rome after the defeat of the Republic, to take refuge as political exiles in Florence and then to return to America, she was a dispossessed empress; and dispossessed emperors or empresses did not expect to live long. 'You speak of my whole future,' she wrote to William Channing. 'That future here on earth now seems to me short . . . Indeed, now I have the child, I am often sad fearing I may not stay long enough.'[1] 'I never think of the voyage without fearing the baby will die in it,'[2] Fuller wrote as early as November 1849.

The Ossolis celebrated their first and only family Christmas in 1849. Margaret described the scene to Caroline Sturgis Tappan:

Christmas day I was just up and Nino all naked on his sofa, when came some beautiful large toys that had been sent him, a bird, a horse, a cat that could be moved to express different things. It almost made me cry to see the kind of fearful rapture with which he regarded them, legs and arms, extended, fingers and toes quivering, mouth made up to a little round O, eyes dilated; for a long time he did not even wish to touch them, after he began to he was different with all the three, loving the bird; very wild and shouting with the horse, with the cat pulling her face close to his, staring in her eyes, and then throwing her away . . . You would laugh to know how much remorse I feel that I never gave children more toys in the course of my life. I regret all the money I ever spent on myself or in little presents for grown people, hardened sinners . . . There is snow all over Florence in our most beautiful piazza. La Maria Novella, with its fair loggia and bridal church is a carpet of snow and the full moon looking down, I had forgotten how angelical all that is, how fit to die by. I have only seen snow in mountain patches for so long, here it is the even, holy shroud of a desired peace. God bless all good and bad tonight and save me from despair.[3]

The sin of despair: Fuller was tempted to it by both immediate circumstances and long-standing premonitions. There was no life for either her or Ossoli in Italy, with his family's enmity and the defeat of republicanism. Mazzini had escaped to England, Garibaldi through the mountains to Venice, losing his wife, and all but a hundred of his original army of 4000. The Ossolis had no income in Florence, and few fellow-sympathisers: the Brownings were hostile to reform.

It was left to Margaret to decide what to do: Ossoli trusted her judgement. There seemed little choice but to return to her writing career in America, where she could publish her history of the Roman Republic and make a living as journalist. This was leaving home, rather than returning to it: 'I leave Italy with most sad and unsatis-fied heart, hoping indeed, to return, but fearing that may not in my 'cross-biased' [life] be permitted till strength of feeling and keenness of perception be less than during these bygone rich, if troubled years . . . I am so sad and weary leaving Italy that I seem paralyzed.'[4] Nor did she have great hopes for a warm welcome from 'those who are inclined to think ill, when they might as well have inclined the other way.'[5] Even Fuller's closest friends, such as the Springs, wrote that she must expect to run the gauntlet if she returned: 'It is because we love you we say stay!'[6] To Emelyn Story Fuller wrote:

> You will not admit for me, as I do not for myself, the rights of the social inquisition of the U.S. to know all the details of my affairs. If my mother is content, if Ossoli and I are content, if our child when grown up is content, that is enough.[7]

Between Fuller and her small hopes came the ocean. In many earlier dreams Fuller had associated water with death: she found herself crossing a bridge to a city on a hill, when the bridge snapped be-neath her. In an 1840 dream about Emerson, she was dying by the sea, and Emerson was all celestial:

> I thought I was with him on the rocks near a castellated place on the sea shore. I was dying and had that transparent spiritual feeling that I do after I have been in great pain, as if separated from the body and yet with memory enough of its pressure to make me enjoy the freedom, Mr E. was in his most angelic mood.[8]

Yet she had escaped the water so far. Her voyage to Liverpool in 1846 was done at record speed, in the comfort which the Springs could afford. Travelling to Naples, her ship collided with another, but she was unharmed. When she returned to Rome from the mountains, after Nino's birth, the diligence in which she had originally booked a place was seized by a mountain torrent; she had arranged at the last moment to travel another way.

This time, in the end, there was only one way to go, the cheapest. That would involve a two-month voyage by the merchantman *Elizabeth*, rather than the ten days she had spent coming over by Cunard steamer. It would require a goat to provide the baby with milk, as well as fresh fruit, water, ample supplies of baby-linen and medicines. Fuller began preparations, still trying to persuade herself that her forebodings were irrational. To her republican friend Costanza Arconati Visconti she wrote:

> I would not for the world have your last thoughts of me mingled with the least unpleasantness, when mine of you must always be all sweet. I say, *last thoughts*. I am absurdly fearful about this voyage. Various little omens have combined to give me a dark feeling. Among others just now, we hear of the wreck of the ship Westmoreland . . . Perhaps we shall live to laugh at these . . .[9]

> I had intended if I went by way of France to take the packet ship 'Argo' from Havre . . . [then] I read of the wreck of the 'Argo' returning from America to France! There were also notices of the wreck of the 'Royal Adelaide', a fine English steamer, and of the 'John Skiddy,' one of the fine American Packets. Thus it seems safety is not to be found in the wisest calculation. I shall embark more composedly in my merchant ship; praying, indeed fervently, that it may not be my lot to lose my babe at sea, either by unsolaced sickness, or amid the howling waves. Or that if I should, it may be brief anguish, and Ossoli, he and I go together.[10]

On 17 May 1850 Margaret, Giovanni and Nino Ossoli sailed on the ship *Elizabeth*. Still in the Mediterranean, the ship's captain, Seth Hasty, fell ill with smallpox; he died off Gibraltar, before the ship had even left Europe. Fuller helped to nurse him, with his wife, in whom she saw 'the heroism of womanly courage'. To Catherine Hasty's parents Fuller sent her closing letter, relying on her final reserves of elevated sentiments:

I want words to tell you how beautiful her conduct has been, so wise, so tender. Such a heroic spirit of Christian love and faith supported her doubts and anguish and enabled her to make exertions that seemed almost miraculous. For ten days and eleven nights she nursed him without an hour that could be called one of refreshment, performing for him the most difficult and repulsive offices with equal judgment, resolution and delicate tenderness. In her desolation she seeks in the same spirit to sustain herself by the Christian's hope. Much as you have prized your child, I am sure that she would be even dearer, could you have seen her on that day.[11]

To Marcus Spring she had admitted despair:

The last days were truly terrible with disgusts and fatigues, for he died, we suppose (no physician has been allowed to come on board to see the body) of confluent small pox. I have seen since we parted great suffering but nothing physical to be compared to this, where the once fair and expressive mould of man is thus lost in corruption before life is fled . . .

It is vain by prudence to seek to evade the stern assaults of Destiny. I submit.[12]

'I accept the universe', Fuller had said to Carlyle's mocking amusement: 'By Gad, she'd better!' Now her universe had shrunk to the ship and death.

The *Elizabeth* was put under quarantine for a week, than allowed to sail under the command of the first mate, Bangs. Nino contracted smallpox two days later, in open sea. Although his father had made great efforts to obtain vaccine for the baby shortly after he was born, it seemed to have had no long-lasting effect. Ossoli did not think Nino would live, but somehow Fuller nursed her son to recovery.

On 18 July the *Elizabeth* was approaching the coast of America, and the passengers were told to get their belongings ready for landing. Bangs, an inexperienced navigator, reckoned to be off the New Jersey shore; in fact they were off Long Island. At 3.30 a.m. the ship struck a sandbar on Fire Island, but did not sink immediately. The passengers' cabin, exposed to the elements on the main deck – one reason for the fare being affordable – was largely flooded, but no one was killed. The crew were isolated in their quarters in the forecastle, supposing the passengers drowned.

When light broke Catherine Hasty saw that the forecastle was intact, the crew alive, and the shore about 50 yards away. Waves were building up, but the sailors were able to help the passengers to the comparative safety of the forecastle while they awaited the help they were sure would come. The crew also made several trips to the cabin in order to rescue wine, figs, jewellery, and money for the passengers. Fuller did not feel she could ask them to risk carrying the heavy trunk with her manuscript history of the Roman Republic. They did rescue the two life belts she had brought, in her dread of drowning. Only one was in usable condition.

One of the sailors decided to try to reach shore using the life belt; he succeeded, and another followed on a spar. A young passenger, Horace Sumner, jumped in on a plank but drowned almost immediately. The cargo was washing up onto the shore, and scavengers arriving; but no rescuers. Later those at the scene – 'nearly a thousand persons . . . and more than half of them were engaged in secreting and carrying off everything that seemed to be of value'[13] – assured Fuller's family that 'if they had known there was anyone important on board, they would have rescued them.'

The ship began to break up about twelve hours after she had first struck the sandbar, in the late afternoon. Catherine Hasty roped herself to a plank, and survived. Wearing a long clumsy watersoaked nightgown, clutching her child, Fuller had no hope of swimming to shore. Ossoli could not swim. At the last moment the steward, Bates, took Nino from Margaret and struck out for shore. The new captain, Bangs, had already abandoned ship, leaving a woman and child on board. Later he was to charge Margaret with wanting to die, in his attempt to excuse himself.

Nino's body was washed up, with the steward's, both heavily bruised and mangled. Of the surviving crew,

the sailors, who had all formed a strong attachment to him during the voyage, wept like children when they saw him. There was some difficulty in finding a coffin, when the time of burial came, whereupon they took one of their chests, knocked out the tills, laid the body carefully inside, locked and nailed down the lid. He was buried in a little nook between two of the sand-hills some distance from the sea.[14]

When the Fuller family arrived, with Thoreau and Ellery Channing, they had the coffin disinterred. It was the first and only time they saw the child. The body was reburied in Mt. Auburn cemetery, Cambridge, under a memorial inscribed to all three: Nino, Giovanni and Margaret.

The bodies of Fuller and Ossoli were probably caught under the foremast of the sunken ship. They never surfaced.

Chronology

1778   Birth of Timothy Fuller (Margaret's father), fourth of eleven children of Rev. Timothy Fuller (1739–1805) and Sarah Williams (d. 1822)

1789   Birth of Margarett Crane, second of four children of Peter Crane (1752–1821) and Elizabeth Jones Weiser (1755–1845)

1801   Timothy Fuller graduates from Harvard

1809   Marriage of Timothy Fuller and Margarett Crane

1810   Birth of Sarah Margaret Fuller (Ossoli), 23 May

1812   Birth of Julia Adelaide Fuller

1814   Death of Julia Adelaide

1815   Birth of Eugene Fuller

1817   Timothy Fuller elected to Congress. Birth of William Henry Fuller

1820   Birth of Ellen Kilshaw Fuller (Channing)

1822   Birth of Arthur Buckminster Fuller

1824   Birth of Richard Frederick Fuller

1825   Timothy Fuller retires from Congress

1826   Birth of James Lloyd Fuller

1828   Edward Breck Fuller born on Margaret's eighteenth birthday, 23 May

1829   Edward dies on 15 September. 'He was some weeks wasting away, and I took care of him always half the night. He was a beautiful child, and became very dear to me then.' (*Letters*, vol. II, p. 187)

1832   Publication of George Sand's *Indiana*

1833   Timothy Fuller moves family to farm in Groton

1835   Death of Timothy Fuller

1836   Fuller teaches in Bronson Alcott's school in Boston

1837   Emerson delivers 'American Scholar' address to Harvard graduating class. Fuller teaches in Greene Street School, Providence

1839   Return to Groton. Sells house there in spring, then moves with mother and younger brothers to Jamaica Plain, Boston. Publication in June of her translation of Eckermann's *Conversations with Goethe*. Begins Boston Conversations

1840   July: first issue of *The Dial*

1841   Longfellow publishes 'Hesperus'; Emerson writes his essay on 'Heroism'

1842 Fuller transfers *The Dial* to Emerson's editorship; he closes it down within the year. Hawthorne publishes *Mosses from an Old Manse*; Thoreau, *Natural History of Massachusetts*; Fuller, her translation of Bettina Brentano's correspondence with Caroline von Gunderode

1843 Publication of 'The Great Lawsuit' (*Dial*, July 1843). May–August: trip to Niagara, Chicago, Illinois prairies, Milwaukee, and Great Lakes

1844 Publication of *Summer on the Lakes*. Birth of Margaret Fuller Channing, Ellen and Ellery Channing's daughter, on Margaret's birthday in May. Fuller offered post as literary editor on Horace Greeley's *New York Daily Tribune*, which she takes up in December. Late summer-autumn: finishes *Woman in the Nineteenth Century* at Fishkill Landing, on the Hudson, where she stays with Caroline Sturgis; makes visits to prostitutes in Sing Sing Prison

1845 Publication of *Woman in the Nineteenth Century* (March). Intense relationship with James Nathan; he leaves New York in June. Fuller publishes some 250 essays in *Tribune* during this year and next. Poe publishes 'The Raven' and *Tales*, Melville *Typee*

1846 Fuller leaves for Europe in spring. Travels in north of England and Scotland, meeting Wordsworth and staying in Martineau's cottage; arrives in London in October, meets Carlyle, Mazzini; leaves for Paris in November. Publication of *Papers on Literature and Art*. French Chamber of Deputies dissolved. Election of initially progressive Pope Pius IX

1847 Meets George Sand, Chopin, Adam Mickiewicz, Lamennais, Pierre Leroux, Béranger in Paris. Departs for Italy in late February; meets Giovanni Angelo Ossoli in April. Travels on with Springs to northern Italy, but decides to return to Rome in autumn while they journey on to Switzerland and Germany

1848 Rebellions in Sicily, Paris, Berlin, Vienna, and Budapest; Mexican–American War ends. Fuller, pregnant by Ossoli, leaves Rome in May for mountains, first Aquila and then Rieti. 5 September: birth of son, Angelo Eugene Philip Ossoli (Nino). November: flight of Pope Pius IX from Rome. December: Fuller returns to Rome, leaving baby behind with nurse

1849 Roman republic proclaimed in February; siege of Rome by French troops; Fuller runs hospital of Bene Fratelli, Ossoli serves as captain in Civic Guard. Rome falls on 1 July. Ossolis, reunited with Nino, flee to Florence. Friendship with Robert and Elizabeth Barrett Browning.

1850 May: Ossolis embark on *Elizabeth* for America. June: Captain Hasty of *Elizabeth* dies of smallpox off Gibraltar; mate takes over vessel. 19 July: *Elizabeth* breaks up on sandbar off Fire Island in storm. Margaret Fuller, Giovanni Ossoli, Nino, and four others drown; five survive

1852 Publication of *Memoirs of Margaret Fuller Ossoli*, edited by James Freeman Clarke, W.H. Channing and Ralph Waldo Emerson

1855 Death from consumption of Ellen Fuller Channing

1859 Deaths of Margarett Crane Fuller and Eugene Fuller (the latter by drowning, like his sister's)

1862 Death of Arthur Fuller in Battle of Fredericksburg

1869 Death of Richard Frederick Fuller. Of the seven Fuller children who survived to adulthood, only two lived past the age of forty-five

1884 Publication of Julian Hawthorne's biography of his father, containing scurrilous remarks about Fuller which receive great publicity

1903 Publication of Henry James's *William Wetmore Story and his Friends*, giving final shape to 'the Margaret myth'.

Works Cited

Ackroyd, Peter, *T.S. Eliot* (London: Hamish Hamilton, 1984).

Allen, James Smith, *Popular French Romanticism: Authors, Readers and Books in the 19th Century* (Syracuse, New York: Syracuse University Press, 1981).

Allen, Margaret Vanderhaar, *The Achievement of Margaret Fuller* (University Park, Pennsylvania: Pennsylvania State University Press, 1979).

Anderson, Bonnie S., and Zinsser, Judith P., *A History of Their Own: Women in Europe from Prehistory to the Present*, 2 vols (New York: Harper & Row, 1988).

Anonymous, 'Death of Margaret Fuller', *New York Daily Tribune*, July 1850, manuscript in the Houghton Library, Harvard University.

Anonymous, review of Margaret Fuller, *Woman in the Nineteenth Century*, *The Broadway Journal*, in Bell Gale Chevigny, *The Woman and the Myth: Margaret Fuller's Life and Writings* (Old Westbury NY: Feminist Press, 1976).

Anonymous, review of Julian Hawthorne, *Nathaniel Hawthorne and His Wife*, *Boston Evening Transcript*, November 1884, manuscript in the Houghton Library, Harvard University.

Anonymous, review of Julian Hawthorne, *Nathaniel Hawthorne and His Wife*, *New York Times*, 23 November 1884, manuscript in the Houghton Library, Harvard University.

Anonymous, review of Julian Hawthorne, *Nathaniel Hawthorne and His Wife*, *Sunday Herald*, 23 November 1884, manuscript in the Houghton Library, Harvard University.

Anonymous, 'The Social Condition of Woman', *North American Review*, no. 42 (1836), p. 513.

Anthony, Katharine, *Margaret Fuller: A Psychological Biography* (London: Jonathan Cape, 1922).

Anthony, Susan B., 'Social Purity', in Aileen S. Kraditor (ed.), *Up from the Pedestal: Selected Writings in the History of American Feminism* (Chicago, 1968).

Arcana, Judith, *Our Mother's Daughters* (London: The Women's Press, 1981).

Astell, Mary, *Reflections upon Marriage* (1700).

Banks, Olive, *Faces of Feminism: A Study of Feminism as a Social Movement* (Oxford: Basil Blackwell, 1981).

Barbour, Frances, 'Margaret Fuller and the British Reviewers', *New England Quarterly*, vol. IX, December 1936.

Barrett Browning, Elizabeth, *Letters*, ed. F.G. Kenyon (London: Macmillan, 1897).

———, *The Letters of Robert Browning and Elizabeth Barrett, 1845–1846*, ed. Elvan Kintner (Cambridge, Massachusetts: Harvard University Press, 1969).

Barry, Brian, 'Nationalism', in David Miller et al. (eds), *The Blackwell Encyclopaedia of Political Thought* (Oxford: Basil Blackwell, 1987).

Baym, Nina, *Woman's Fiction: A Guide to Novels by and about Women in America, 1820–1870* (Ithaca: Cornell University Press, 1978).

Berg, Barbara, *The Remembered Gate: Origins of American Feminism. The Woman and the City 1800–1860* (Oxford: Oxford University Press, 1978).

Blake, Millie Devereux, letter of 15 July 1901 to Miss Fuller, manuscript in the Houghton Library, Harvard University (Box B).

Blanchard, Paula, *Margaret Fuller: From Transcendentalism to Revolution* (New York: Delacorte Press/Seymour Lawrence, 1978, reprinted 1987 by Addison-Wesley, Reading, Massachusetts, with foreword by Carolyn G. Heilbrun).

Bloom, Harold, *The Anxiety of Influence: A Theory of Poetry* (Oxford/New York: Oxford University Press, 1973).

Booth, Charles, *Charles Booth's London: A Portrait of the Poor at the Turn of the Century drawn from His Life and Labour of the People in London*, eds. Albert Fried and Richard Elman (Harmondsworth: Penguin, 1971).

Briggs, Charles F., review of *Woman in the Nineteenth Century* in *The Broadway Journal*, 22 March 1845, in Joel Myerson (ed.), *Critical Essays on Margaret Fuller* (Boston: G.K. Hall, 1980).

Brockden Brown, Charles, *Alcuin: A Dialogue*, ed. Lee R. Edwards (New York, 1970).

Brownson, Orestes A., 'Miss Fuller and Reformers', *Brownson's Quarterly Review*, April 1845, no. 7, pp. 249–57.

'B.T.', report on death of Margaret Fuller, *New York Daily Tribune*, 23 July 1850, manuscript in the Houghton Library, Harvard University (Box B).

Buell, Lawrence, *Literary Transcendentalism: Style and Vision in the American Renaissance* (Ithaca: Cornell University Press).

Butler, Charles, *The American Lady* (1836).

Campbell, Joseph, *The Hero with a Thousand Faces* (Princeton, New Jersey: Princeton University Press, 1949).

Caplan, Paula, *Barriers between Women* (Lancaster: MTP Press, 1981).

Cate, Curtis, *George Sand: A Biography* (London: Hamish Hamilton, 1975).

Chapman, John Jay, 'Emerson', in *The Shock of Recognition: The Development of Literature in the United States Recorded by the Men who Made It*, ed. Edmund Wilson (New York: Doubleday, 1943).

Cheney, Ednah Dow, *Reminiscences* (Boston: Lee & Shepard, 1902).

Chevigny, Bell Gale, *The Woman and the Myth: Margaret Fuller's Life and Writings* (Old Westbury, NY: Feminist Press, 1976).

Cheyfitz, Eric, *The Trans-Parent: Sexual Politics in the Language of Emerson* (Baltimore: Johns Hopkins, 1981).

Chodorow, Nancy, *The Reproduction of Mothering* (Berkeley: University of California Press, 1978).

Clark, David, 'Death in Straithes', *Between Pulpit and Pew* (Cambridge: Cambridge University Press, 1982).

Clarke, James Freeman, letter of 1 March 1838 to Margaret Fuller, in *Letters of James Freeman Clarke*, ed. John Wesley (Hamburg: Cram, de Gruyter, 1957.

——, reply to Julian Hawthorne, *Boston Evening Transcript*, 2 January 1885, manuscript in the Houghton Library, Harvard University.

Clarke, Sarah Ann, reply to Julian Hawthorne, *Boston Evening Transcript*, 12 December 1884, manuscript in the Houghton Library, Harvard University.

Cocks, Joan, *The Oppositional Imagination: Feminism, Critique and Political Theory* (London: Routledge, 1989).

Conrad, Susan Phinney, *Perish the Thought: Intellectual Women in Romantic America 1830–1860* (New York: Oxford University Press, 1976).

Cott, Nancy F., *The Bonds of Womanhood: 'Woman's Sphere' in New England 1780–1835* (New Haven: Yale University Press, 1977).

———, 'Passionlessness: An Interpretation of Victorian Sexual Ideology, 1790–1850', in Nancy F. Cott and Elizabeth H. Pleck (eds), *A Heritage of Her Own* (New York, 1979).

Cranch, Christopher P., letter to the *Boston Evening Transcript*, 9 January 1885, manuscript in the Houghton Library, Harvard University.

Culverwell, R.J., *On Single and Married Life, or the Institutions of Marriage; Its Intentions, Obligations, and Physical and Constitutional Disqualifications Anatomically, Physiologically and Medically Considered; with an Exposition of the Structure and Purpose of the Reproductive System, the Hereditary Transmission of Qualities, and the Accidents and Infirmities Incident to Youth, Maturity and Old Age* (1847?).

David, Deirdre, *Intellectual Women and Victorian Patriarchy: Harriet Martineau, Elizabeth Barrett Browning, George Eliot* (London: Macmillan, 1987).

Deiss, Joseph Jay, *The Roman Years of Margaret Fuller* (New York: Thomas Y. Crowell, 1969).

de Beauvoir, Simone, *The Second Sex*, tr. and ed. H.H. Parshley (New York: Bantam, 1952).

de Staël, Germaine, *Corinne, ou l'Italie* (Paris: Librairie Stéreotype, 1807).

de Tocqueville, Alexis, *Democracy in America*, tr. Henry Reeve (New York: Vintage Books, 1945).

D'Emilio, John, and Freedman, Estelle B., *Intimate Matters: A History of Sexuality in America* (New York: Harper & Row, 1988).

Dickenson, Donna, *Emily Dickinson* (Leamington Spa, Warks./New York: Berg/St. Martin's, 1985).

———, *George Sand: A Brave Man, The Most Womanly Woman* (Oxford/New York: Berg/St. Martin's, 1988).

——— (ed.), *Woman in the Nineteenth Century and Other Writings by Margaret Fuller* (Oxford/New York: Oxford University Press, World's Classics Series, 1993).

Dickinson, Emily, *Selected Poems*, ed. Ted Hughes (London: Faber, 1968).

———, *The Poetry of Emily Dickinson*, ed. Thomas H. Johnson, variorum edition (Cambridge, Massachusetts: Harvard University Press, 1955).

Dijkstra, Bram, *Idols of Perversity: Fantasies of Feminine Evil in Fin-de-Siècle Culture* (Oxford/New York: Oxford University Press, 1986).

Donald, David Herbert, *Look Homeward: A Life of Thomas Wolfe* (Boston: Little, Brown, 1987).

Douglas, Ann, *The Feminization of American Culture* (New York: Alfred Knopf, 1977).

Drysdale, George, *Physical, Sexual and Natural Religion* (1855).

Dworkin, Andrea, *Right-Wing Women: The Politics of Domesticated Females* (London: The Women's Press, 1983).

Eagleton, Mary (ed.), *Feminist Literary Theory: A Reader* (Oxford: Basil Blackwell, 1986).

Earnest, Ernest, *Silas Weir Mitchell* (Philadelphia: University of Pennsylvania Press, 1950).

Eliot, George, 'Margaret Fuller and Mary Wollstonecraft', *The Leader*, 13 October 1855, in *The Essays of George Eliot*, ed. Thomas Pinney (London: Routledge & Kegan Paul, 1983).

Emerson, Ralph Waldo, 'Heroism', in *Collected Works of Ralph Waldo Emerson*, ed. Joseph Slater (Cambridge, Massachusetts: Belknap Press, 1983).

———, *Journals and Miscellaneous Notebooks*, ed. A.W. Plumstead, William H. Gilman, and Ruth H. Bennett, vol. XI, *1848–51* (Cambridge, Massachusetts: Belknap Press, 1975).

———, *Journals and Miscellaneous Notebooks*, ed. Merton M. Sealts Jr (Cambridge, Massachusetts: Harvard University Press, 1979).

———, *Nature*, in *Complete Essays and Other Writings of Ralph Waldo Emerson*, ed. Brooks Atkinson (New York: Random House, 1950).

Faderman, Lillian, *Surpassing the Love of Men* (London: The Women's Press, 1985).

Faludi, Susan, *Backlash: The Undeclared War against American Women* (New York: Crown, 1991).

Flexner, Eleanor, *A Century of Struggle* (Cambridge, Massachusetts: Belknap Press, 1959).

Foucault, Michel, *The History of Sexuality*, vol. I, *An Introduction* (Harmondsworth: Penguin, 1981).

Fourier, Charles, *Théorie des Quatre Mouvements*, in *The Utopian Vision of Charles Fourier: Selected Texts on Work, Love and Passionate Attraction*, tr. and ed. J. Beecher and R. Bienvenue (Boston, 1971).

Fuller, Frederick T., 'Hawthorne and Margaret Fuller', *The Literary World*, 10 January 1885.

Fuller, Sarah Margaret (Ossoli), 'Aglauron and Laurie,' manuscript in the Houghton Library, Harvard University (*Works* III).

———, 'American Literature: Its Position in the Present Time, and Prospects for the Future', in Mason Wade (ed.), *The Writings of Margaret Fuller* (Clifton, New Jersey: Augustus M. Kelley, 1973, reprint of 1941 Viking edition).

———, 'Carlyle's *Cromwell*', *New York Daily Tribune*, 19 December 1845.

———, 'Emerson's Essays', *New York Daily Tribune*, 7 December 1844.

———, 'French Novelists of the Day', *New York Daily Tribune*, 1 February 1845.

———, 'The Great Lawsuit' (excerpts), in Perry Miller (ed.), *The Transcendentalists: An Anthology* (Cambridge, Massachusetts: Harvard University Press, 1950).

———, *The Letters of Margaret Fuller*, ed. Robert N. Hudspeth, 6 vols. (Ithaca, New York: Cornell University Press, 1983–93).

———, 'Modern British Poets', in *Papers on Literature and Art* (London: Wiley & Putnam, 1846).

———, 'Mrs. Jameson's Memoirs', *New York Daily Tribune*, 24 July 1846.

———, 'Our City Charities', *New York Daily Tribune*, 19 March 1845, manuscript in the Houghton Library, Harvard University.

———, *Papers on Literature and Art* (London: Wiley & Putnam, 1846).

———, 'Poe's Poems', *New York Daily Tribune*, 26 November 1845.

——, 'Poe's Tales', *New York Daily Tribune*, 11 July 1845.

——, 'Prison Discipline', *New York Daily Tribune* (1845), manuscript in the Houghton Library, Harvard University (*Works* IV, pp. 153–5).

——, review of *Narrative of the United States Exploring Expedition* (1844) by Commander Charles Wilkes, *New York Daily Tribune*, 28 June 1845.

——, review of *Ormond* by Charles Brockden Brown, *New York Daily Tribune*, 21 July 1846.

——, *Summer on the Lakes in 1843: with Autobiography and Memoir by Ralph Waldo Emerson, W.H. Channing and Others* (London: Ward and Lock, 1861, reprint of 1844 edition with excerpts from *Memoirs* added).

——, *'These Sad but Glorious Days': Dispatches from Europe, 1846–1850*, eds Larry J. Reynolds and Susan Belasco Smith, (New Haven: Yale University Press, 1991).

——, *Woman in the Nineteenth Century* (New York: Greenwood Press, 1968, reprint of 1845 edition).

Gay, Peter, *The Bourgeois Experience: Victoria to Freud*, vol. I, *Education of the Senses* (Oxford: Oxford University Press, 1984).

Gilbert, Sandra M., and Gubar, Susan, *No Man's Land: The Place of the Woman Writer in the Twentieth Century*, vol. I, *The War of the Words* (New Haven/London: Yale University Press, 1988).

——, *The Madwoman in the Attic* (New Haven: Yale University Press, 1979).

Gilligan, Carol, *In a Different Voice: Psychological Theory and Women's Development* (Cambridge, Massachusetts: Harvard University Press, 1982).

Hartsock, Nancy, 'The Feminist Standpoint: Developing the Ground for a Specifically Feminist Historical Materialism', in Sandra Harding (ed.), *Feminism and Methodology: Social Science Issues* (Milton Keynes: Open University Press, 1987).

Hawthorne, Julian *Nathaniel Hawthorne and His Wife* (Boston, 1884).

Hawthorne, Nathaniel, *American Notebooks*, ed. Claude M. Simpson (Columbus, Ohio: Ohio State University Press, 1972).

——, *The Blithedale Romance*, in *The Complete Novels and Selected Tales of Nathaniel Hawthorne* (New York: Modern Library, 1965).

——, *The Scarlet Letter*, ed. Harry Levin (Boston: Houghton Mifflin, 1960).

Hawthorne, Sophia Peabody, letter to her mother on 'The Great Lawsuit', in Julian Hawthorne, *Nathaniel Hawthorne and his Wife*, above, p. 258.

Heilbrun, Carolyn G., *Writing a Woman's Life* (New York/London: W.W. Norton, 1988).

Held, David, *Models of Democracy* (Cambridge: Polity Press, 1987).

Helsinger, Elizabeth K., Sheets, Robin Lauterbach, and Veeder, William, *The Woman Question: Society and Literature in Britain and America 1837–1883*, vol. I, *Defining Voices* (Chicago: University of Chicago Press, 1989).

Higginson, Thomas Wentworth, 'An Open Portfolio', prefatory essay to *The Poems of Emily Dickinson* (Boston, 1891), reprinted in C.R. Blake and C.F. Wells (eds), *The Recognition of Emily Dickinson* (Ann Arbor, Michigan: University of Michigan Press, 1964).

——, *Margaret Fuller Ossoli* (Boston: Houghton Mifflin, American Men of Letters Series, 1884).

Higginson, Thomas Wentworth (presumed author), review of Julian Hawthorne, *Nathaniel Hawthorne and His Wife* (Boston, 1884), in *Atlantic Monthly*, February 1885, pp. 259–65.

Holyoake, George Jacob, *Sixty Years of an Agitator's Life* (London, 1892).

Howe, Julia Ward, *Margaret Fuller (Marchesa Ossoli)* (London: W.H. Allen, Eminent Women Series, 1883).

Huntingdon, Frederic Dan, review of *Woman in the Nineteenth Century*, *The Christian Examiner*, May 1845, no. 38, pp. 416–7, in Joel Myerson (ed), *Critical Essays on Margaret Fuller* (Boston: G.K. Hall, 1980).

James, Henry, *The Bostonians* (New York: Penguin, 1983).

——, *Letters*, ed. P. Lubbock (London, 1920).

——, *William Wetmore Story and His Friends* (Boston: Houghton Mifflin, 1903).

Jameson, Anna, *Memoirs of Celebrated Female Sovereigns* (London: George Routledge, 1831).

——, *Memoirs of the Loves of the Poets: Biographical Sketches of Women Celebrated in Ancient and Modern Poetry* (Boston: Houghton Mifflin, 1900, reprint of 1829 edition).

——, *Winter Studies and Summer Rambles in Canada* (London: Saunders & Otley, 1838).

Johnson, Douglas, 'Managing the Great Man's Memory', review of Simone de Beauvoir's *Adieux: A Farewell to Sartre*, *New York Times Book Review*, 6 May 1984.

Keohane, Nannerl O., 'But for Her Sex...The Domestication of Sophie', in MacAdam, Neumann and Lafrance (eds), *Trent Rousseau Papers* (Ottawa: University of Ottawa Press, 1980).

Lacan, Jacques, *Écrits: A Selection*, tr. Alan Sheridan (New York: W.W. Norton, 1977).

Lange, Lynda, 'Rousseau and Modern Feminism', in Mary Landon Shanley and Carole Pateman (eds), *Feminist Interpretations and Political Theory* (Cambridge: Polity Press, 1991).

Lawrence, David Herbert, *Studies in Classic American Literature* (Harmondsworth: Penguin, 1977, reprint of 1923 edition).

Lecky, W.E.H., *The History of European Morals*, 2 vols. (1869).

Lowell, Amy, 'A Critical Fable', in *Complete Poetical Works* (Boston: Houghton Mifflin, 1955).

Lowell, James Russell, 'A Fable for Critics', in *Poetical Works* (Boston: Houghton Mifflin, 1904).

Macintyre, Alasdair, *After Virtue* (London: Duckworth, 1981).

Malraux, André, *The Voices of Silence*, tr. S. Gilbert (London, 1954).

Martineau, Harriet, *Autobiography*, ed. Maria Weston Chapman (Boston: James R. Osgood, 1877).

——, *Household Education* (Philadelphia: Lea & Blanchard, 1849).

——, *Society in America* (New York: Saunders, Otley, 1837).

Memoirs of Margaret Fuller Ossoli, eds Ralph Waldo Emerson, James Freeman Clarke, and William Henry Channing (London: Richard Bentley, 1852).

Miller, Perry, *Margaret Fuller: American Romantic* (New York: Doubleday, 1963).

Morgan, Robin, *Sisterhood is Global* (Harmondsworth: Penguin, 1985).

Mossberg, Barbara Antonina Clarke, *Emily Dickinson: When a Writer is a Daughter* (Bloomington, Indiana: Indiana University Press, 1982).

Murdock, Maureen, *The Heroine's Journey* (Boston: Shambhala, 1990).

Nead, Lynda, *Myths of Sexuality: Representations of Women in Victorian Britain* (Oxford: Basil Blackwell, 1988).

Neal, John, letter to Margaret Fuller on *Woman in the Nineteenth Century*, 4 March 1845, in Bell Gale Chevigny, *The Woman and the Myth: Margaret Fuller's Life and Writings* (Old Westbury, N.Y.: Feminist Press, 1976).

Noddings, Nel, *Caring: A Feminine Approach to Ethics and Moral Education* (Berkeley and Los Angeles: University of California Press, 1984).

———, *Women and Evil* (Berkeley: University of California Press, 1989).

Nussbaum, Martha Craven, *The Fragility of Goodness: Luck and Ethics in Greek Tragedy and Philosophy* (Cambridge: Cambridge University Press, 1986).

Okin, Susan Moller, *Women in Western Political Thought* (Princeton, New Jersey: Princeton University Press, 1979).

Ordon, Edmund, 'Mickiewicz and Emerson', *University of Buffalo Studies*, no. 1 (July 1956).

Orga, Ates, *Chopin* (London: Omnibus Press, 1976).

Ostriker, Alicia Suskin, *Stealing the Language: The Emergence of Women's Poetry in America* (London: The Women's Press, 1986).

Pateman, Carole, *The Sexual Contract* (Cambridge: Polity Press, 1988).

Poe, Edgar Allan, *Complete Works* (New York: G.P. Putnam's Sons, 1902).

Pritchett, V.S., *The Myth Makers* (London: Chatto & Windus, 1979).

Prochaska, F.K., 'Women in English Philanthropy 1790–1830', *International Journal of Social History*, vol. 19 pp. 426–45.

Rawls, John, *A Theory of Justice* (Cambridge, Massachusetts: Harvard University Press, 1971).

Raymond, Janice, *A Passion for Friends: Toward A Philosophy of Female Affection* (London: The Women's Press, 1986).

Reid, Marion, *A Plea for Women* (Edinburgh: William Tait, 1843).

Rendall, Jane, *The Origins of Modern Feminism: Women in Britain, France and the United States 1780–1860* (London: Macmillan, 1985).

Ross, Mrs, *Hesitation: or, To Marry, or Not to Marry?* (London, 1819).

Sand, George, *Lettres d'un voyageur* (Paris: Garnier-Flammarion, 1971).

Sewall, Richard, *The Life of Emily Dickinson* (New York: Farrar, Straus, Giroux, 1974).

Showalter, Elaine, Clarendon Lectures, Oxford University, 2–11 May 1989.

———, *Sexual Anarchy: Gender and Culture at the* Fin de Siècle (London: Bloomsbury, 1991).

Smith, Page, *Daughters of the Promised Land: Women in American History* (Boston: Little, Brown, 1970).

Spender, Dale, *Women of Ideas, and What Men Have Done to Them* (London: Routledge & Kegan Paul, 1982).

Stanton, Elizabeth Cady, *Eighty Years and More: Reminiscences 1815–1897* (New York: Schocken Books, 1971, reprint of T. Fisher Unwin edition of 1898).

———, and Anthony, Susan B., *History of Woman Suffrage* (1881).

Sturgis, Caroline, letter to Margaret Fuller on publication of *Woman in the Nineteenth Century*, 4 March 1845, manuscript in the Houghton Library, Harvard University.

Swann, Charles, *Nathaniel Hawthorne: Tradition and Revolution* (Oxford: Oxford University Press, 1991).

Tait, Dr William, *Magdalenism* (1840).

Taylor, Barbara, *Eve and the New Jerusalem* (London: Virago, 1983).
———, 'Mary Wollstonecraft,' entry in *The Blackwell Encyclopaedia of Political Thought*, eds. David Miller et al. (Oxford: Basil Blackwell, 1987).
Thomas, Clara, *Love and Work Enough: The Life of Anna Jameson* (Toronto: University of Toronto Press, 1967).
Thompson, William, *Appeal of One-Half the Human Race, Women, against the Pretensions of the Other Half, Men, to Retain Them in Political, and thence in Civil and Domestic, Slavery* (London: Virago, 1983, reprint of 1825 edition).
Thomson, Patricia, *George Sand and the Victorians: Her Influence and Reputation in 19th-Century England* (London: Macmillan, 1977).
Thoreau, Henry David, 'Essay on Civil Disobedience', in *The Portable Thoreau*, ed. Carl Bode (New York: Viking Press, 1947).
———, *Walden*, ibid.
———, *A Week on the Concord and Merrimack Rivers*, ibid.
Ticknor, Caroline, *Hawthorne and His Publishers* (Boston: Houghton Mifflin, 1913).
Urbanski, Marie Mitchell Olesen, *Margaret Fuller's Woman in the Nineteenth Century: A Literary Study of Form and Content, of Sources and Influence* (Westport, Connecticut: Greenwood Press, 1980).
———, 'The Genesis, Form, Tone and Rhetorical Devices of *Woman in the Nineteenth Century*', in Joel Myerson (ed.), *Critical Essays on Margaret Fuller* (Boston: G.K. Hall, 1980).
Vogel, Ursula, 'Rationalism and Romanticism: Two Strategies for Women's Liberation', in Judith Evans et al., *Feminism and Political Theory* (London: Sage, 1986).
von Frank, Albert, *The Sacred Game: Provincialism and Frontier Consciousness in American Literature, 1630–1860* (New York: Cambridge University Press, 1985).
Wade, Mason, *Margaret Fuller: Whetstone of Genius* (New York: Viking, 1940).
——— (ed.), *The Writings of Margaret Fuller* (Clifton, New Jersey: Augustus M. Kelley, 1973, reprint of 1941 Viking edition).
Wakerman, Elyce, *Father Loss: Daughters Discuss the Man that Got Away* (New York: Henry Holt, 1984).
Watson, David, *Margaret Fuller: An American Romantic* (Oxford/New York: Berg/St. Martin's, 1987).
Wecter, Dixon, *The Hero in America: A Chronicle of Hero-Worship* (New York: Scribner's, 1941).
Welter, Barbara, *Dimity Convictions: The American Woman in the Nineteenth Century* (Athens, Ohio: Ohio University Press, 1976).
Winegarten, Renée, *Mme de Staël* (Leamington Spa, Warks./New York: Berg/St. Martin's, 1985).
Wollstonecraft, Mary, *A Vindication of the Rights of Woman*, ed. C.W. Hagelman jr. (New York: W.W. Norton, 1967 reprint of 1792 text).
Woody, Thomas, *A History of Women's Education in the United States* (New York: Science Press, 1929).
Woolf, Virginia, 'Professions for Women', in *Women and Writing* (London: The Women's Press, 1988).
Ziff, Larzer, *The American 1890s: Life and Times of a Lost Generation* (New York: Viking, 1966).

Notes

PREFACE

1. Sandra M. Gilbert and Susan Gubar, *No Man's Land: The Place of the Woman Writer in the Twentieth Century*, vol. I, *The War of the Words* (New Haven/London: Yale University Press, 1988).
2. In the Clarendon lectures, delivered May 2–11 1989 at Oxford.
3. *In a Different Voice: Psychological Theory and Women's Development* (Cambridge, Massachusetts: Harvard University Press, 1982).
4. Carolyn G. Heilbrun, *Writing a Woman's Life* (New York/London: W.W. Norton, 1988).
5. Donna Dickenson, *Emily Dickinson* (Leamington Spa, Warwickshire/New York: Berg Publishers/St. Martin's Press).
6. Donna Dickenson, *George Sand: A Brave Man, The Most Womanly Woman* (Oxford/New York: Berg Publishers/St. Martin's Press).
7. Cambridge: Polity Press, 1988.

CHAPTER 1: 'MY GOD, HOW I HATED HER!'

1. Amy Lowell, 'A Critical Fable' (1922), *Complete Poetical Works* (Boston: Houghton Mifflin, 1955), p. 409, quoted in Gilbert and Gubar, *War of the Words*, p. 205. Interestingly, Charlotte Perkins Gilman's husband tried – and failed – to cure her of post-partum depression by reading to her from Fuller's *Woman in the Nineteenth Century* – in addition to administering the horrific treatment fictionalised in her story 'The Yellow Wallpaper'.
2. Bell Gale Chevigny, *The Woman and the Myth: Margaret Fuller's Life and Writings* (Old Westbury, NY: Feminist Press, 1976), p. 9.
3. Gilbert and Gubar, *War of the Words*, p. 86.
4. V.S. Pritchett's derogatory reference to George Sand as a 'thinking bosom' in *The Myth Makers* (London: Chatto & Windus, 1979), p. 124; Dickenson, *George Sand*, p. 143.
5. Margaret Fuller, *Woman in the Nineteenth Century* (New York: Greenwood Press, 1968, reprint of 1845 edition).
6. Quoted by Elaine Showalter, 'Miranda's Story,' third Clarendon Lecture, delivered 4 May 1989, Oxford University.
7. Gilbert and Gubar, *War of the Words*, p. 142, citing Nina Baym, *Woman's Fiction: A Guide to Novels by and about Women in America, 1820–1870* (Ithaca: Cornell University Press, 1978).
8. James's attitude as described by Larzer Ziff in *The American 1890s: Life and Times of a Lost Generation* (New York: Viking, 1966), p. 275, quoted in Gilbert and Gubar, *No Man's Land*, p. 142.
9. Eric Cheyfitz, *The Trans-Parent: Sexual Politics in the Language of Emerson* (Baltimore, Johns Hopkins, 1981), p. 98.

10. Quoted in Ernest Earnest, *Silas Weir Mitchell* (Philadelphia: University of Pennsylvania Press, 1950), p. 174, and in Elaine Showalter, *Sexual Anarchy: Gender and Culture at the* Fin de Siècle (London: Bloomsbury, 1991), p. 77.
11. Quoted in Gilbert and Gubar, *War of the Words*, p. 142.
12. The title of Ann Douglas's influential book (New York: Alfred Knopf, 1977).
13. Quoted in Gilbert and Gubar, *War of the Words*, p. 143.
14. Gilbert and Gubar, *War of the Words*, p. 142.
15. Quoted in Showalter, first Clarendon Lecture, 2 May 1989.
16. Emerson, cited in Gilbert and Gubar, *War of the Words*, p. 227.
17. Cheyfitz, *The Trans-Parent: Sexual Politics in the Language of Emerson*, p. xi. A similar position is taken by John Jay Chapman in his essay, 'Emerson', in Edmund Wilson (ed.) *The Shock of Recognition: The Development of Literature in the United States Recorded by the Men Who Made It* (New York: Doubleday, 1943). Harold Bloom, in *The Anxiety of Influence: A Theory of Poetry* (Oxford/New York: Oxford University Press, 1973), presents Emerson as obsessed with the son's fall from perfect unity with the father, and an ensuing quest for male identity, which must be defined in opposition to the fallen feminine world which he now inhabits.
18. Chapman, 'Emerson', quoted in Cheyfitz, p. 82.
19. This view still surfaces, even in our supposedly sexually liberated time. For example, David Watson writes in his 1987 study *Margaret Fuller: An American Romantic* (Oxford/New York: Berg/St. Martin's Press): 'That the failures of this rapidly constructed (and somewhat reluctant) editorial team are now so transparent must not be allowed to disguise their success in protecting the good name of their subject for well over half a century.' (p. 91)
20. Quoted in Elizabeth K. Helsinger, Robin Lauterbach Sheets and William Veeder, *The Woman Question: Society and Literature in Britain and America 1837–1883*, vol. I, *Defining Voices* (Chicago/London: University of Chicago Press, 1989), p. 129, fn. 4.
21. Quoted in Marie Mitchell Olesen Urbanski, *Margaret Fuller's Woman in the Nineteenth Century: A Literary Study of Form and Content, of Sources and Influence* (Westport, Connecticut: Greenwood Press, 1980), p. 36.
22. Indeed, the male critic in Lowell's 'Critical Fable' who confesses to despising Fuller goes on to turn the tables on the female narrator: 'But have you no women, whom you must hate too?/ I shall think all the better of you if you do./ And of them, I may add.' She replies: 'A few./ But I scarcely think man feels the same contradictory/Desire to love them and shear them of victory?' (Lowell, *Collected Poems*, p. 409, quoted in Gilbert and Gubar, *No Man's Land*, p. 205).
23. E.g. in the report, 'Death of Margaret Fuller,' *New York Tribune*, July 1850, Houghton Library manuscript.
24. Robert N. Hudspeth (ed.) *The Letters of Margaret Fuller* (hereafter cited as *Letters*) (Ithaca/London: Cornell University Press, 1988), vol. V, p. 291.
25. Letter of 18 July 1845, in *Letters*, vol. IV, p. 145, fn. 2.

26. Ralph Waldo Emerson, *The Journals and Miscellaneous Notebooks of Ralph Waldo Emerson*, vol. XI, *1848–51*, eds A.W. Plumstead, William H. Gilman and Ruth H. Bennett (Cambridge, Massachusetts: Belknap Press, 1975), p. 258, cited in *Letters*, vol. I, *1817–38*, p. 60.

27. *Memoirs of Margaret Fuller Ossoli* (hereafter referred to as *Memoirs*) (London: Richard Bentley, 1852), vol. I, p. 270.

28. Ibid., p. 73.

29. *Letters*, vol. I, pp. 61–2 (note by Hudspeth, 'The Sources').

30. For example, in the fanciful letter which Fuller wrote to Beethoven as her 'master' (25 November, 1843): her original phrase, 'no heavenly sweetness of Jesus', is altered, probably by Channing, to 'no heavenly sweetness of saint or martyr'.

31. Quoted in Chevigny, *Woman and Myth*, p. 155.

32. Ted Hughes, introduction to *Selected Poems of Emily Dickinson* (London: Faber, 1968), p. 11.

33. This is confirmed by an entry in Bronson Alcott's journal of March 8th, 1877, cited as a footnote in Urbanski, *Fuller's Woman in the Nineteenth Century*, p. 43.

34. Emerson, ed. Plumstead et al., *Journals*, vol. II, p. 500, quoted in Urbanski, *Fuller's Woman in the Nineteenth Century*, p. 41, fn.

35. *Memoirs*, p. 259.

36. Both quoted in Urbanski, *Fuller's Woman in the Nineteenth Century*, p. 37.

37. Joseph Jay Deiss, *The Roman Years of Margaret Fuller* (New York: Thomas Y. Crowell, 1969), pp. 13–14.

38. *Memoirs*, p. 116.

39. Emerson, notebook on Fuller used in preparation of *Memoirs*, quoted in Chevigny, *Woman and Myth*, p. 35.

40. Letter of 1 February 1835 to Frederic H. Hedge, *Letters*, vol. I, p. 224.

41. *Letters*, vol. I, p. 64.

42. *Memoirs*, vol. I (American edition), p. 227, original emphasis, quoted in Chevigny, *Woman and Myth*, p. 33.

43. *Memoirs*, p. 99.

44. *Memoirs*, p. 174.

45. Cited in Urbanski, *Fuller's Woman in the Nineteenth Century*, p. 11 (from the American edition of the *Memoirs*, vol. I, pp. 321–2.)

46. Ibid., p. 171.

47. David Watson, *Margaret Fuller: An American Romantic*.

48. One story, probably apocryphal, claims that Fuller's and Ossoli's bodies *were* washed up on Fire Island several days after the wreck but buried surreptitiously at Coney Island. Emerson sent Thoreau to the scene of the accident, to search for the trunk with the Italian manuscript, but he had no success.

49. Letter of 1 February 1835 to Frederic H. Hedge, *Letters*, vol. I, p. 224.

50. Cheyfitz, *Trans-Parent*, p. 82. The second quotation in this passage is from Chapman, 'Emerson', p. 657.

51. Quoted in Urbanski, *Fuller's Woman in the Nineteenth Century*, p. 13.

52. *Memoirs*, p. 287.

53. This view is taken by Watson in his *Fuller*, p. 95 ff.

54. Chevigny, *Woman and Myth*, p. 10.
55. Emerson, in *Memoirs*, vol. I (American edition), pp. 227–9, quoted in Chevigny, *Woman and Myth*, pp. 32–3.
56. *Memoirs*, vol. II (English edition), pp. 1, 3 and 42–3, quoted in Watson, *Fuller*, p. 97.
57. Bram Dijkstra, *Idols of Perversity: Fantasies of Feminine Evil in Fin-de-Siècle Culture* (New York/Oxford: Oxford University Press, 1986), pp. 122–3, 127.
58. *Memoirs*, vol. I, p. 303.
59. Ibid., p. 270.
60. James Russell Lowell, 'A Fable for Critics,' in *Poetical Works* (Boston: Houghton Mifflin, 1904), vol. IV, pp. 62–4, reprinted in Chevigny, *Woman and Myth*, pp. 163–5.
61. Ralph Waldo Emerson, *Letters*, vol. IV, p. 222, reprinted in Chevigny, *Woman and Myth*, p. 415.
62. (Fuller's) *Letters*, vol. III, p. 91.
63. Mason Wade, *Margaret Fuller: Whetstone of Genius* (New York: Viking, 1940), p. 113, quoted in Chevigny, *Woman and Myth*, p. 160.
64. A comment made in 1855, quoted by Caroline Ticknor in *Hawthorne and His Publishers* (Boston: Houghton Mifflin, 1913), p. 142, and reproduced in Gilbert and Gubar, *War of the Words*, p. 142.
65. Nathaniel Hawthorne, *American Notebooks*, ed. Claude M. Simpson (Columbus, Ohio: Ohio State University Press, 1972), pp. 342–3, quoted in Chevigny, *Woman and Myth*, pp. 160–1.
66 Nathaniel Hawthorne, *The Blithedale Romance*, in *The Complete Novels and Selected Tales of Nathaniel Hawthorne* (New York: Modern Library, 1965), p. 465.
67. Hawthorne, journal entry of April 3, 1858, quoted in Chevigny, *Woman and Myth*, p. 418.
68. Charles Swann, *Nathaniel Hawthorne: Tradition and Revolution* (Oxford: Oxford University Press, 1991).
69. Gilbert and Gubar, *War of the Words*, p. 25.
70. In *Studies in Classic American Literature* (1923: New York, Penguin, 1977), p. 10, quoted in Gilbert and Gubar, *War of the Words*, p. 145.
71. In the final revels on the evening of her death Zenobia takes the part of a queen. Hawthorne's wife, Sophia Peabody, referred contemptuously to Fuller as 'Queen Margaret' on the publication of the precursor to *Woman in the Nineteenth Century*, 'The Great Lawsuit' – punning on the book's epigraph. 'The Earth waits for her Queen'.
72. Cited in an anonymous review, presumed to be by Thomas Wentworth Higginson, of Julian Hawthorne's biography, *Nathaniel Hawthorne and His Wife* (Boston, 1884), in *The Atlantic Monthly*, February 1885, pp. 259–65. By permission of the Houghton Library, Harvard University.
73. Frederick T. Fuller, 'Hawthorne and Margaret Fuller Ossoli', *The Literary World*, 10 January 1885. By permission of the Houghton Library.
74. Ibid.
75. Swann, *Hawthorne*, passim.
76. Nathaniel Hawthorne, *The Scarlet Letter*, ed. Harry Levin (Boston: Houghton Mifflin, 1960), p. 261.

77. Helsinger, Sheets and Veeder, *Woman Question:* vol. I, *Defining Voices,* p. xv.
78. Fuller, *Woman in the Nineteenth Century,* in Chevigny, *Woman and Myth,* p. 256.
79. Fuller, 'French Novelists of the Day', published in *New York Tribune,* 1 February 1845, reproduced in Mason Wade (ed.), *The Writings of Margaret Fuller* (Clifton, New Jersey: Augustus M. Kelley, 1973, reprint of 1941 Viking edition), p. 306.
80. *Letters,* vol. IV, p. 268, 18 April 1847.
81. Fuller, 'French Novelists of the Day', pp. 305–6.
82. Fuller, 'French Novelists of the Day', quoted in Dickenson, *George Sand,* p. 157.
83. Ibid.
84. Cited by Frederick T. Fuller in 'Hawthorne and Margaret Fuller Ossoli'. By permission of the Houghton Library.
85. Ibid.
86. Cited by James F. Clarke, *Evening Transcript,* 2 January 1885. By permission of the Houghton Library.
87. Anonymous review, presumed to be by Thomas Wentworth Higginson, of *Nathaniel Hawthorne and His Wife, The Atlantic Monthly,* February 1885, pp. 259–65. By permission of the Houghton Library.
88. Chevigny, *Woman and Myth,* pp. 417–18. The passage from the notebooks, reproduced on pp. 418–19 of Chevigny, is taken from Malcolm Cowley (ed.), *The Portable Hawthorne* (New York: Viking Press, 1948, pp. 594–7).
89. Anonymous review of *Nathaniel Hawthorne and His Wife* in the *Boston Evening Transcript,* November 1884. By permission of the Houghton Library.
90. Anonymous review in the *New York Times,* 23 November 1884. By permission of the Houghton Library.
91. In 'Hawthorne and Margaret Fuller Ossoli'. By permission of the Houghton Library.
92. E.g. replies by Sarah Ann Clarke (*Boston Evening Transcript,* 12 December 1884) and her brother James (*Boston Evening Transcript,* 2 January 1885).
93. Christopher P. Cranch, letter to *Boston Evening Transcript,* 9 January 1885. By permission of the Houghton Library.
94. Reply to Julian Hawthorne by James F. Clarke, *Boston Evening Transcript,* 2 January 1885. By permission of the Houghton Library.
95. Anonymous review in the *Sunday Herald,* 23 November 1884. By permission of the Houghton Library.
96. Thomas Wentworth Higginson, 'An Open Portfolio', prefatory essay to the first edition of Emily Dickinson's poems (Boston: 1891), reprinted in C.R. Blake and C.F. Wells (eds), *The Recognition of Emily Dickinson* (Ann Arbor, Michigan: University of Michigan Press, 1964), p. 3.
97. Higginson, *Margaret Fuller Ossoli,* American Men of Letters Series (Boston: Houghton Mifflin, 1884), pp. 4–5.
98. Ibid., p. 58.

99. *Letters*, vol. I, p. 327.
100. Higginson, *Margaret Fuller Ossoli*, pp. 88–9.
101. Ibid., p. 11.
102. Ibid., p. 84.
103. E.g. on p. 233, referring to a previous love affair, probably her possible romance with Samuel G. Ward – about which Higginson prefers to keep silent.
104. Ibid., p. 247, quoting from a letter written by the American counsel in Rome, Kinney, to Emerson on 2 May 1851, but apparently suppressed by him in the *Memoirs*.
105. Ibid., p. 314.
106. Showalter, *Sexual Anarchy*, p. 79.
107. Ibid., pp. 82–3.
108. Chevigny, *Woman and Myth*, pp. 7–8.
109. Henry James, *The Bostonians* (New York: Penguin, 1983) pp. 121–1, quoted in Gilbert and Gubar, *War of the Words*, p. 24.
110. Gilbert and Gubar, *No Man's Land*, p. 25.
111. In *Sexual Anarchy*, p. 34.
112. Henry James, *William Wetmore Story and his Friends* (Boston: Houghton, Mifflin, 1903), vol. I, pp. 127–31, reproduced in Chevigny, *Woman and Myth*, pp. 420–1.
113. '[Women writers] are impeded by the extreme conventionality of the other sex. For though men sensibly allow themselves great freedom in these respects, I doubt that they realise or can control the extreme severity with which they condemn such freedom in women.' (Virginia Woolf, 'Professions for Women,' in *Women and Writing*, London, The Women's Press, 1988, p. 62).
114. Report, 'Death of Margaret Fuller', July 1850, *New York Tribune*. By permission of the Houghton Library.
115. Edgar Allan Poe, *Complete Works* (New York: Putnam, 1902), vol. IX, pp. 13–14, quoted in Chevigny, *Woman and Myth*, p. 161.
116. Quoted in Margaret Vanderhaar Allen, *The Achievement of Margaret Fuller* (University Park, Pennsylvania: Pennsylvania State University Press, 1979), p. 149.
117. That this is a common assumption about women writers is argued in Dickenson, *Emily Dickinson*, and *George Sand*.
118. Poe, *Complete Works*, vol. IX, pp. 17–19, quoted in Chevigny, pp. 162–3.
119. Ibid.
120. Henry James, *Notes on Novelists*, p. 130, quoted in Patricia Thomson, *George Sand and the Victorians: Her Influence and Reputation in 19th-Century England* (London: Macmillan, 1977), p. 227, emphasis added.
121. *Letters of Henry James*, ed. P., Lubbock (London, 1920), vol. I, p. 363, quoted in Thomson, *Victorians*, p. 185.
122. Anonymous review in *Sunday Herald*, 23 November 1884. By permission of the Houghton Library.
123. In addition to Chevigny, other feminist-inspired biographies and studies which attempt to resuscitate Fuller's reputation include: Urbanski, *Fuller's Woman in 19th Century*; Dale Spender's account drawn largely

from Urbanski, 'Margaret Fuller', in *Women of Ideas, and What Men Have Done to Them* (London: Routledge and Kegan Paul, 1982); Paula Blanchard, *Margaret Fuller: From Transcendentalism to Revolution* (New York: Delacorte Press/Seymour Lawrence, 1978); Susan Phinney Conrad, *Perish the Thought: Intellectual Women in Romantic America 1830–1860* (New York: Oxford University Press, 1976); Helsinger, Sheets and Veeder, 'Margaret Fuller and *Woman in the Nineteenth Century*', in *Defining Voices*; Jane Rendall, *The Origins of Modern Feminism: Women in Britain, France and the United States, 1780–1860* (London: Macmillan, 1985), pp. 280–4; and Margaret Vanderhaar Allen, *The Achievement of Margaret Fuller* (University Park, Pennsylvania: Pennsylvania State University Press, 1979). Watson's *Margaret Fuller* uses feminist scholarship, but from a generally anti-feminist perspective, and one somewhat unsympathetic to Fuller.

124. Gilbert and Gubar, *War of the Words*, p. 149.

125. Elizabeth Barrett Browning, *Letters*, ed. F.G. Kenyon (New York: Macmillan, 1898), vol. II, pp. 59–60, quoted in Chevigny, *Woman and Myth*, pp. 413–14.

126. *Letters of Elizabeth Barrett Browning*, ed. F.G. Kenyon, vol. I, pp. 459–60, reprinted in Chevigny, *Woman and Myth*, p. 414.

127. *Letters of Elizabeth Barrett Browning*, vol. I, p. 452, quoted in Deirdre David, *Intellectual Women and Victorian Patriarchy: Harriet Martineau, Elizabeth Barrett Browning, George Eliot* (London: Macmillan, 1987), pp. 134–5.

128. George Jacob Holyoake, *Sixty Years of an Agitator's Life* (London, 1892), vol. I, p. 244, mentioned in *Letters*, vol. IV, p. 250, fn. 5.

129. Quoted in Frances M. Barbour, 'Margaret Fuller and the British Reviewers', *New England Quarterly*, vol. IX (Dec. 1936), pp. 622–3, and in Blanchard, *Margaret Fuller*, pp. 342–3.

130. Quoted in Barbour, 'British Reviewers', p. 622, and in Blanchard, *Margaret Fuller*, p. 341.

131. Blanchard, *Margaret Fuller*, p. 341.

132. In the *Leader*, vol. VI (13 Oct. 1855), pp. 988–9, reprinted in Thomas Pinney (ed.) *The Essays of George Eliot* (London: Routledge and Kegan Paul, 1983), pp. 199–206.

133. Ibid., p. 203.

134. Ibid., p. 200.

135. In Pinney, *Essays of George Eliot*, p. 199.

136. Quoted in Dickenson, *George Sand*, p. 165.

137. *Letters*, vol. I, p. 307 (tentatively dated by Hudspeth as November 1837).

138. Ibid.

139. *Harriet Martineau's Autobiography*, ed. Maria Weston Chapman (Boston: James R. Osgood, 1877), vol. II, pp. 381–3, reprinted in Chevigny, *Woman and Myth*, pp. 228–30.

140. Fuller, journal of 1835, reprinted in *Memoirs*, vol. I, p. 109.

141. Martineau, *Autobiography*, vol. I, pp. 189–90, in David, *Intellectual Women and Patriarchy*, p. 87.

142. David, *Intellectual Women and Patriarchy*, pp. 22–3.

143. Ibid., p. 27 ff.
144. Martineau, *Autobiography*, vol. I, pp. 400–1, quoted in David, *Intellectual Women and Patriarchy*, pp. 46–7.
145. Ibid., p. 47.
146. David, *Intellectual Women and Patriarchy*, p. xi.
147. Martineau, *Household Education* (Philadelphia: Lee & Blanchard, 1849), quoted in David, *Intellectual Women and Patriarchy*, p. 55.
148. Ibid., p. 46.
149. Ibid.
150. Elaine Showalter's term, in *Sexual Identity*, p. 59.
151. David, *Intellectual Women and Patriarchy*, p. 229.

CHAPTER 2: FATHER'S LANGUAGE, MOTHER'S NAME

1. Henry David Thoreau, quoted in Gilbert and Gubar, *War of the Words*, p. 227.
2. Nancy Chodorow, *The Reproduction of Mothering* (Berkeley: University of California Press, 1978); Carol Gilligan, *In a Different Voice* (Cambridge, Mass.: Harvard University Press, 1982).
3. *Memoirs*, vol. I (American edition), pp. 13–14, quoted in Blanchard, *Margaret Fuller*, p. 18.
4. Blanchard, *Margaret Fuller*, p. 19.
5. Elyce Wakerman, *Father Loss: Daughters Discuss the Man that Got Away* (New York: Henry Holt, 1984), pp. 253, 256.
6. For further detail, see Rendall, *Origins of Modern Feminism*, ch. 2.
7. Dickenson, *Emily Dickinson*, p. 34.
8. Samuel Fowler Dickinson, grandfather of Emily Dickinson, quoted in Richard B. Sewall, *The Life of Emily Dickinson* (New York: Farrar, Straus & Giroux, 1974), vol. I, p. 37.
9. Quoted in Blanchard, *Margaret Fuller*, p. 11.
10. Alicia Suskin Ostriker, *Stealing the Language: The Emergence of Women's Poetry in America* (London: The Women's Press, 1986), p. 23.
11. Ibid., pp. 25–6.
12. Rendall, *Origins of Modern Feminism*, pp. 38–9.
13. Quoted in Higginson, *Margaret Fuller Ossoli*, p. 47.
14. Jacques Lacan, *Écrits: A Selection*, tr. Alan Sheridan (New York: W.W. Norton, 1977).
15. *Letters*, vol. I, p. 81 (13 January 1818).
16. Letter from Timothy to Margaret Fuller, 22 February 1820, in *Letters*, vol. I, p. 97, fn. 7.
17. *Memoirs*, vol. I (American edition), pp. 17–18.
18. *Memoirs*, vol. I (English edition), p. 26. This is part of the autobiographical fragment which Fuller wrote in 1840; there is a great deal of debate over how much of it is true, how much fantasy.
19. *Memoirs*, vol. I (English edition), pp. 12–13.
20. Barbara Welter, *Dimity Convictions: The American Woman in the Nineteenth Century* (Athens, Ohio: Ohio University Press, 1976), p. 146 ff.

21. In *The Presence of the Word: Some Prolegomena for Cultural and Religious History* (New Haven: Yale University Press, 1967).
22. *Memoirs*, vol. I (American edition), p. 56, quoted in Chevigny, *Woman and Myth*, p. 24.
23. Gilbert and Gubar, *War of the Words*, p. 243.
24. *Memoirs*, vol. I (English edition), pp. 13–14.
25. See Alasdair MacIntyre, *After Virtue* (London: Duckworth, 1981) and Martha Craven Nussbaum, *The Fragility of Goodness: Luck and Ethics in Greek Tragedy and Philosophy* (Cambridge: Cambridge University Press, 1986).
26. Conrad, *Perish the Thought*, p. 12.
27. Ostriker, *Stealing the Language*, p. 28 ff.
28. Quoted in Ann Douglas, *The Feminization of American Culture* (New York: Knopf, 1977), p. 46.
29. Chevigny, *Woman and Myth*, pp. 18–19.
30. The Rev. John Todd, quoted on p. 24 of Thomas Woody, *A History of Women's Education in the United States* (New York: Science Press, 1929), vol. I, pp. 154–5, cited by Conrad, *Perish the Thought*, p. 23.
31. *Letters*, vol. I, p. 137, 19 April 1824, original emphasis.
32. Quoted in Blanchard, p. 42.
33. *Letters*, vol. I, p. 139, 21 May 1824, original emphasis. Fuller later came to adore Miss Prescott, but she would not admit as much to her father – only to her uncle Abraham (in letters of 14 July and 29 September 1824). After all, Timothy was the one who had taught her never to say, 'I am mistaken.'
34. *Letters*, vol. I, p. 107, 5 January 1821.
35. Ibid., p. 132, 23 December 1823.
36. Ibid., p. 149, 14 February 1825.
37. *Memoirs*, vol. I (English edition), p. 28.
38. Mary Eagleton (ed.), *Feminist Literary Theory: A Reader* (Oxford: Basil Blackwell, 1986), introduction, section 3.
39. Mrs. Ross, *Hesitation: or, To Marry, or Not to Marry?* (London, 1819, published in New York the same year).
40. *Letters*, vol. I, p. 91.
41. Ibid., p. 94.
42. Ibid., p. 95.
43. Ibid., pp. 105–6, 4 December 1820.
44. Ibid., p. 107, 5 January 1821.
45. Ibid., pp. 101–2, 7 August 1820.
46. According to Hudspeth, this was probably Thomas Redman, who married Mary Elizabeth Messinger in 1821.
47. *Letters*, vol. I, p. 101.
48. Ibid.
49. *Letters*, p. 89, 20 November 1819.
50. *Memoirs*, vol. I (American edition), pp. 35, 38–9, quoted in Blanchard, *Margaret Fuller*, p. 27.
51. Watson, *Margaret Fuller*, p. 4.
52. Chevigny, *Woman and Myth*, pp. 19–20.

53. Katherine Anthony, *Margaret Fuller: A Psychological Biography* (London: Jonathan Cape, 1922).

54. Margarett Crane Fuller to Margaret Fuller, undated reply to the latter's letter of 8 January 1842, Houghton manuscript, quoted in *Letters*, vol. III, p. 37, fn. 3. Margaret had rebuked her mother mildly for underestimating the kindness of her aunt, with whom she was staying, 'Uncle H. [Henry Holton Fuller] and Aunt M. [Mary Stone Fuller] are most kind to me, considering my comfort in every way and doing little things for me. I think you, usually too indulgent, are not sufficiently so in your estimate of Aunt M.' Roused, no doubt, by Margaret's tendency to lecture, Mrs Fuller replied somewhat snappishly: 'You judge from your experience, and I from mine. I do know that never any person had less of *personal kindness*, I will not say *heart felt sympathy* than I have received from my husband's family since his death.'

55. Quoted in Frederick T. Fuller, 'Hawthorne and Margaret Fuller Ossoli'.

56. *Memoirs*, vol. I. (English edition), pp. 21–2.

57. Quoted in Higginson, *Margaret Fuller Ossoli*, p. 21.

58. Judith Arcana, *Our Mother's Daughters* (London: The Women's Press, 1981).

59. Diary of 1844, quoted in Higginson, *Margaret Fuller Ossoli*, p. 23.

60. *Letters*, vol. I, p. 113, emphasis added.

61. Ibid., p. 116, 9 December 1821.

62. This is Chevigny's view, for example.

63. Ibid., p. 117, 23 December 1821.

64. Chodorow, *The Reproduction of Mothering* (cited at 2 above).

65. Nancy Hartsock summarising Chodorow in 'The Feminist Standpoint: Developing the Ground for a Specifically Feminist Historical Materialism,' (1983) reprinted in Sandra Harding (ed.) (1987) *Feminism and Methodology: Social Science Issues*, Open University Press, Milton Keynes, p. 168.

66. Maureen Murdock, *The Heroine's Journey* (Boston: Shambhala, 1990), p. 17.

67. Letter of 17 April 1834 to James F. Clarke, forthcoming in *Letters*, vol. VI.

68. Undated letter to Margarett C. Fuller, forthcoming in *Letters*, vol. VI, as no. 919.

69. Gilligan, *In a Different Voice* (cited at 2 above).

70. Hartsock, 'Feminist Standpoint', p. 169.

71. *Letters*, vol. II, p. 219, 29 July 1841.

72. Cited in Blanchard, *Margaret Fuller*, pp. 30–1.

73. Chevigny, *Woman and Myth*, pp. 22–3.

74. Quoted in Dickenson, *Emily Dickinson*, p. 10.

75. Barbara Antonina Clarke Mossberg, *Emily Dickinson: When a Writer is a Daughter* (Bloomington, Indiana: Indiana University Press, 1982).

76. Heilbrun, *Writing a Woman's Life*, pp. 64–5.

77. Showalter, Clarendon lectures, 4 May.

CHAPTER 3: 'WHERE CAN I HIDE TILL I AM GIVEN TO MYSELF?'

1. Margaret Fuller quoted in Conrad, *Perish the Thought*, p. 12.
2. See Chapter 2 for examples. The cult of True Womanhood was simultaneously accepted and challenged – much as Fuller did – by Sophia Ripley's essay for *The Dial* which ends, 'Is this the ideal of a perfect woman, and if so, how does it differ from a perfect man?' (quoted in Urbanski, *Fuller's Woman in 19th Century*, p. 118.)
3. Letter of 19 November 1830 to Almira P. Barlow, *Letters*, vol. I, p. 171.
4. *Memoirs*, vol. I (American edition), p. 75, quoted in Blanchard, *Margaret Fuller*, p. 59.
5. Heilbrun, *Writing a Woman's Life*, p. 51.
6. Ibid., p. 48.
7. Ibid.
8. Ibid., p. 49.
9. Chevigny, *Woman and Myth*, p. 6.
10. Dixon Wecter, *The Hero in America: A Chronicle of Hero-Worship* (New York: Scribner's, 1941).
11. Conrad, *Perish the Thought*, chapter 1.
12. Fuller did have religious experiences of some sort in 1831 and 1840.
13. Julia Ward Howe, *Margaret Fuller (Marchesa Ossoli)* (London: W.H. Allen, Eminent Women Series, 1883).
14. Heilbrun, *Writing a Woman's Life*, p. 52.
15. Sandra M. Gilbert and Susan Gubar, *The Madwoman in the Attic* (New Haven: Yale University Press, 1979), p. 483.
16. Letter tentatively dated 16 November 1846, *Letters*, vol. IV, pp. 239–40.
17. *Letters*, vol. I, p. 151. Fuller may have been trying to impress her old teacher, Susan Prescott, to whom this letter is written. But this account of her zeal tallies with that of later letters to other correspondents.
18. *Memoirs*, vol. I (English edition), pp. 67–8.
19. Page Smith, *Daughters of the Promised Land: Women in American History* (Boston: Little Brown, 1970), p. 91.
20. Alexis de Tocqueville, *Democracy in America*, tr. Henry Reeve (New York: Vintage Books, 1945, vol. II, p. 223), quoted in Chevigny, *Woman and Myth*, p. 4.
21. Harriet Martineau, *Society in America* (New York: Saunders & Otley, 1837), vol. II, p. 226, quoted in Chevigny, p. 5.
22. Renée Winegarten, *Mme de Staël* (Leamington Spa, Warks.: Berg Publishers, 1985), p. 66.
23. Ibid., p. 87.
24. Germaine de Staël, *Corinne ou l'Italie* (Paris: Librairie Stéréotype, 1807), quoted in Winegarten, *Mme de Staël*, p. 83.
25. *Letters*, vol. I, pp. 166–7, 4 May 1830.
26. Heilbrun, *Writing a Woman's Life*, pp. 38–9; Peter Ackroyd, *T.S. Eliot* (London: Hamish Hamilton, 1984).
27. I had the same sense as Heilbrun in reading David Herbert Donald's *Look Homeward: A Life of Thomas Wolfe* (Boston: Little Brown, 1987). Wolfe played the hard-drinking, rebellious outsider to society while

wheedling success after success from the 'establishment': university at 15, last-minute admission to a prestigious playwriting workshop at Harvard despite failure to register for it in time, 'adoption' by a series of wealthy and powerful mother and father figures, bestsellerdom at 29. Perhaps it was his success in playing that intensely masculine role of the rebel which assured him of professional triumph.

28. Donald, *Look Homeward*, p. 102.
29. Letter to Frederic H. Hedge, 4 July 1833, in *Letters*, vol. I, p. 189.
30. A daunting account of what women's everyday work entailed is found in Blanchard, *Margaret Fuller*, pp. 77–8. The judgement that Fuller pursued as extensive a programme of education as Gibbon's is Emerson's (*Memoirs*, vol. I, p. 309). It need hardly be said that Gibbon did not do a great deal of housework.
31. Letter to Amelia Greenwood, 20 March 1834, *Letters*, vol. I, pp, 201–2. Material in square brackets was added by the editors of the *Memoirs*. The original is badly damaged.
32. Letter to Arthur B. Fuller, 31 December 1837, *Letters*, vol. I, p. 320.
33. Letter to Eliza R. Farrar, 25 April 1833, *Letters*, vol. I, p. 180.
34. Letter to Frederic H. Hedge, *Letters*, vol. I, p. 188.
35. André Malraux, *The Voices of Silence*, tr. S. Gilbert (London, 1954).
36. Letter of 1 February 1835 to Frederic H. Hedge, *Letters*, vol. I, p. 223..
37. Quoted in Blanchard, *Margaret Fuller*, pp. 83–4.
38. Expressed by Goethe in *Wilhelm Meisters Lehrjare*: 'Das Sicherste bleibt immer, nur das Näschte zu tun was vor uns liegt.' (footnote by Hudspeth in *Letters*, vol. I, p. 175).
39. Letter to James F. Clarke, tentatively dated 20 May 1833 by Hudspeth, *Letters*, vol. I, p. 182.
40. *Memoirs*, vol. I (English edition), p. 157.
41. *The Poetry of Emily Dickinson*, ed. Thomas H. Johnson, variorum edition (Cambridge, Mass.: Harvard University Press, 1955), no. 863.
42. *Memoirs*, vol. I (English edition), p. 202.
43. Letter to Almira P. Barlow, 1 February 1836, *Letters*, vol. I, p. 243. This is particularly poignant because Fuller *was* needed when she *did* die: she was correct that 'there never could come a time when my departure would be easier to myself, or less painful to others' – though for a 25-year-old to say that is deeply affecting.
44. *Memoirs*, vol. I (American edition), p. 154, quoted in Blanchard, *Margaret Fuller*, pp. 92–3, original emphasis.
45. Letter of 4 March 1839 to Charles K. Newcomb, *Letters.*, vol. II, p. 57.
46. Letter to Frederic H. Hedge, 1 February 1835, *Letters*, vol. I, p. 223.
47. Letter to Timothy and Margarett C. Fuller, 2 June 1835, *Letters*, vol. I, p. 230, original emphasis.
48. Letter to Margarett C. Fuller, 5 September 1837, *Letters*, vol. I, p. 300.
49. *Letters*, vol. I, p. 237, recipient unknown, 3 November 1835.
50. Letter to Frederic H. Hedge, 6 March 1835, *Letters*, vol. I, p. 226. There is some indication that the 'bigwig from Salem' was Hawthorne.
51. *Letters*, vol. I, p. 241. This manuscript is not folded, which indicates it may not be a letter; nor is it dated, although Hudspeth thinks it probably dates from 1836. It is a prayer, I believe.

52. *Memoirs*, vol. I (English edition), p. 48.
53. Perry Miller, *Margaret Fuller: American Romantic* (New York: Doubleday, 1963), p. 5, quoted in Blanchard, *Margaret Fuller*, p. 44.
54. Margaret Fuller Ossoli, *Summer on the Lakes in 1843*, 1844, in edition of 1861 with excerpts from *Memoirs* (London: Ward and Lock), p. 97.
55. Ibid., p. 98.
56. Letter to A. Bronson Alcott, 27 June 1837, *Letters*, vol. I, p. 287.
57. Quoted in Blanchard, *Margaret Fuller*, p. 121.
58. Quoted in Conrad, *Perish the Thought*, p. 61.
59. Emerson, *Journals*, vol. VI, p. 366, quoted in Blanchard, p. 100.
60. *Letters*, vol. I, pp. 162–3, tentatively dated by Hudspeth as 28 March 1830.
61. *Memoirs*, vol. I (English edition), p. 128. A similar androgyny is found in Fuller's journal comment about her capacity for friendship with Emerson: 'I am bent on being his only friend myself. There is enough of me would I but reveal it. Enough of woman to sympathize with all his feelings, enough of man to appreciate all thoughts.' (quoted in Chevigny, *Woman and Myth*, pp. 76–7).
62. Letter to Arthur B. Fuller, 5 July 1837, *Letters*, vol. I, p. 289.
63. Sarah Ann Clarke, quoted in Higginson, *Margaret Fuller Ossoli*, pp. 117–8.
64. Chevigny, *Woman and Myth*, pp. 70–1.
65. Letter to Caroline Sturgis, tentatively dated 1840 by Hudspeth, *Letters*, vol. II, p. 105. Another letter to Sturgis, probably also dating from the same year, uses the same phrase (*Letters*, vol. II, p. 107).
66. Emerson, *Nature*, in *Complete Essays and Other Writings of Ralph Waldo Emerson*, ed. Brooks Atkinson (New York: Random House, 1950), p. 25, quoted in Chevigny, *Woman and Myth*, p. 66.
67. *Memoirs*, vol. I (English edition), pp. 284–5, 291.
68. Sarah Ann Clarke, quoted in Higginson, *Margaret Fuller Ossoli*, p. 118.
69. Blanchard, *Margaret Fuller*, p. 130. George Sand could be added to that list: in much of her most productive period the engraver Alexandre Manceau, seventeen years her junior, filled this 'wifely' function. But Sand also managed to maintain an intense level of work during her time with the far more demanding Chopin and Musset.
70. Emerson, *Journals*, vol. IV, p. 238, quoted in Blanchard, *Margaret Fuller*, p. 119.
71. Letter to William Henry Channing, 10 December 1840, *Letters*, vol. II, pp. 191–2.
72. Letter to the editor who had requested her translations, John S. Dwight, 31 May 1837, *Letters*, vol. I, p. 281.
73. Letter to Jane F. Tuckerman, 16 June 1837, *Letters*, vol. I, p. 284.
74. Letter to Emerson of 14 August 1837, *Letters*, vol. I, p. 294.
75. Letter to Margarett C. Fuller, 18 November 1837, *Letters*, vol. I, p. 314.
76. Letter to Caroline Sturgis, July 1838, *Letters*, vol. I, p. 338.
77. Letter to Ralph Waldo Emerson, 1 March 1838, *Letters*, vol. I, p. 327.
78. Henry David Thoreau, *Walden*, in *The Portable Thoreau*, ed. Carl Bode (New York: Viking Press, 1947), p. 266.
79. Gilligan, *In a Different Voice*, p. 35.

80. Letter to Caroline Sturgis, 14 October 1837, *Letters*, vol. I, p. 303.
81. In Emerson's quotation book 'Encyclopedia,' referring to Montaigne's 'On Friendship' (quoted by Fuller in her letter to Emerson of 14 August 1837). There is also a reference to Aristotle's doctrine that 'the friend is another self'; this is why there is no friend but the self. Janice Raymond offers an interesting gloss on this Aristotelian idea in *A Passion for Friends: Toward a Philosophy of Female Affection* (London: The Women's Press, 1986): 'Female friendship begins with the companionship of the Self. Aristotle maintained that 'the friend is another self.' Until the self is another friend, however, women can easily lose their Selves in the company of others.' (p. 6).
82. *In a Different Voice*, summarised briefly in the previous chapter.
83. Douglas Johnson, 'Managing the Great Man's Memory', review of *Adieux: A Farewell to Sartre* by Simone de Beauvoir, *New York Times Book Review*, 6 May 1984, quoted in Raymond, *Passion for Friends*, p. 4.
84. James Freeman Clarke, letter of 1 March 1838 to Fuller, in *Letters of James Freeman Clarke*, ed. John Wesley Thomas (Hamburg: Cram, de Gruyter, 1957), p. 129, quoted in Chevigny, *Woman and Myth*, pp. 67–8.
85. Raymond, *Passion for Friends*, p. 5, a gloss on Simone de Beauvoir's statement that 'if [woman] did not exist, men would have invented her. But she exists also apart from their inventiveness.' (*The Second Sex*, tr. and ed. H.H. Parshley (New York: Bantam, 1952), p. 174).
86. The subtitle of Raymond's *A Passion for Friends*.
87. E.g. Raymond, *Passion for Friends*; Lillian Faderman, *Surpassing the Love of Men* (London: The Women's Press, 1985); Paula Caplan, *Barriers between Women* (Lancaster: MTP Press, 1981); and Robin Morgan, *Sisterhood is Global* (Harmondsworth: Penguin, 1985).
88. Hudspeth, introduction to vol. II of *Letters*, p. 6.
89. Higginson, *Margaret Fuller Ossoli*, p. 137.
90. Letter to William H. Channing, 22 March 1840, *Letters*, vol. II, p. 126.
91. *Letters*, vol. II, p. 146, 5 July 1840.
92. Letter to William H. Channing, probably 2 February 1841, *Letters*, vol. II, p. 201.
93. Letter to William H. Channing, 19 April 1840, *Letters*, vol. II, p. 131.
94. Lawrence Buell, *Literary Transcendentalism: Style and Vision in the American Renaissance* (Ithaca: Cornell University Press), p. 18, quoted in Larry J. Reynolds and Susan Belasco Smith (eds), *'These Sad but Glorious Days': Dispatches from Europe, 1846–1850, by Margaret Fuller* (New Haven: Yale University Press, 1991), p. 8, fn 27. © 1991 Yale University Press. Quoted by permission.
95. Buell, *Literary Transcendentalism*, p. 16, quoted ibid.
96. Letter to Caroline Sturgis, 4 March 1839, *Letters*, vol. II, p. 58.
97. *Letters*, vol. II, p. 82, 11 July 1839.
98. *Letters of Ralph Waldo Emerson*, vol. II, p. 197, quoted in Hudspeth (ed.), *Letters* (of Fuller), p. 70, fn. 2.
99. Higginson, *Margaret Fuller Ossoli*, p. 159.
100. *Dial*, number 2, p. 409, quoted in Higginson, *Margaret Fuller Ossoli*, p. 166.

101. Letter to William H. Channing, 22 March 1840, in *Letters*, vol. II, p. 126.
102. Dickenson, *Emily Dickinson*, p. 21.
103. Sewall, *Life of Emily Dickinson*, vol. II, p. 400.
104. Letter to Samuel G. Ward, July 1839, in *Letters*, vol. II, p. 81.
105. Letter to Samuel G. Ward, 15 October 1839, *Letters*, vol. II, pp. 95–6.
106. For example Hudspeth's notes on this letter, which he actually heads 'To Samuel G. Ward' (*Letters*, vol. II, pp. 90–1.) Hudspeth has generously acknowledged to me, 'You may be right that I jumped too quickly to the conclusion that the letter in 2:90–91 was addressed to Sam Ward . . . While Ward still seems right to me, I should at least have made it a questionable attribution in the headnote rather than the self-confident "To Samuel G. Ward"!' (private correspondence, 4 February 1992).
107. In a letter to Caroline Sturgis, 7 October 1839, *Letters*, vol. II, p. 93.
108. Dickenson, *Emily Dickinson*, pp. 24–5.
109. Emerson and George Ripley, who was in charge of the journal's finances, differed frequently. In April 1840 Fuller complained to Emerson, 'I shall show Mr R. what you have written and talk with him once more – Those parts you thought too fierce, he thought not sufficiently so. I know not whether I can find the golden mean between you.' (*Letters*, vol. II, p. 132.)
110. Letter to Ralph Waldo Emerson, 26 December 1839, *Letters*, vol. II, p. 104.
111. Letter to Ralph Waldo Emerson, 29 September 1840, *Letters*, vol. II, p. 160.
112. Letter to Ralph Waldo Emerson, 23 February 1840, *Letters*, vol. II, p. 122.
113. Emerson, *Letters*, vol. II, pp. 384–5, quoted in Blanchard, *Margaret Fuller*, p. 151.
114. Letter to Ralph Waldo Emerson, 20 January 1840, *Letters*, vol. II, p. 116. The quotation is from *Much Ado about Nothing*, III, ii, 70–3.
115. Letter to Caroline Sturgis, probably 25 October 1840, *Letters*, vol. II, p. 170.
116. Letter to Frederic H. Hedge, 10 March 1840, *Letters*, vol. II, p. 125.
117. *Memoirs*, vol. I (English edition), pp. 121–2.
118. Letter to Ralph Waldo Emerson, 12 April 1840, in *Letters*, vol. II, p. 128.
119. Letter to William H. Channing, 25 October 1840, *Letters*, vol. II, p. 171.
120. See note 6 above.
121. Conrad, *Perish the Thought*, p. 32.
122. This is Chevigny's argument in *Woman and Myth*, examined in Chapter 4.

CHAPTER 4: WRITING A LIFE FOR WOMEN

1. In Perry Miller (ed.), *Margaret Fuller: American Romantic* (Ithaca, NY: Cornell University Press, 1963), p. 192.

2. Margaret Fuller, *Woman in the Nineteenth Century* (New York, 1845), excerpted in Chevigny, *Woman and Myth*, p. 277.

3. To varying degrees this is true of Blanchard, Chevigny, and Margaret Vanderhaar Allen in her *The Achievement of Margaret Fuller* (Pennsylvania: Pennsylvania State University Press, 1977). Although Allen, for example, calls Fuller's feminism a 'bold, uncompromising challenge to society', (p. 132) she later backtracks, judging Fuller's acceptance of separate male and female natures an unfortunate but understandable confusion. Susan Phinney Conrad (in *Perish the Thought*) likewise deplores Fuller's adhesion to the True Woman cult, though she is pleased to note that Fuller eventually grew out of it.

4. See Susan Faludi, *Backlash: The Undeclared War against American Women* (New York: Crown, 1991).

5. Charles Butler, *The American Lady* (1836), p. 18, quoted in Bram Dijkstra, *Idols of Perversity: Fantasies of Feminine Evil in Fin-de-siècle Culture* (Oxford/New York: Oxford University Press, 1986), p. 111.

6. David, *Intellectual Women and Victorian Patriarchy*, pp. 3–6.

7. Ibid., p. 230.

8. Marie Mitchell Olesen Urbanski, *Margaret Fuller's Woman in the Nineteenth Century: A Literary Study of Form and Content, of Sources and Influence* (Westport, Connecticut: Greenwood Press, 1980), p. 109.

9. 'This essay, "The Great Lawsuit: Man versus Men, Woman versus Women," was her most Transcendentalist work . . .' (Chevigny, *Woman and Myth*, p. 215.)

10. Howe, *Margaret Fuller*, p. 83 ff.

11. 'On a Columnar Self-/ How ample to rely/ In Tumult- or Extremity . . ./Suffice Us- for a Crowd-/ Ourself- and Rectitude-/ And that Assembly- not far off/ From furthest Spirit- God.' (Thomas H. Johnson [ed.], *Collected Poems of Emily Dickinson*, Harvard University Press, 1955, no. 789).

12. Carole Pateman, *The Sexual Contract* (Cambridge: Polity Press, 1988).

13. Chevigny, *Woman and Myth*, p. 222. In using the term feminism, I realise that I am being somewhat anachronistic. The word was not in general use until the late nineteenth century. However, it seems hopelessly cumbersome to replace 'feminism' with 'concern for women,' 'interest in the Woman Question', or whatever, every time I need to refer to Fuller's beliefs. Although the term was not available in Fuller's time, the attitude which it represents was, and is better depicted by the term 'feminism' than by any substitute, I think. Barbara Taylor follows the same strategy in *Eve and the New Jerusalem* (London: Virago, 1983), p. x, fn.

14. Quoted in Eleanor Flexner, *A Century of Struggle* (Cambridge, Massachusetts: Belknap Press, 1959), p. 68, and in Allen, *Achievement of Margaret Fuller*, p. 139.

15. Heilbrun, *Writing a Woman's Life*, p. 53.

16. To William H. Channing, *Letters*, vol. II, p. 202, 19 February 1841.

17. For example, in a letter of 5 April 1841 ('When he [Theodore Parker] came down, he was in a fine glow; *you* would have said he looked *manly*') (*Letters*, vol. II, p. 206), and throughout *Summer on the Lakes*.

18. *Woman in the Nineteenth Century*, in Chevigny, *Woman and Myth*, p. 251.
19. Letter to George T. Davis, 17 December 1842, *Letters*, vol. III, p. 105.
20. I think this is less true of Thoreau, but her relationship with Emerson was far more important to Fuller, and longer-standing. To Thoreau she wrote, 'If intercourse should continue, perhaps a bridge may be made between the minds so widely apart, for I apprehended you in spirit, and you did not seem to mistake me as widely as most of your kind do.' (*Letters*, vol. II, p. 243, 18 October 1841). Hudspeth judges that Thoreau was referring to Fuller in the section of his *Week on the Concord and Merrimack Rivers* which runs, 'I know a woman who possesses a restless and intelligent mind, interested in her own culture, and earnest to enjoy the highest possible advantages, and I meet her with pleasure as a natural person who not a little provokes me, and I suppose is stimulated in turn by myself. Yet our acquaintance plainly does not attain to that degree of confidence and sentiment which women, which all, in fact, covet. I am glad to help her, as I am helped by her; I like very well to know her with a sort of stranger's privilege'. (p. 279) A degree of that strangeness between them was due to Thoreau's friendship with Ellery Channing, Margaret's brother-in-law. In some instances she felt that Thoreau took Ellery's part against her sister Ellen. However, Thoreau – who, according to Emerson, never liked anything – had a good opinion of Fuller's essay 'The Great Lawsuit.' And it was Thoreau who was dispatched to look for Fuller's body, and the missing trunk with the manuscript of the Italian history, when the *Elizabeth* went down off Fire Island.
21. Letter to Emerson, 8 September 1841, *Letters*, vol. II, p. 230, emphasis added. 'Festus', the poem by Philip Bailey (1816–1902), was published in 1839 and finally reviewed in the October 1841 *Dial*.
22. Rusk, *Letters of Emerson*, vol. III, p. 8, quoted in *Letters*, vol. III, p. 43, fn. 1.
23. Letter possibly addressed to William H. Channing, February 1842, *Letters*, vol. III, p. 43.
24. Letter to Elizabeth Hoar, possibly 8 March 1842, in *Letters*, vol. III, p. 47.
25. Letter to Elizabeth Hoar, 20 March 1842, *Letters*, vol. III, p. 55.
26. Clara Thomas, *Love and Work Enough: The Life of Anna Jameson* (Toronto: University of Toronto Press, 1967), p. 60.
27. Anna Jameson, *Memoirs of Celebrated Female Sovereigns* (London: George Routledge, 1831), preface, quoted in Urbanski, *Margaret Fuller's Woman*, p. 74.
28. Jameson, *Memoirs of the Loves of the Poets: Biographical Sketches of Women Celebrated in Ancient and Modern Poetry* (Boston: Houghton Mifflin, 1900 reprint of 1829 text), preface, quoted in Urbanski, *Margaret Fuller's Woman*, p. 74.
29. *Woman in the Nineteenth Century*, p. 172 of original 1845 edition, quoted in Marie Mitchell Olesen Urbanski, 'The Genesis, Form, Tone and Rhetorical Devices of Woman in the Nineteenth Century,' in Joel

Myerson (ed.), *Critical Essays on Margaret Fuller* (Boston: G.K. Hall, 1980), p. 277.

30. Elizabeth K. Helsinger, Robin Lauterbach Sheets and William Veeder, *The Woman Question: Society and Literature in Britain and America 1837–1883* (Chicago/London: University of Chicago Press, 1989), vol. I, *Defining Voices*, p. 45.

31. Higginson, *Margaret Fuller Ossoli*, p. 198 ff. Julia Ward Howe thinks that the subtitle "means to her the leading idea and ideal of humanity, as wronged and hindered from development by the thoughtless and ignorant action of the race itself' (*Margaret Fuller*, p. 118).

32. Douglas, *Feminization of American Culture*, pp. 10–11.

33. Quoted in Nancy F. Cott, *The Bonds of Womanhood: 'Woman's Sphere in New England, 1780–1835* (New Haven: Yale, 1977), p. 148, and in Rendall, *Origins of Modern Feminism*, p.78.

34. Rendall, *Origins of Modern Feminism*, p. 79.

35. *Woman in the Nineteenth Century*, in Chevigny, *Woman and Myth*, p. 243.

36. Ibid., p. 247, original emphasis.

37. Ibid., pp. 258–9.

38. Quoted in Conrad, *Perish the Thought*, p. 29.

39. F.K. Prochaska, 'Women in English philanthropy 1790–1830', *International Journal of Social History*, vol. 19, pp. 426–45, cited in Olive Banks, *Faces of Feminism: A Study of Feminism as a Social Movement* (Oxford: Basil Blackwell, 1981), p. 14.

40. In Page Smith, *Daughters of the Promised Land* (Boston and Toronto: Little, Brown, 1970), p. 125, cited in Nel Noddings, *Women and Evil* (Berkeley: University of California Press, 1989), pp. 80–1.

41. Quoted in Helsinger, Sheets and Veeder, *Woman Question*, vol. I, *Defining Voices*, p. 14.

42. Rendall, *Origins of Modern Feminism*, pp. 38–9.

43. Bonnie S. Anderson and Judith P. Zinsser, *A History of Their Own: Women in Europe from Prehistory to the Present*, (New York: Harper & Row, 1988) vol. II, pp. 143, 148.

44. Elizabeth Cady Stanton, *Eighty Years and More: Reminiscences 1815–1897* (New York: Schocken Books, 1971, reprint of T. Fisher Unwin edition of 1898), pp. 31–2.

45. *Woman in the Nineteenth Century*, in Chevigny, *Woman and Myth*, pp. 245–6.

46. Ibid., p. 248.

47. Ibid., p. 253, emphasis added.

48. William Thompson, *Appeal of One-half the Human Race, Women, against the Pretensions of the Other Half, Men, to Retain Them in Political, and thence in Civil and Domestic, Slavery* (London: Virago, 1983 reprint of 1825 edition), pp. 56–7.

49. Charles Brockden Brown, *Alcuin: A Dialogue*, ed. Lee R. Edwards (New York, 1970), cited in Rendall, *Origins of Modern Feminism*, p. 41.

50. Fuller reviewed Brockden Brown's novel *Ormond* in a *New York Tribune* article of 21 July 1846, but I am unaware of any positive evidence that she had read *Alcuin* before.

51. Margaret Fuller Ossoli, *Summer on the Lakes in 1843: with Autobiography and Memoir by Ralph Waldo Emerson, W.H. Channing and Others* (London: Ward and Lock, 1861, reprint of the 1844 edition with selections from the *Memoirs*), p. 110.
52. Ibid., p. 31.
53. Ibid., p. 6.
54. Ibid., p. 18.
55. Rendall, *Origins of Modern Feminism*, p. 24.
56. *Summer*, pp. 167–8.
57. Ibid., p. 229.
58. *Woman in the Nineteenth Century*, in Chevigny, *Woman and Myth*, p. 260.
59. Ibid., p. 60.
60. Ibid., p. 65.
61. Ibid., p. 59.
62. Ibid., pp. 174–5.
63. Ibid., p. 187.
64. *Woman in the Nineteenth Century*, in Chevigny, *Woman and Myth*, p. 256.
65. Welter, *Dimity Convictions*, p. 146.
66. Conrad, *Perish the Thought*, p. 25.
67. Quoted in Conrad, *Perish the Thought*, p. 27.
68. *Woman in the Nineteenth Century*, in Chevigny, *Woman and Myth*, p. 263.
69. Letter written by Sand in April 1848, quoted in Curtis Cate, *George Sand: A Biography* (London: Hamish Hamilton, 1975), p. 419.
70. Elizabeth Cady Stanton and Susan B. Anthony, *History of Woman Suffrage* (1881), quoted in Helsinger, Sheets and Veeder, *Woman Question*, vol. I, *Defining Voices*, p. 40.
71. *Woman in the Nineteenth Century*, in Chevigny, *Woman and Myth*, pp. 250–1.
72. Letter to W.H. Channing, no date, forthcoming in *Letters*, vol. VI as no. 908.
73. *Reminiscences of Ednah Dow Cheney* (Boston: Lee & Shepard, 1902), pp. 205, 193–4, reproduced in Chevigny, *Woman and Myth*, pp. 230–1.
74. Letter written by Fuller on 13 July 1844, *Letters*, vol. III, p. 209.
75. Ursula Vogel, 'Rationalism and Romanticism: Two Strategies for Women's Liberation,' in Judith Evans et al., *Feminism and Political Theory* (London: Sage Publications, 1986), pp. 17–46.
76. This is the argument put forward by Susan Phinney Conrad in the opening pages of *Perish the Thought*.
77. Marion Reid, *A Plea for Woman* (Edinburgh: William Tait, 1843).
78. Barbara Taylor, entry on Wollstonecraft in *The Blackwell Encyclopaedia of Political Thought*, eds David Miller et al. (Oxford: Basil Blackwell, 1987).
79. 'The Social Condition of Woman,' *North American Review* (1836), no. 42, p. 513.
80. Noddings, *Women and Evil*, pp. 2–3.

81. *Woman in the Nineteenth Century*, in Chevigny, *Woman and Myth*, p. 265, original emphasis.

82. Andrea Dworkin, *Right-Wing Women: The Politics of Domesticated Females* (London: The Women's Press, 1983), p. 57.

83. Houghton manuscript (*Works* III, p. 677 ff.). By permission of the Houghton Library.

84. *Woman in the Nineteenth Century*, in Chevigny, *Woman and Myth*, p. 250.

85. Henry David Thoreau, 'An Essay on Civil Disobedience,' in *The Portable Thoreau*, ed. Carl Bode (New York: Viking, 1947), p. 110.

86. Carole Pateman, *The Sexual Contract* (Cambridge: Polity Press, 1987), p. 41.

87. This is still true in modern neo-liberal works such as John Rawls's influential *A Theory of Justice* (Cambridge, Massachusetts: Harvard University Press, 1971).

88. Mary Astell, *Reflections upon Marriage* (1700), quoted in Taylor, *Eve and the New Jerusalem*, p. 32.

89. Joan Cocks, *The Oppositional Imagination: Feminism, Critique and Political Theory* (London: Routledge, 1989), pp. 129–30.

90. Gilligan, *In a Different Voice*, p. 100. See also Nel Noddings, *Caring: A Feminine Approach to Ethics and Moral Education* (Berkeley and Los Angeles: University of California Press, 1984).

91. *Woman in the Nineteenth Century*, in Chevigny, *Woman and Myth*, p. 241.

92. Charles F. Briggs, review in the *Broadway Journal*, 22 March 1845, in Myerson (ed.), *Critical Essays on Margaret Fuller*, p. 14.

93. *Woman in the Nineteenth Century*, in Chevigny, *Woman and Myth*, p. 278.

94. Ibid.

95. Letter from Sophia Peabody Hawthorne to her mother, July 1843, on 'The Great Lawsuit,' in Julian Hawthorne, *Nathaniel Hawthorne and His Wife*, vol. I, p. 258, reproduced in Chevigny, *Woman and Myth*, p. 231.

96. Letter of 4 January 1846, in Elvan Kintner (ed.), *The Letters of Robert Browning and Elizabeth Barrett, 1845–1846* (Cambridge, Massachusetts: Harvard University Press, 1969) p. 361, in *Letters*, vol. IV, p. 220, fn. 1. The mass of British readers of *Woman* were more favourably impressed. On her arrival in London, Fuller wrote that 'I find a surprizing [sic] number of persons who not only receive me warmly, but have a preconceived strong desire to know me. This is founded mostly on their knowledge of "Woman in the Nineteenth etc."' (Letter to Richard Fuller, 27 September 1846, *Letters*, vol. IV, p. 228).

97. Mary Wollstonecraft, *A Vindication of the Rights of Woman*, ed. C.W. Hagelman Jr, (New York: W.W. Norton, 1967 reprint of the 1792 text), p. 17.

98. Frederic Dan Huntingdon, review in the *Christian Examiner* (May 1845), no. 38, pp. 416–7, in Myerson, *Critical Essays*, pp. 26–7.

99. Anonymous review of *Woman in the Nineteenth Century* in the *Broadway Journal*, quoted in Chevigny, *Woman and Myth*, p. 232.

100. Edgar Allan Poe, review of August 1846, in *Complete Works of Edgar*

Allan Poe (New York: G.P. Putnam's Sons, 1902), vol. IX, pp. 7–8, reproduced in Chevigny, *Woman and Myth*, pp. 222–3.

101. Orestes A. Brownson, 'Miss Fuller and Reformers,' *Brownson's Quarterly Review* (April 1845), no. 7, pp. 249–57, in Myerson, *Critical Essays*, p. 19.
102. Miller, *Margaret Fuller: American Romantic*, quoted in Urbanski, *Margaret Fuller's Woman*, p. 37.
103. Letter to James Freeman Clarke, 17 April 1834, forthcoming in *Letters*, vol. VI.
104. Ibid., pp. 124–5.
105. Thoreau, 'Civil Disobedience,' p. 127.
106. *Woman in the Nineteenth Century*, in Chevigny, *Woman and Myth*, pp. 264–5.
107. Brownson, 'Miss Fuller and Reformers', in Myerson, *Critical Essays*, p. 23.
108. Letter from Neal to Fuller, 4 March 1845, quoted in Chevigny, *Woman and Myth*, p. 235, original emphasis.
109. Caroline Sturgis to Margaret Fuller, 4 March 1845, Houghton manuscript, quoted in *Letters*, vol. IV, p. 64. Fuller wrote to her brother Richard that Sturgis had upset her: 'The newspaper sallies are dying away about my book; many expressions of feeling from private sources come in; here as often before I have found the stranger more sympathizing and in my belief intelligent than some of my private friends.' (Letter of 27 March 1845)
110. Urbanski, *Margaret Fuller's Woman*, p. 6.

CHAPTER 5: 'TO DRINK THE AIR AND LIGHT'

1. Margaret Fuller, dispatch 20, 30 December 1847, in Larry J. Reynolds and Susan Belasco Smith (eds) *'These Sad but Glorious Days': Dispatches from Europe, 1846–1850* (New Haven: Yale University Press, 1991), p. 177. © 1991 Yale University Press. Quoted with permission.
2. As with 'feminism,' I use this term 'sexual politics' in the full knowledge that it may be anachronistic; but again, devising a substitute is hopelessly clumsy.
3. John D'Emilio and Estelle B. Freedman, *Intimate Matters: A History of Sexuality in America* (New York: Harper & Row, 1988), p. 8.
4. Blanchard, *Margaret Fuller*, p. 229.
5. Letter to George T. Davis, 1 February 1836, forthcoming in *Letters*, vol. VI, as no. 120a.
6. Lynda Nead, *Myths of Sexuality: Representations of Women in Victorian Britain* (Oxford: Basil Blackwell, 1988), pp. 110–11.
7. Fuller, *Woman in the Nineteenth Century*, in Chevigny, *Woman and Myth*, p. 267.
8. Anna Jameson, *Winter Studies and Summer Rambles in Canada* (London: Saunders & Otley 1838), vol. I, p. 112, quoted in Urbanski, *Margaret Fuller's Woman*, p. 75.

9. This summary is based on Banks, *Faces of Feminism*, pp. 15–16, in turn drawing on Barbara Berg, *The Remembered Gate: Origins of American Feminism, The Woman and the City 1800–1860* (Oxford: Oxford University Press, 1978).
10. D'Emilio and Freedman, *Intimate Matters*, p. xix.
11. Ibid., p. 23.
12. Ibid., p. 29.
13. Ibid., p. 50.
14. Ibid., p. 133.
15. Ibid., illustration 15, following p. 108.
16. Ibid., p. 51.
17. Ibid., p. 58.
18. Ibid., p. 65.
19. Ibid., p. 41.
20. Quoted in D'Emilio and Freedman, *Intimate Matters*, p. 70.
21. Quoted ibid.
22. R.J. Culverwell, *On Single and Married Life, or the Institutions of Marriage; Its Intentions, Obligations, and Physical and Constitutional Disqualifications Anatomically, Physiologically and Medically Considered; with an Exposition of the Structure and Purpose of the Reproductive System, the Hereditary Transmission of Qualities, and the Accidents and Infirmities Incident to Youth, Maturity and Old Age* (1847?), p. 85, quoted in Nead, *Myths of Sexuality*, p. 20.
23. George Drysdale, *Physical, Sexual and Natural Religion* (1855), quoted in Nead, *Myths of Sexuality*, p. 21.
24. Peter Gay, *The Bourgeois Experience: Victoria to Freud*, vol. I., *Education of the Senses* (Oxford/New York: Oxford University Press, 1984).
25. Bram Dijkstra, *Idols of Perversity: Fantasies of Feminine Evil in Fin-de-Siècle Culture* (New York/Oxford: Oxford University Press, 1986), p. 3.
26. W.E.H. Lecky, *The History of European Morals*, vol. II (1869), p. 299, quoted in Nead, *Myths of Sexuality*, p. 51.
27. Nancy F. Cott, 'Passionlessness: An Interpretation of Victorian Sexual Ideology, 1790–1850,' in Nancy F. Cott and Elizabeth H. Pleck, eds, *A Heritage of Her Own* (New York, 1979), p. 165, quoted in D'Emilio and Freedman, *Intimate Matters*, p. 45.
28. *Woman in the Nineteenth Century*, quoted in Blanchard, *Margaret Fuller*, p. 218.
29. For example Dr William Tait's *Magdalenism* (1840): 'A man may by industry, perseverance, and determination, raise himself from any rank of society to another; but this is not the case with a woman who forsakes the path of virtue, and prostitutes her body for the love of gain. The general law in regard to them appears to be, like that of gravitation, always pressing downwards . . . till they sink into the lowest state of degradation into which it is possible for a human being to fall . . . the general law by which the fate of prostitutes is regulated.' (Quoted in Nead, *Myths of Sexuality*, p. 146.)
30. Fuller, 'Prison Discipline', *New York Daily Tribune*, 1845, Houghton MS. (*Works* IV, pp. 153–5). By permission of the Houghton Library.
31. Letter to Georgiana Bruce, 15 August 1844, in *Letters*, vol. III, p. 223.

32. Fuller, *Tribune* article of 19 March 1845. By permission of the Houghton Library.
33. Letter to James Nathan, 24 June 1845, *Letters*, vol. IV, p.121.
34. Fuller, *Woman in the Nineteenth Century*, in Chevigny, *Woman and Myth*, pp. 268–9.
35. Ibid., pp. 270–1.
36. *Memoirs*, vol. II (American edition), pp. 157–60, quoted in Chevigny, *Woman and Myth*, p. 306.
37. Emerson, *Journals*, vol. VIII, p. 95, quoted in Allen, *Achievement of Margaret Fuller*, p. 191.
38. Susan B. Anthony, 'Social Purity', in Aileen S. Kraditor, ed., *Up from the Pedestal: Selected Writings in the History of American Feminism* (Chicago, 1968), quoted in D'Emilio and Freedman, *Intimate Matters*, p. 149.
39. Fuller, *Woman in the Nineteenth Century*, in Chevigny, *Woman and Myth*, pp. 267–8.
40. Fuller, 'Mrs. Jameson's Memoirs', *New York Tribune*, 24 July 1846, quoting from Jameson.
41. Michel Foucault, *The History of Sexuality*, vol. I, *An Introduction* (Harmondsworth: Penguin, 1981).
42. Letter to James Nathan of 24 June 1845 (no. 2), in *Letters*, vol. IV, p. 122. An unintentionally hilarious account of Fuller's relationship with Nathan is provided in Joseph Jay Deiss's *The Roman Years of Margaret Fuller*. Deiss speculates, offensively to all concerned: 'What would his orthodox Mama back in Hamburg have said of his marriage to a *goy*?' Indeed: since *goy* is only applied to men, she would have been more than a little surprised, I suppose.
43. Chevigny, *Woman and Myth*, p. 7.
44. Letter to James Nathan, 15 April 1845, *Letters*, vol. IV, pp. 77–8.
45. Letter to James Nathan, 19 April 1845, *Letters*, vol. IV, pp. 82–3.
46. Letter tentatively dated 31 August 1845, *Letters*, vol. IV, p. 158.
47. Letter to James Nathan, 22 July 1845, *Letters*, vol. IV, p. 137.
48. Dated as 25 November 1843 in the *Memoirs*, vol. I (English edition), pp. 311–14. This letter may not be authentic; it does not appear in the Hudspeth edition of the *Letters*.
49. George Sand, *Letters d'un voyageur* (Paris: Garnier-Flammarion, 1971), p. 51, translation mine.
50. *Letters*, vol. IV, pp. 162–3.
51. Ralph Waldo Emerson, 'Heroism,' in *Collected Works of Ralph Waldo Emerson*, ed. Joseph Slater (Cambridge, Massachusetts: Belknap Press, 1983), vol. II, p. 147–8.
52. Ibid., p. 154.
53. Letter to James Nathan, 9 April 1845, *Letters*, vol. IV, p. 72.
54. Letter to James Nathan, 9 May 1845, *Letters*, vol. IV, p. 98.
55. Letter to James Nathan, 5 June 1845, *Letters*, vol. IV, p. 113.
56. Letter of James Nathan, 27 April 1845, *Letters*, vol. IV, p. 91.
57. Letter of James Nathan, tentatively dated as 4 May 1845, *Letters*, vol. IV, pp. 95–6.

58. Charles Fourier, *Théorie des Quatre Mouvements*, quoted in Barbara Taylor, *Eve and the New Jerusalem: Socialism and Feminism in the Nineteenth Century* (London: Virago, 1983), p. 29.
59. Anonymous article of 13 January 1840 in the Fourierite journal *The Morning Star*, quoted in Taylor, *Eve and the New Jerusalem*, p. 29.
60. Rendall, *Origins of Modern Feminism*, p. 295.
61. Taylor, *Eve and the New Jerusalem*, p. 31.
62. Undated letter (recipient unknown) forthcoming in *Letters*, vol. VI, as no. 955.
63. *Memoirs*, vol. II (American edition), pp. 64–5, reproduced in Chevigny, *Woman and Myth*, p. 311.
64. Fuller, dispatch 36, 15 November 1849, in Reynolds and Smith (eds), *Sad but Glorious Days*, p. 317.
65. Quoted in Chevigny, *Woman and Myth*, p. 289.
66. Emerson, *Dial*, no. 3, p. 101, quoted in Higginson, *Margaret Fuller Ossoli*, p. 176.
67. Undated letter to Mary G. Ward, forthcoming in *Letters*, vol. VI as no. 944.
68. *New York Tribune*, 8 September 1845, in Chevigny, *Woman and Myth*, p. 290.
69. Letter to James Freeman Clarke, 1 May 1835, forthcoming in *Letters*, vol. VI.
70. Fuller, preface to *Papers on Literature and Art* (London: Wiley & Putnam, 1846), p. vi.
71. *Spectator*, 26 September 1846, pp. 930–1, quoted in *Letters*, vol. IV, p. 230, fn. 2.
72. Ibid., pp. vi–vii.
73. Quoted in Higginson, *Margaret Fuller Ossoli*, p. 210.
74. 'T.L.', *Morning Courier and New-York Enquirer*, 7 March 1846, excerpted in Chevigny, *Woman and Myth*, pp. 307–8.
75. Fuller, review of Commander Charles Wilkes, *Narrative of the United States Exploring Expedition* (1844), in *New York Daily Tribune*, 28 June 1845, excerpted in Chevigny, *Woman and Myth*, pp. 343–4.
76. 'Modern British Poets,' from *Papers on Literature and Art* (1846), in Mason Wade (ed.), *The Writings of Margaret Fuller* (Clifton, New Jersey: Augustus M. Kelley, 1973, reprint of 1941 Viking edition), p. 331.
77. Fuller, 'American Literature: Its Position in the Present Time, and Prospects for the Future' (1846) in Wade (ed.), *Writings of Margaret Fuller*, p. 383.
78. Howe, *Margaret Fuller*, p. 132.
79. Fuller, 'Poe's Poems,' *New York Tribune*, 26 November 1845, in Wade (ed.), *Writings of Margaret Fuller*, p. 399.
80. Fuller, 'Poe's Tales,' *New York Tribune*, 11 July 1845, in Wade (ed.), *Writings of Margaret Fuller*, pp. 396–7.
81. Fuller, 'American Literature', in Wade (ed.), *Writings of Margaret Fuller*, p. 371.
82. Fuller, 'Emerson's Essays,' *New York Tribune*, 7 December 1844, in Wade (ed.), *Writings of Margaret Fuller*, pp. 393–4.

83. Quoted in Dijkstra, *Idols of Perversity*, p. 11.
84. A view of Fuller also taken by Albert von Frank in *The Sacred Game: Provincialism and Frontier Consciousness in American Literature, 1630–1860* (Cambridge University Press, 1985).
85. Reynolds and Smith, introduction to *Sad but Glorious Days*, p. 2.
86. Letter to Samuel G. and Anna B. Ward, 3 March 1846, *Letters*, vol. IV, p. 193.
87. Reynolds and Smith, introduction to *Sad but Glorious Days*, p. 9.
88. Ibid., p. 8.
89. Fuller, dispatch 1 (23 August 1846) to the *New York Tribune*, in Reynolds and Smith (eds), *Sad but Glorious Days*, pp. 41–2.
90. Ibid., p. 47.
91. Letter to Caroline Sturgis, tentatively dated 16 November 1846, *Letters*, vol. IV, p. 240.
92. Letter to Emerson, 16 November 1846, *Letters*, vol. IV, p. 245.
93. Fuller, dispatch 5 (30 September 1846), in Reynolds and Smith (eds), *Sad but Glorious Days*, p. 76. Hudspeth thinks that Fuller may have been trying to kill herself: she had just received news of Nathan's engagement. I think she is probably telling the truth in this account, that she wanted to survive and saved herself. My interpretation is borne out, I think, by a letter to her favourite brother Richard, to whom she rarely lied (if anything, she was typically tactlessly frank with him.) 'On the lofty Ben Lomond, I got lost, and passed the night out on a heathery Scotch mountain, alone, and only keeping my life, by exertions to ward off the effects of the cold and wet, to which I should have feared my bodily strength and mental patience alike unequal, *if* I had not tried.' (letter of 27 September 1846, *Letters*, vol. IV, p. 228, original emphasis.) – 'Ossian' was the fictive Gaelic poet whose *Fingal* (1762) and *Temora* (1763) – actually written by James Macpherson (1736–96) – enjoyed great vogue among the Romantics.
94. Fuller, dispatch 2 (27 August 1846), in Reynolds and Smith (eds), *Sad but Glorious Days*, p. 57.
95. Fuller, 'Carlyle's Cromwell', *New York Tribune*, 19 December 1845, in Wade (ed.), *Writings of Margaret Fuller*, p. 297.
96. *The Journals and Miscellaneous Notebooks of Ralph Waldo Emerson*, ed. Merton M. Sealts Jr (Cambridge, Massachusetts: Harvard University Press, 1973), vol. X, p. 551, quoted in Reynolds and Smith (eds), *Sad but Glorious Days*, p. 256, fn. 6.
97. Fuller, dispatch 9 (undated), in Reynolds and Smith (eds), *Sad but Glorious Days*, p. 100.
98. Ibid., pp. 100–1.
99. David Clark, 'Death in Staithes,' *Between Pulpit and Pew* (Cambridge University Press, 1982).
100. Fuller, dispatch 1, in Reynolds and Smith (eds), *Sad but Glorious Days*, p. 48.
101. Fuller, dispatch 10 (undated), in Reynolds and Smith (eds), *Sad but Glorious Days*, pp. 102–3.
102. Albert Fried and Richard Elman (eds), *Charles Booth's London: A Por-*

trait of the Poor at the Turn of the Century drawn from his Life and Labour of the People in London* (Harmondsworth: Penguin, 1971), p. 89.

103. James Smith Allen, *Popular French Romanticism: Authors, Readers and Books in the 19th Century* (Syracuse, New York: Syracuse University Press, 1981), p. 153 ff.
104. Quoted ibid., p. 153.
105. Fuller, dispatch 12 (undated), in Reynolds and Smith (eds), *Sad but Glorious Days*, pp. 124–5.
106. Ibid., pp. 120–1.
107. See, for example, Pateman, *Sexual Contract*, pp. 96–102; Susan Moller Okin, *Women in Western Political Thought* (Princeton, NJ: Princeton University Press, 1979); Nannerl O. Keohane, 'But for Her Sex . . . The Domestication of Sophie', in MacAdam, Neumann and Lafrance (eds), *Trent Rousseau Papers* (Ottawa: University of Ottawa Press, 1980); and David Held, *Models of Democracy* (Cambridge: Polity Press, 1987), p. 72 ff. An unconventional estimate of Rousseau's thought as enhancing feminism is given in Lynda Lange's 'Rousseau and Modern Feminism', in Mary Lyndon Shanley and Carole Pateman (eds), *Feminist Interpretations and Political Theory* (Cambridge: Polity Press, 1991), pp. 95–111.
108. Rendall, *Origins of Modern Feminism*, p. 17.
109. Fuller, 'French Novelists of the Day,' *New York Tribune*, 1 February 1845, in Wade (ed.), *Writings of Margaret Fuller*, pp. 303–6.
110. *Memoirs*, vol. I (American edition), pp. 194–9, reprinted in Chevigny, *Woman and Myth*, pp. 360–3.
111. Ates Orga, *Chopin* (London: Omnibus Press, 1976), p. 104.
112. Edmund Ordon, 'Mickiewicz and Emerson,' *University of Buffalo Studies* no. 1 (July 1956), p. 43, quoted in Chevigny, *Woman and Myth*, p. 300.
113. Letter from Adam Mickiewicz to Margaret Fuller, February 1847, in *Letters*, vol. V, p. 175–6, fn. 2.
114. Letter to Emerson, 15 March 1847, *Letters*, vol. IV, pp. 261–2.
115. Letter to Marcus and Rebecca Spring, 10 April 1847 (incorrectly dated by Fuller 1846), *Letters*, vol. IV, p. 263.
116. For more detail, see Rendall, *Origins of Modern Feminism*, p. 168ff.
117. Fuller, dispatch 13 (undated), in Reynolds and Smith (eds), *Sad but Glorious Days*, pp. 119, 128.
118. Fuller, dispatch 13, pp. 129, 131.
119. Fuller, dispatch 14 (May 1847), in Reynolds and Smith (eds), *Sad but Glorious Days*, p. 131.
120. Letter to Evert A. Duyckinck, 23 May 1847, in *Letters*, vol. IV, p. 272.
121. Fuller, dispatch 14, in Reynolds and Smith, *Sad but Glorious Days*, pp. 136–7.
122. Reynolds and Smith, *Sad but Glorious Days*, fn. 11 to dispatch 20, p. 184.
123. Fuller, dispatch 18 (undated), in Reynolds and Smith (eds), *Sad but Glorious Days*, p. 165.
124. A letter of 19 January 1849 to her brother Richard is actually quite

congratulatory about the fruits of the war, however. 'I thought of the new prospects as to wealth opened to our countrymen by this acquisition of New Mexico and California, the vast prospects of our country every way, so that it is in self *[sic]* a vast blessing to be born in America . . .' (*Letters*, vol. V, p. 179).

125. Letter to Caroline Sturgis, 13 March 1845, *Letters* IV, p. 59.
126. Brian Barry, 'Nationalism,' in David Miller et al. (eds). *The Blackwell Encyclopaedia of Political Thought* (Oxford: Basil Blackwell, 1987), p. 354.
127. Giuseppe Mazzini, letter of 8 September 1847 to Pope Pius IX, reproduced by Fuller in dispatch 21, 31 December 1847, in Reynolds and Smith (eds), *Sad but Glorious Days*, pp. 194–5.
128. Letter to William C. Russell, 30 October 1846, forthcoming in *Letters*, vol. VI as no. 996a.
129. Letter to Richard Fuller, 29 October 1847, *Letters*, vol. IV, p. 310.
130. Letter to Marcus Spring, 9 August 1847, *Letters*, vol. IV, p. 285.
131. Letter of 11 January 1848, *Letters*, vol., pp. 41–3.
132. Fuller's letter to Tappan of 16 March 1849 (*Letters*, vol. V, p. 207 ff.) compares Tappan's baby with her own, in a manner which indicates that a previous lost letter must have imparted the news of Angelino's birth.
133. Letter of April 1848, *Letters*, vol. V, p. 60.
134. In a letter of 3 April 1849, Ossoli, on duty with the Civic Guard, wrote, 'Dear, how much I wish to spend tomorrow with you, since I well believe you will remember that it is the 4th April.' Hudspeth thinks this means they were married on 4 April 1848, a plausible view.
135. Letter to Caroline Sturgis Tappan, 16 March 1849, *Letters*, vol. V, p. 210.
136. Letter to Ellen Fuller Channing, 11 December 1849, *Letters*, vol. V, p. 292.
137. Letter to Arthur Hugh Clough, 18 February 1850, forthcoming in *Letters*, vol. VI as no. 865. By permission of the Bodleian Library, Oxford. MS.Eng.lett.d.176.
138. Letter of 8 January to Richard F. Fuller, forthcoming in *Letters*, vol. VI, as no. 856. By permission of the Houghton Library.
139. Letter to Marcus and Rebecca Spring, 5 January 1850, forthcoming in *Letters* vol. VI as no. 860. By permission of the Houghton Library.
140. Quoted in Curtis Cate, *George Sand: A Biography* (London: Hamish Hamilton, 1975) p. 622.
141. Letter to Giovanni Angelo Ossoli, 22 August 1848, *Letters*, vol. V, p. 109.
142. Letter to Charles King Newcomb, 22 June 1848, *Letters*, vol. V, pp. 77–8.
143. Letter to Richard F. Fuller, 17 March 1849, *Letters*, vol. V, p. 213.
144. Fuller, dispatch 32, 10 June 1849, in Reynolds and Smith (eds), *Sad but Glorious Days*, pp. 293–4.
145. Fuller, dispatch 34, 6 July 1849, in Reynolds and Smith (eds), *Sad but Glorious Days*, p. 310.

146. Fuller, dispatch 35, 31 August 1849, in Reynolds and Smith (eds), *Sad but Glorious Days*, p. 316.
147. Joseph Campbell, *The Hero with a Thousand Faces* (Princeton, New Jersey: Princeton University Press, 1949); *The Power of Myth* (New York: Doubleday, 1988); and interview with Maureen Murdock, 15 September 1981, reported in Murdock, *Heroine's Journey*, p. 2.
148. Higginson, *Margaret Fuller Ossoli*, p. 5.
149. Letter to Ralph Waldo Emerson, 20 December 1847, *Letters*, vol. IV, p. 315.
150. Letter to Lewis Cass Jr, forthcoming in *Letters* vol. VI as no. 868.

CHAPTER 6: DREAMING A WOMAN'S DEATH

1. Letter of 17 December 1849, *Letters*, vol. V, p. 301.
2. Letter to unknown correspondent, 29 November 1849, *Letters*, vol. V, p. 283.
3. Letter of 29 December 1849, *Letters*, vol. V, pp. 305–6.
4. Letter to William Wetmore Story, 10 May 1850, forthcoming in *Letters*, vol. VI, as no. 881. The reference to 'cross-biased' comes from George Herbert's poem 'The Church': 'Thus doth thy power crosse-bias me, not making/ Thine own gift good, yet me from my wayes taking.'
5. Letter to Emelyn Story, 16 April 1850, forthcoming in *Letters*, vol. VI, as no. 877.
6. Letter from Rebecca Spring to Margaret Fuller, 14 April 1850, forthcoming in *Letters*, vol. VI, no. 883, fn. 1.
7. Letter to Emelyn Story, 30 November 1849.
8. Letter to Caroline Sturgis Tappan, 26 May 1840, forthcoming in *Letters*, vol. VI, as no. 260a.
9. Letter of 6 April, 1850, forthcoming in *Letters*, vol. VI, as no. 875.
10. Letter to Costanza Arconati Visconti, 21 April 1850, forthcoming in *Letters*, vol. VI, as no. 878.
11. Letter to Samuel and Hannah Fogg Thompson, June 1850, forthcoming in *Letters*, vol. VI, as no. 886.
12. Letter to Marcus Spring, 3 June 1850, forthcoming in *Letters*, vol. VI, as no. 885.
13. Report signed 'B.T.' in *New York Daily Tribune*, 23 July 1850, Box B, Houghton Library. By permission of the Houghton Library.
14. Ibid. There were speculations, based on conflicting accounts by a lighthouse keeper, Captain Dominy, and a passer-by named Dow, that the bodies of Margaret and Giovanni were recovered and buried secretly in the potter's field, but 'they are of the character of those floating fancies which are apt to arise after such a disaster.' (Letter of 15 July 1901 from Millie Devereux Blake, president of the Margaret Fuller Memorial Committee, to Miss Fuller, Box B, Houghton Library.)

Index

STALKY & CO.